OUTSIDE THE LAW:
A THIEF'S PRIMER

OUTSIDE THE LAW
A THIEF'S PRIMER

□ □ □

BRUCE JACKSON

Transaction Books
Rutgers University
New Brunswick, New Jersey

For my mother

CONTENTS

ACKNOWLEDGMENTS

THIS IS ONE BOOK of a group resulting from a continuing study of prison and criminal culture that was supported for several years by the Harvard Society of Fellows. To the Senior Fellows, who for that period granted without question what must have seemed peculiar requests at times, my thanks.

For friendship and counsel, I want particularly to thank Dr. George Beto, Director of the Texas Department of Corrections; Professor John Gagnon, formerly Senior Research Sociologist at the Institute for Sex Research and presently on the faculty of the State University of New York at Stony Brook; the Honorable Charles Wyzanski, Jr., Chief Judge, U.S. District Court, Massachusetts; Professor Aidan Gough of the University of Santa Clara; Professor Frederic J. Fleron, Jr., of the University of Kentucky.

In addition, I should like to thank Billy Brammer, intermittently of Austin, Texas, for havens from grimness; Mr. Jack Heard, Assistant Director of the Texas Department of Corrections, for his careful reading of the manuscript and his many comments; Mrs. Julie Sparkman, of Huntsville, Texas, for super services; Mr. Herald Price Fahringer, of

Buffalo, for counsel; Warden Sidney Lanier, Warden Howard Sublett, Warden Carl Luther McAdams, Warden Terill Hutto, and the other Texas correctional officials who offered such memorable hospitality; "Kid," "Wilson," and the other people whose real names I couldn't use either, for various kinds of help; and Barbara Bator, Linda Wachob, and Gail Barrett for their aid back in Buffalo.

Most important, of course, is Sam himself. This book uses him as an exemplar of a kind, but he was obviously a collaborator as well. I regret that necessity requires me to obscure the identity of a partner. He taught me much, for which I am grateful, and wherever he is now—greetings, and hang loose.

And, especially, thanks to Sue, who put up with it all.

Note: The sources of a number of quotations in the footnotes, identified as "Wilson," "Kid," etc., were working and incarcerated thieves who read the manuscript in its original form. *Convict ms.* in the text and notes refers to an unpublished essay by two inmates of the Texas Department of Corrections which discussed aspects of the inmate social system; the authors of the essay requested, as did Wilson and Kid, that their names not be used here.

BRUCE JACKSON

CHARACTER: N. (colloq. Texas, derives from *police character*, *i.e.*, a person whose criminal *modus vivendi* is known to the police)

(1) "I think a character is somebody that makes his living completely outside the law but yet has some principles about it." (Sam)

(2) "I believe a character is a dyed-in-the-wool burglar, a thief, someone that's making his living solely on others, on society itself." (Wilson, another one)

Sam said: I don't know, maybe it's a sense of resentment because they make it. I watch them from across the street and hope they have a good day. Today it's theirs, tonight it's mine.

and: I just dig stealing. I *like* it.

OUTSIDE THE LAW:
A THIEF'S PRIMER

THE CONTEXT:

AN INTRODUCTION

The day after Sam got out of prison we drove through a recently developed section of Houston. He pointed to one shiny new building, all metal and glass. "Boy, if that had been here five years ago, we'd have had a relationship."

"Hard," Kid said. "They're all floodlit inside."

"You can get around that. What kinda boxes they got in those places?"

"Tin cans," Kid said.

"I don't like tin cans. I like real boxes. On tin cans you can cut your fingers."

I

THIS BOOK is composed of statements made by a moderately successful thief who was, when I first met him, midway in a five-year residency in a Texas state prison. He had done time once before, a two-year sentence that terminated a ten-year career as check forger; between the two prison terms he had supported himself by opening other people's safes.

Sam's story presents neither a theoretical discussion of the general category of behavior our society accepts as criminal nor a portrait of a perfect representative of that category.

No single career could be adequate for such a portrait. His statements form, rather, an attempt by one kind of thief to describe the kind of world in which he thinks he moved, and the relationships he thinks he had with it and its actors. The statements try to describe what he did, but more important, they try to put into a balance satisfactory for *him* the roles he enacted and the roles to which he aspired.

Most of what he says is true. I have checked out what I could by talking with other thieves who knew him on the streets and with convicts who knew him in prison, and by spending considerable time with him in both prison and the free world. Individual chapters, and in some cases the entire manuscript, were read by a number of consultants, including the former Houston police chief, Mr. Jack Heard (now Assistant Director of the Texas Department of Corrections), a Texas warden, lawyers, some pulled-up and some working thieves in various parts of the country, and some convicts; several of these people knew Sam. A few of them made remarks about the manuscript, and these have been included in the notes.

We cannot, of course, assume that the Sam with whom I spoke was the same person as (or revealed all the goals and anguish of) Sam the thief. When he and I first met, he was in prison and I was someone from the square world, a difference in status not immediately conducive to mutual soul-baring. But there were certain mediating factors that minimized the distortions. Most important was that Sam and I did not work together on anything having to do with his own career until after we had known each other for over a year, by which time he and a number of people he trusted had decided I was someone it was safe to talk to. I was at first working on a collection of Negro convict work songs, and our early talks resulted from his curiosity about that project. He did not perceive me as a potential threat, and there was no feeling that he was a potential subject. He worked in the only air-conditioned office inside the prison, and I would frequently go there to hide from the outrageous summer weather of the Texas Gulf; on those occasions we talked about a number of things. Later, when I started working on inmate acculturation and criminal learning, he helped me select interviewees; he was particularly helpful with autobiographical and analytical comments made by other inmates that I thought odd or wrong. Sometimes, so I wouldn't have to take notes, I used a tape recorder while we talked. These first tapings were about other people, other situations. Later, when I realized how articulate he was, I tried to focus our discussions on his own experiences. That phase covered about two years. Whenever I visited the prison system, we taped. Later, when he was out, we talked more. By the time we were consciously working on his career, I knew him rather well and it was possible to talk without much of the posing sometimes natural to such situations. Because of the way the book developed, I think it is more honest than it might have been had we started out with it as our goal. The image he offers is not one made to suit a traveling sociologist. Over a relatively long period I was able to observe him with other convicts and with other criminals in Texas and Mexico, and neither his style of presenting himself nor his method of conversation changed appreciably.

In any autobiographical account there are amounts of distortion, inflation, and rationalization. As a partial check on those, I sometimes asked the same questions or led the conversation to the same topic after a year or so had elapsed. When inconsistencies were revealed, I tried to determine whether they were deliberate or unconscious, whether they revealed a lapse of memory, remission in honesty, or gap in perception, whether they were designed to make Sam more acceptable to me or himself, and whether they revealed more than they concealed (for what one chooses to dissimulate about is often more telling than the particular truth in question). The words are all Sam's. I have rearranged the order of many statements, I have deleted most of my questions, and I have edited his prose only to the extent of removing the false starts and repetitions common to speech but annoying in print.

The career of thief comprises not only acts of theft but a style of living. Distortion in any thief's account of himself tends to occur when he relates aspects of his relationship with the style. The acts of theft are themselves verifiable (with minor discrepancies allowed: a thief may claim more jobs than he actually pulled, he might exaggerate the size of his income, he might minimize his fears), and the crafts involved in obtaining other people's money without their consent are fairly well known. What cannot be known is how a particular thief really relates to the perquisites and requisites of the life situation in which his occupation sets him: there is not only the question of his relationship with his listener, but also that of his honesty with himself.

A man says, "I did this because . . ." or "I felt this way . . ." and we infer an attitude or set of attitudes toward behavior or things. Behind that rests a more basic and more problematic set: the attitudes or values that make the *surface* attitudes attractive.

Sam, a thief, tells about the facts of his working life and the way he would like us to perceive his attitudes toward those facts. He is presenting the self he considers or wants considered his outside self, and that is a *fact*, one not open to adjudication. What we can wonder about is why he really says he wants those things, why he really felt the need to do the things he did. That act of speculation you can do as well as I, so I will not attempt it. But I will try to tell a bit more about the parameters of Sam's world.

There are many different types of criminal actors. Some are not at all involved in the criminal world, and they earn the label of "criminal" by an act that is in their experience anomalous, resulting from extraordinary conditions; these are usually called *impulse criminals*. There is a large group of technical offenders who might be called *service criminals*; I say technical offenders because their activities have no victims in the usual sense of the word; though the activities are proscribed by law, the lawbreaker works with the consent and at the request of the citizenry he services. In this group would be bookies, prostitutes, pimps, dope pushers, etc. There is of course a group that offends against morality, which in America means sexual morality, with or without the consent of the other person or persons involved; in this group would be the homosexuals, rapists, fondlers, etc.

The people who make their living by criminal acts of other kinds may be classified in four categories: *habitual* or *compulsive*, *organized*, *professional*, and *career*.

The *habitual* or *compulsive criminal* or *thief* is one who steals but for whom neither the acquisition of property nor the style of criminal life is particularly important. For this person, the *act* is an end in itself.

Organized crime covers an extremely wide range of behavior. It includes everything from the so-called Mafia or Syndicate operation to price-fixing by large, otherwise respectable, industrial concerns. The term refers to the *mode* of business activity.

Professional crime refers to the nature of the individual actor's commitment. The standard description of this kind of actor has been given in *The Professional Thief*, which consists of an autobiographical account by one thief and an interpretation of that account by Edwin H. Sutherland. The core of Sutherland's definition is this: "The hypothesis may be taken that professional thieves constitute a group which has the characteristics of other groups and that these group characteristics are in no sense pathological. Also, the hypothesis may be taken that tutelage by professional thieves and recognition as a professional thief are essential and universal elements in the definition, genesis, and continued behavior of the professional thief. No one is a professional thief unless he is recognized as such by other professional thieves. Tutelage by professional thieves is essential for the development of the skills, attitudes, codes, and connections which are required in professional theft."[1]

There is a problem with this definition: it excludes the full-time thief who was self-taught. It excludes check writers who work alone (as most do) and armed robbers. Most armed robbers do not stay active long enough to acquire any kind of real occupational role, but some do. Consider the

following comments by two California robbers I know, the
Bobbsey Twins, who had in one eighteen-month period committed nearly two hundred robberies in the Los Angeles
area:

"When my partner and I decided to go into crime," one
said, "the first thing we had to decide next was just what
branch of crime to go into. You've got car theft, burglary,
stealing, stealing money or rolling drunks, armed robbery,
other things. . . ."

"We weren't broke," his partner said, "we weren't down
and out. We had a little bit of money, and I had a job at the
time. But the job prospects weren't very good, and I don't
dig that type of manual work, so when we got together and
talked it over, we decided that to get the amount of money
we wanted in the shortest time, that crime was the way to
get it. Now crime, we feel, is just like any other business.
In other words, there's setbacks in crime and there's deficits.
Just as if you run a business, you might go bankrupt, or your
employee might embezzle every dime you've got without the
insurance to cover it. It's the same with crime. Of course the
penalty for going bankrupt in crime is much stiffer than—
but at the same time your material gain is much greater
than—in a regular business."

"So we decided to go into crime, and, in order to decide
which branch we wanted to go into, since we were both
inexperienced criminals at the time, we decided to do as
much research as we could and find out which made the
most money the fastest and that percentagewise was the
safest. I think you'll find that every public library in a city
has statistics on the number of crimes committed the previous year, how much money each crime was, and you could
figure out, from the amount stolen, the number of crooks
caught, and the number of convictions, what you wanted to
know. We spent four days at the public library and we re-
searched, and we came up with armed robbery as the most
likely for us."

"There are things you have to take into consideration.
A crime is pulled and got away with, say, but one man might

have pulled twenty armed robberies before he's caught, so they got him on one but there's nineteen that they have unsolved. Statisticswise it looks like everybody's getting away, but it's actually not that way. You've got to take that into consideration when you check in."

"We found, though, that armed robbery is by far the best as getting away with it is concerned because, unlike burglary or breaking and entering, you don't take anything that you have to convert into cash, thereby putting something in somebody else's hands, and you're taking nothing but *money*, which is spendable any damned place. I don't care where you go, the money's going to be good. And unlike stealing cars, you don't have to worry about transporting the car to wherever you're going to sell it. And unlike strong-armed robbery, which I tried once, you don't have to worry about knocking some sonofagun in the head and maybe causing him a hell of an injury or maybe even killing him when you didn't even intend to. But there's that possibility in armed robbery too—of having to shoot somebody."

"We discussed this a great deal. What we would do, if and when. Luckily, in all this time, there's only been one or two slight instances where we've had to worry about it. And I think we came out with flying colors. We could have very easily killed someone."

"We made up our minds to begin with, if we ever got surrounded in the position where the police said, 'Come out with your hands up,' that we would come out with our hands up. None of this Custer's Last Stand bit. If I walked into a place and the man actually got the drop on me, where I knew if I tried to shoot him he was going to shoot me, then I'm giving up, because I can see no point in getting killed. I'm not the hero type. I'm somewhat of a physical coward, or I wouldn't pick up a gun in the first place. That's the way I look at it."

"Of course if it's a situation where it's going to be them or us, it's going to be someone else."

"Of course," his partner said.

"I think the main thing that kept us out of trouble those

years was we *never* went back to any old hangout. We never went back to the old bunch we used to hang around with."

"See, you'll find in crime you move in different circles. When you first start off, you're a working man and you're accustomed to the $70- or $100-a-week paycheck, and when you get the extra amount to where you can afford to spend $200 a week, you're way up. But it don't last long. Maybe six weeks or two months. And then you get accustomed to this, and then you start looking for something a little bigger and better to hit. Which you do. And then you move up into the $300-a-week spending bracket. And this continues; there's no stoppage. It's a plane that just keeps advancing. And as you advance, your mode of living, your clothes change in accordance. Your apartment changes. You can't go back.

"If we had gone to the first places we hung out, the cock-tail lounges and places like that where we went when we were making a hundred a week, if we started going in there in a $500 suit, wearing tailor-made clothes, monogrammed silk shirts, right away you get raised eyebrows. Somebody says, 'Hmmm, what's going on here?' So you got to drop your friends, too. What friends you make at each level you got to leave at that level. And that's just what we did, and I think that's one of the things that kept us out of trouble for so long.

"But the stage we were living at when we left Los Angeles, about the only way we could have got any higher was to rob Fort Knox. But I couldn't find a way to get in there."

"We *never* associated with thieves or anything like that. If we *had* to have anything to do with them, we did it and that was it. But we never ran around with them."

Sutherland's definition of *professional thief* requires two essential elements: recognition and tutelage. The Bobbsey Twins taught themselves, and once they had learned the ropes, they avoided criminals. In Sam's case there was both recognition and tutelage, but neither was essential to his criminal self-identification; both came quite late in his career. By the time Sam learned about safes, he had been a full-time criminal for over ten years.

He was first a check writer, which is a craft requiring little or no tutelage. It takes no great flash of wisdom to realize that people will give you money for a slice of paper or to realize that if you are going to depend on that for your liveli-hood, it might be more pleasant to use names other than your own. Highly skilled craft aspects, such as check rais-ing, are now fairly rare. The problem in check passing is handling the person with the money you want, and that is dependent on personal style rather than technical skill. Check writing is a solitary profession, it is better done alone, it is one in which the worst thing that can happen is to become well-known. Check writers do not socialize very well; they may meet in jail, but they do not tend to hang around together outside.

Safecracking is usually quite the opposite. There is con-siderable mechanical craft involved, and the rudiments are often learned by watching someone who knows how to do it well. I know a few who managed to teach themselves and who went for many years without knowing another criminal, but I suspect these are rare. Most seem to have apprenticed the craft, as Sam did.[2]

The term *professional thief* has come to have certain unfortunate applications, not so much because Sutherland unreasonably limited or obfuscated the meaning or activity, but rather because he wrote about a specific kind of criminal actor and did not have to distinguish among the other actors. If we are to keep Sutherland's characteristics of tutelage and peer recognition as the qualifications of a professional thief, and if we want to continue using the term, we need another term for relatively successful thieves like the Bobbsey Twins and Sam, a term that will distinguish them from the rums, the incompetents, the career convicts, the amateurs, the impetuous.

So, to maintain Sutherland's usage and have a descriptive term for someone like Sam, I am going to call his role that of *career* thief or criminal. The term is certainly not new, but the above discussion indicates its most useful limits. Most easily, I'd like to be able to say, A career thief is a thief like Sam.

Sam is a man somewhere between real success and mild failure in crime. He is not so committed to the thief or character role or so sociopathic that he can ignore his status; his partial commitment to middle-class norms causes him to spend a considerable amount of time justifying himself to himself.

He tends to idealize the character life, but it is important to realize that criminals like Sam *do* idealize it. Most characters do not help one another very much, except when profit is involved, but Sam helps others; most characters do not give anything away, but Sam is generous; the average character will snitch as soon as he is asked, but Sam will submit to torture before he admits knowing anything about himself or anyone else, even when he knows that what he is asked to admit is already known. That most characters, that the most successful of them will snitch, hoard, cheat on colleagues, and do whatever else they have to do or want to do to get along doesn't matter. It is *because* Sam is not all the way there, because he is not completely alienated from his earlier middle-class aspirations, that he is far more conscious of what he calls the "qualifications."

Life, for this sort of offender, is extremely discontinuous, more so than it is for the organized criminal or vice offender. Organized criminals have life continuity the same as any other businessmen; addicts and prostitutes have sustaining symbiotic relationships with police and other criminals with whom they must deal, and the very nature of their illegal acts demands a certain regularity of movement and perhaps even clients. The prostitute has a relationship—albeit antagonistic—with her customers; the addict has to maintain his connections, has to have his daily shots, has to deal with the police. But the safe-cracker never confers with his victim, and the check writer confers a brief and artificial moment only; both are highly mobile; neither deals with the police except when he is arrested, and any relationships developing then are transitory. They may frequent character joints, bars where criminals congregate, but meetings in such places are usually rare and unplanned. At most, the working safe-cracker or check writer has sustained contact with a few people with whom he may be working at a particular time and with his lawyer. This relative isolation contributes to his dependence on externals for status, his tendency to spend a great deal of money quickly and obviously, his attempt to make an expensive rather than "good" appearance.[3]

The role of character is one of *expression;* the role of thief, one of *action.* Sam is triangulated by those two roles and his role of middle-class Texan. He is perfectly at home in none of them; he is perfectly free of none of them.

This triangulation creates a certain role ambiguity. Sam wants to make it in the society of thieves (however amorphous an entity that may be), which requires a certain style and the establishment of certain skills; he also wants to make it in (or can't escape from) the same middle-class box he sees his family in. Both contexts are acquisitive, but display and dispensation of acquisitions vary enough to delineate a pair of very different life styles.

In the middle-class world, money is spent on things that are permanent (house in a "good" section of town, art) or socially approved (gifts to charity, vacations, private schools for the children, a few clubs); the character world, as Sam points out, "high plays," it spends quickly and obviously.

Part of the difference results from exigencies of the acquisition processes: the successful square must be relatively stationary to make his money and exercise his class options, and his job is related to his status (money isn't enough, he must make it in a "correct" way); the thief must be mobile and ungrounded if he is to survive. The square evidences his success, and concomitantly his status, by his occupational role and his concrete possessions; the thief, by visible spending. Half the thief's status parameters are not verifiable (he cannot brag too much about his jobs, he cannot have witnesses to his expertise), while the square can have his professional status inspected at any time (*e.g.*, the doctor with all his diplomas and certificates and licenses arrayed for your view, or the professor with his list of publications; thieves have no offices, they don't get certificates for jobs well done, and they don't write for professional journals).

In the world of the career criminal, as in the middle class, the *sine qua non* of status is the ability to make money. In both, there are secondary qualifications by which the individual is evaluated, but before he is eligible for the evaluation process, he must pass the income test. Without the income qualification, one cannot play the social game at all. The career thief, remember, has referents in our world as much as his, and for some the incentive to steal is acquisitive purely: they want things or the status things seem to represent. Other values are subsumed in the quest, sometimes quite consciously. These points were summed up by one professional killer who said to me, "In my walk of life you've got to use a certain amount of cold calculation, at times animal cunning, and brute force to survive. And in doing so, you leave a certain amount of your feelings buried deep, and you keep them that way. . . . I'm not interested in being tough. Every act I have committed to an extent has been made on the basis of the buck. 'Cause I've learned that the buck is what makes you an American citizen as well as a person that can be respected. A broke man is like a dead man. No one wants to hear what he got to say, 'cause what the hell, he must not be of any value if he's not using it for his own benefit. . . ."

The word *criminal* identifies not a specific kind or style of behavior but rather the way certain actions and kinds of actions are formally evaluated in a particular culture at a particular time. *Crime* is not so much a physical fact as it is a relationship, one that signalizes an attitude. The label of *criminal* is affixed to the actor because of his *presumed* mental set and not because he acted in a certain way.

This is most clearly illustrated by the various ways our society regards the killing of one human being by another.

Killing is murder in a narrowly defined set of circumstances only; in most cases it occurs with the endorsement of one's society and is regarded as a proper, and perhaps laudable, act; in many cases it is considered an unavoidable accident and no culpability follows.

If one kills another person without intent and through no fault or carelessness of one's own (a drunk runs into the road from between two parked cars on a rainy night while you are driving under the speed limit; a boxer kills his opponent; a construction worker dumps a load of steel on a place where a fellow worker wasn't supposed to be standing; a doctor makes a defensible error in judgment in the operating room that is perceived as an error only after the death of his patient), our society does not hold one liable. There are many circumstances in which one may fully intend to kill the other person but that killing is defined as justifiable or even socially desirable (the police officer defending himself or others against an armed felon, the homeowner shooting an armed intruder, the husband shooting his wife and her lover *in medias res*, the pilot dumping high explosive and jellied gasoline on what he has been told are enemy camps, the state's professional executioner killing a condemned man). Other kinds of killing, depending on the intentions of the killer and the postures of the killed, may be negatively sanctioned by our society in a variety of ways, ranging from relatively brief or suspended jail terms (for vehicular homicide, say) to execution (for premeditated murder, which is deliberately causing the death of another person without legal justification). The specific *act* in all these situations is the same—one individual directly causes the death of another—but because of the perpetrator's intentions, the victim's actions, both persons' roles in society, and the circumstances of the death, society attaches different weights and offers different responses.

We often read or talk about the *criminal* as if this were some homogeneous category, as if the word defined a personality type. It is no more useful than the word *killer*, which could, given the proper circumstances, cover any of us. And it hides an important point of discrimination: one man might be noncriminal his entire life but for two minutes (when he decided to dip into the till or shoot his wife) and earn that brand; another might engage in activity defined as criminal from the onset of puberty through senility, and earn the same brand.

We might question also the notion that on the streets there exists an entity that can be called a *society* of thieves. There is clearly a society of convicts (which Sam discusses at some length; it has also been the subject of several studies[4]), but the thief's working context is quite different. The professional criminal or career thief has none of the institutional status and concomitant role perquisites that he might have in prison or that the organized criminal, who is by definition part of a hierarchical structure, has outside. The working thief may display the marks of affluence (by his clothes, by "high playing," by ostentatious spending, etc.), but he cannot openly display proficiency at his trade. This latter factor exists not only because of the risk of arrest, but also, and more importantly, because the trade itself is rarely perceived as an end in itself. Characters rarely brag about technical elements well handled, but they do brag about big scores; covert thieves brag about nothing, of course.

The character world is one that exists in default rather than because of a positive function: its members are those who have in one way or another been stigmatized as members of a vaguely defined deviant category, and who have accepted that stigma and in one way or another chose to make the most of it. When one examines it as a *culture*, one finds that the only real constant is the lip service paid the Code. Usually, the Code is something one should observe, but not me in these circumstances right now; when someone does not inform, the odds are it is because of fear of personal revenge rather than moral interdiction.

The *Assessment of Crime* task-force report of the President's Crime Commission commented: "The shifting, transitory pattern of most professional criminals' working relationships was found to be accompanied by the absence of any strong ethical codes. Few seemed to feel bound by any 'no ratting' rule. Typically, they appeared to take it for granted that others would do whatever necessary to protect themselves—to avoid imprisonment or reduce a sentence—and that they, therefore, should do likewise. As one professional criminal commented: 'The one who gets his story told first gets the lightest sentence.' There was little resentment expressed about this. It was treated like the weather—a fact of life. Further, criminals expected to be cheated by their colleagues, or by most colleagues. Many of those interviewed reported having been cheated by fences and even by their partners in a particular venture. Victimization of one professional group by another is also fairly common, limited only by fear of reprisal.

"There were exceptions to this general pattern, however. Some professional criminals stated that they had worked with certain individuals whom they trusted completely. And relative stability was found among the really successful professional criminals in New York and Chicago. In Chicago, for example, there is a group of between 50 and 200 'heavy' professional thieves who concentrate on such criminal activities as burglary, robbery, and cartage theft. It is said that this group, or at least the core members of the group, are quite stable and quite highly organized, and apparently they exert a considerable amount of control over their own regular members, as well as over persons who work with them only on occasional jobs."[5]

What we must bear in mind here is that few thieves *are* organized in any sense of the word, and that the group the Crime Commission refers to above is minute.

Other than this peculiar Code, it is hard to find functions or goals of the supposed society. It has no lobby to agitate for benefits for members; it has no newspaper to pass around notes of interest; it has no pension fund, no annual meetings, no group insurance, no lapel pin; it offers no gain to potential members (other than the gains of any business relationship: a hijacker should know who will take ten thousand cartons of cigarettes off his hands quickly, just as a

tie manufacturer should know who will take ten thousand
neckties; in neither case do these temporary dyadic relationships form a society); it prescribes no penalties for non-
members (it cannot punish scabs, it cannot refuse licenses);
it can elect no officers, and even if it could, there is little
it could do because there is no way to discipline the membership when there is no way to insure the monopolistic
assignment of territories that could be the only organiza-
tional benefit. It is here, in fact, where organized and professional crime are most highly polarized: organized criminals
avoid safes and checks not because they find such
activities inherently loathsome, but because there is no way
to insure even a modicum of safety and monopoly. Running
whores or gambling establishments requires the cooperation
of law enforcement officials, the cooperation necessary to
stay open and the cooperation necessary to destroy com-
petition.

Working criminals such as Sam do not form a society or
even a group; they do form a category. The distinction between the two terms has been well made by Erving Goffman:
"The term 'category' is perfectly abstract and can be applied
to any aggregate, in this case, persons with a particular
stigma. A good portion of those who fall within a given
stigma category may well refer to the total membership by
the term 'group' or an equivalent, such as 'we' or 'our people.'
Those outside the category may similarly designate those
within it in group terms. However, often in such cases the
full membership will not be part of a single group, in the
strictest sense; they will neither have a capacity for collective
action, nor a stable and embracing pattern of mutual interaction. What one does find is that the members of a particular stigma category will have a tendency to come together
into small social groups whose members all derive from the
category, these groups themselves being subject to over-
arching organization to varying degrees. And one also finds
that when one member of a category happens to come into
contact with another, both may be disposed to modify their
treatment of each other by virtue of believing that they each

belong to the same 'group.' Further, in being a member of the category, an individual may have an increased probability of coming into contact with any other member, and even forming a relationship with him as a result. A category, then, can function to dispose its members to group-formation and relationships, but its total membership does not thereby constitute a group. . . ."[6]

Even though thieves like Sam sometimes work in small firms of two or three, they are essentially loners. There is no love of craft, no allegiance to guild. Success is often dependent upon being able to look square and honest, the opposite of what one really is. Work is separted from the goal of work; it is as anomic as college sociology. Social relationships are highly transitory.

Once one has met a number of professionals or career thieves in situations in which rapport may be established, one discovers they are frequently middle-class in background and often quite articulate. These are the two qualifications that open the standard channels of economic advancement in the noncriminal world. Many of the better thieves one meets are agile enough to make as much money legally. And they often know it. One said to me, only half joking, "I bet you wonder why a bright clean-cut kid like me from a good family turned to crime." I said I had indeed wondered about that. "I like the life," he said, meaning the romantic business of spending big, carrying an automatic pistol in a special shoulder holster, moving in two worlds at once.

He liked the life. And so does Sam. Jack Heard wrote at one point: "This section where he says that if the fee was $5,000 or $25,000 to get out of jail, that he would go out and rob a bank rather than come to the penitentiary . . . he doesn't place much value on money, but sees it as a means of being able to operate, being able to go back and rob and stay on the streets and party. Money is strictly a medium of exchange for freedom, not for any value the money has itself."

Sam liked to steal,[7] and he liked being a thief, a character. About the rest, he will tell you himself.

II

Most prisons are organized nominally to handle the personalities who fit the public's image of the Criminal—that nefarious deviant who supplies such fine copy for scandal sheets and television script-writers—but only rarely do prison staffs have an opportunity to deal with that sort of offender. The deliberate and intelligent criminals—the professional killer, the high-level narcotics distributor, the fraudulent corporation executive, the thoughtful burglar, the physician salting away money which ought to be paid to the I.R.S.— go to prison so rarely they hardly affect the statistics. And when they do go, they do not stay very long. Prison population reflects only that part of the criminal world that isn't smart, rich, dishonest, or lucky enough to stay out of jail.[8]

Largely, a state prison is populated by people who are not too bright (and who, therefore, don't steal very well); impulse criminals (whose offending act reflects not a life pattern but a set of extreme circumstances—most murderers are in this category); chronic convicts (a large group of men who stay out for short periods only because they don't know how to get along anywhere *but* in prison, and who seem to spend their criminal hours out of prison not seeking profit so much as prestigious reincarceration); some habitual offenders (those who can't manage to stay out of trouble but who still base their value systems in the world outside); and a rather small number of competent working criminals who had a run of bad luck or a moment of carelessness.

As a culture, prison seems to structure itself into three fairly clear components: *noncriminal*, *thief*, and *convict*.

The *noncriminal* group is composed of men under sentence for a crime, naturally, but whose attitude and orientation are directed toward the values and goals of a noncriminal society. This includes the impulse criminals, certain vice offenders (such as students caught with marijuana), embezzlers, and others. Sometimes the political prisoners are part of this group, though they may form a fourth group standing apart from the other three in order to proselytize among them (political prisoners in federal institutions, civil rights organizers in southern prisons, at one time labor unionizers in both sets of institutions, and presently Black Muslims in both, etc.). These men have little to do with underworld society, inside or out. They often avoid the politics of inmate society and either steer clear or are kept out of the various prison rackets. They try to do their time as quietly as possible. Sometimes a member of this group may go over to one of the others, especially if he is on a long sentence.

The *thief* culture is composed of those who were working criminals on the outside. Numerically, it is probably the smallest of the three. Its members engage in a variety of illegal activities in the free world, ranging from floating phony stocks to commercial assassination; they are so engaged for the high profits primarily, and in some cases for the style of criminal life as well. This group also has its referents in the free world, not in prison, but because of experience it tends to get along very well in prison. One member said, "In here, I go along with all the rules and regulations. I don't ever resist things even. It's something I've never understood: on the street I've done everything and anything, but when I come to the penitentiary, I never get into trouble, I never have been in trouble, I'm never arrested in here, I never have to be breaking out, I do my work. I get on the streets and I go to robbing and stealing. But in here, it seems like I'm just a different character, a different person."

The *convict* group is the one that supplies the largest portion of the recidivist and the prison populations. "The hard core member of the convict subculture," write Irwin and Cressey, "finds his reference groups inside the institutions and . . . seeks status through means available in the prison environment."[9] The thief wants leisure time, "things that will make prison life a little easier. . . . The convict seeks privileges which he believes will enhance his position in the inmate hierarchy."[10] Members of the convict group frequently get in trouble immediately on release, for they are dependent on authority imposed by the administration and other convicts, and their goals are conceived in terms of the prison and cannot be fulfilled in the free world. This group includes those sometimes called *habitual convicts*, persons for whom the criminal act itself means little; what does matter is that the act is committed in a way that will get them into prison. These are often men who *need* prison, and their reasons vary considerably: some appreciate the security and regimentation and don't have the qualifications necessary to get into the Army or join a police department; some have been introduced to homosexual roles during previous confinements and don't know how to be homosexual on the streets. Whatever their reasons, they get into jail and prison with depressing regularity.

When Sam discusses prison society, he does it from the point of view of a person involved in both the thief and the convict cultures. He is not, of course, a habitual convict, but he knows that to make it comfortably in prison he has to deal in terms of the internal culture, and that requires that he understand the two most important elements in it.

Prison is more likely to create a culture than free-world criminal contexts, and for obvious reasons: prison is a cultural isolate, it is a continuing society set off from other societies, it has needs that are not met by the free society's equipment, so it develops things of its own, both material and verbal. Probably the most frequently articulated element is the Code.

It is moot whether the Code receives more reinforcement from prison exigencies or Burt Lancaster movies. An old inmate at the penitentiary in Huntsville told me that a man who followed the Code was called *convict* by the other inmates, and it was a term of respect. "*Convict*," he said, "means that you're supposed to be a good people. To the inmate body, wherever you might meet 'em, inside or outside. If they call you *convict*, why that means it's qualified as you keep your mouth shut and tend to your own business, and you're not a snitch and don't meddle in other people's business or things like that."

"Don't inform, don't meddle, don't bring heat" says the

Code.[11] The latter two items are usually respected, and hostility is accorded violators; the first is the most discussed and the most violated. "Though there is little group loyalty in total institutions," writes Erving Goffman, "the expectation that group loyalty should prevail forms part of the inmate culture and underlies the hostility accorded those who break inmate solidarity."[12] This does not mean informing does not occur; it does mean that it generally occurs *in camera*. The members of this society got where they are by breaking laws, and only a few bother to distinguish between laws made by squares and laws made by convicts, however much their movie counterparts might assert otherwise.

The "don't inform" section of the Code may be a joke to the noncriminals and those members of the thief group who choose to remain aloof, but to some of the other inmates it is as venerable as motherhood. In a Massachusetts state prison I was told of an inmate who was in solitary confinement when the other man in that row of cells cursed the guard through the door. The guard assumed the first inmate, Joe, was the one who had shouted, and told him to stop. The second inmate did it again, and Joe was awarded an extra five days' punishment. He couldn't say, "It wasn't me," he said, because that would have been informing by implication. On the other hand, there is a well-traveled story about a warden who broke up a dining hall riot by promising to come in there with all the snitch-kites (informing letters) he had received in the last month if the hall wasn't cleared in five minutes.

Old-timers insist there is far more informing nowadays, that in the old days punishment was swift and sure. But every contemporary account I have found, going back over seventy years, says the same thing. The fact is that informing is now and always has been part of the *modus vivendi*. Characters have to live in the prison, so they strike a balance: they inform only when it seems they'll get enough concessions in return to make it worth-while. The no-snitch rule would be powerful if everyone obeyed it, but as soon as a few break the rule, the whole structure crumbles, and the result is like a political convention where all the delegates rush to be on the winning side, whether they like the candidate or not. Attitude and act differ.

Like most human organizations, formal and informal, prison society is imperfectly structured. One of the things that prevents its becoming monolithic is the existence of alternate kinds of status, some free-world and some penitentiary, that are extra-structural and role-conferring. These status elements are related to the kind and quality of criminal activity one engaged in on the streets, one's physical size, one's sexual role in the prison, etc. Here are some illustrative comments from inmates in several state institutions:

"One of the things that most affects your prestige in here is the size of the robbery, what you've done. Someone who was arrested for stealing a car to joy-ride around town, why he isn't considered to be anything. You know he really can't caper; in other words, he doesn't know how to thieve, he just stole the car and drove it around a few blocks, you know. Whereas the guy that hit a supermarket who at one time in his possession had maybe $200,000—whether it was for five minutes or two days, he had it—he's considered to be a good operator, because he's willing to go out after the big stuff. I'll agree, it doesn't make sense, but that's the consensus. This makes a difference, and also if he has friends outside that send him money and he always has commissary, always has cigarettes, he's considered to be all right and most generally can get what he wants in the prison." (Missouri)

"The great common denominator is money. The amount taken in a single robbery or the total amount earned or retained by a particular member is a powerful influence in the social strata. With money, even the fink can buy superficial respect and hire simple friends to do his bidding. He can command considerable influence over the clans or influence convict opinion. He can purchase creature comforts and buy immunity from threatening groups. Everyone caters, to a greater or lesser degree, to the wealthy inmate. His money freely in circulation contributes greatly to the welfare of the populace." (Texas *Convict ms.*)

"Most of the guys that are here are way below the ordinary educational level. Even their crimes aren't anything spectacular. They'll get money without thinking—"

"At the back door or something."

"—and the embezzler is completely incomprehensible to them."

"A burglar, he's just a run-of-the-mill boy. A car thief, a man who steals a car for a specific crime, this isn't bad, but we have a lot of joy riders."

"If you want a best reputation when you come to this penitentiary, which is no worse than a lot of others, is if you've done time in Alcatraz. That there is the tall one, the medal of honor. They even write it up in the prison newspaper."

"Sure, it's silly. Anybody who can't get along in Leavenworth or Atlanta, who is so maladjusted that he can't put up with a few little restrictions, is sent to the fuckin' Rock. As far as I'm concerned, I'd hate to go to the Rock because it must be full of bugs; it must be a bunch of nuts and rats." (Two Missouri robbers)

"Cop killers and those who engage in gun duels with the minions of the law comand due respect. Murderers rate fairly high, except those who've killed women or children. A burglar is a good middle-of-the-road profession. Hijackers are a respectable lot, whereas rape fiends fall in the social caste. Child molesters are the most loathed, as are sodomites and homosexuals, although the latter two are tolerated as a relative necessity in a world without women. Dope fiends and pimps are a fairly easygoing group and fit in easily with various other groups." (Texas *Convict ms.*)

"Being a cop killer will hurt you more than it'll ever help you. The first time when you get out, if you get out, the first thing police do if they run upon you is kill you, because you've already killed one of theirs, one of their men. They'll not just murder you, but if they ever caught you in a joint, they'd do it." (Texas burglar)

"Physical physique is an important factor in seeking a slot on the higher rungs of the social ladder. The tall, muscular individual commands respect because all convicts are great respecters of brute force. The adept behavior of the brute receives distant and quiet courtesy because it is terribly face-losing to be pummeled into the ground before many witnesses who may hold one in high esteem solely on the basis of one's physical prowess. The top braves carefully avoid fighting among themselves because of the fear of losing the battle to a more proficient man." (Texas *Convict ms.*)

"The man that pays his debts and someone knows that if this man borrows from him he'll pay it back, why he's all right. If he knows he doesn't have to watch what he says or does in that man's presence, that he won't snitch, this insures him to be a good person. And of course who you associate with has a bearing: if you associate with someone that has a bad reputation, there's going to be an element that does talk about you to a certain extent. It's a very touchy thing, you know. And there are some, you always have in an institution a group that will keep themselves aloof from the over-all population. They don't have too much to do with anybody. I try to be one of these. I have a lot of acquaintances, but I have very few friends. Mainly because friendship in here can fall out over the slightest thing: it can fall out over a pack of cigarettes or a candy bar. They become important things. Most of the guys in here don't have any money, and they don't even have razor blades. If they don't have a job and they don't earn any money in here, they don't have anything. They can't buy a toothbrush, tooth powder, razor blades, anything. Consequently commissary is a means of exchange. If somebody beats somebody out of a dollar, it's about like beating someone out of $50 outside." (Missouri)

One of the most important intramural factors affecting status and role is prison sex. Though the number of inmates participating at any particular time may be relatively small, it seems that somewhere between 30 per cent and 50 per cent of the population participate in one of the available sex roles sometime in their incarceration career. Prison sex is important not because it consumes so much of anyone's time and energy, but because it consumes considerable interest and concern. It is like a city's crime rate: very few people are affected by it directly, but there is a lot of talk by insiders and outsiders regarding the threat it poses.

There are three basic participating sexual roles in prisons for men: *stud* (or *daddy, jocker, wolf*; the person who plays the "active"[13] or inserting role); *punk* (*penitentiary punk, penitentiary turnout, kid*; the person who plays the "passive" or insertee role and who adopts that role in prison only); and *queen* (*free-world punk*; person who plays the same role as the punk but who is actively homosexual in the free world as well). Both queens and punks are sometimes referred to as *gals*. Some punks submit to anal coitus only, others perform fellatio as well; queens are expected to do both. Punks have considerably lower status in the hierarchy than do queens. When I asked why, one Texas inmate said, "Because the penitentiary turnouts aren't man enough to admit what they are," which struck me as an interesting inversion. A Missouri convict said, "You hate a son of a bitch who tries to act like you do and then turns tricks. But a person who just happens to have a different psychological make-up than you and has brought it in with him, well, hell, we all have psychological problems."

The worst places for sexual abuses seem to be the temporary detention centers, such as county jails. These are populated by an uncomfortable conglomerate: the innocent too broke to afford bail before trial, minor offenders serving out a short sentence, inmates awaiting transfer to state prisons, defendants in serious trials. Much of the population is in for morals and disorderly conduct charges. The cell blocks are often run by a strong inmate or inmate gang. Into this mess are thrown first offenders and often boys who would not be there at all if they were adults (such as one Ohio youth recently incarcerated because his school principal objected to his long hair).

A man just out of the Harris County Jail in Houston said, "They always try to talk you into it, and if that don't work, they just take it anyway. When I was over there, there was a lot of them that was tore up and beat up and had broken ribs and black eyes and cuts and bruises. They always used to take them out and put them someplace else then." Another man told of an experience he had had as a youth: "I was fifteen and in Oakland, California. I was put in the Juvenile Detention Home. My one experience there was gang rape until I passed out. And I spent three months in a hospital after that and required seven stitches. In the beginning four people held me down. And then I lost count and I lost consciousness and everything. Then I woke up in the hospital. And I was only doing thirty days."

Some inmates disagree; they insist one can fight off assault: "Everybody says you can get screwed with enough people ganging up, but I think somebody wouldn't give in if he didn't want to. There's a punk up there in the tank for protection because twelve guys rushed at him in the county jail where I was and he got a razor and cut one of 'em's foot clean off. Sliced another one's head open. He didn't get fucked. But these other punks, they do it because they want everybody to leave them alone or they like it.

"The guy who's hogged, he's just a laughingstock after that. The ones that fuck him, they always say he wasn't no good anyway. There was one poor little old guy, he couldn't speak English and he couldn't talk anyway because they had a belt around his neck choking him and one of them fucked him and then he took the little boy's hat and wiped his peter off on it and put it back on the boy's head. And this other one, the one that had already fucked him, he held him down while this other boy was getting on. And that's when the boss come up there and caught them. He went up to the boss with his pants down crying and telling what happened. He disappeared after that. We don't know what happened to him. You never know around this place."

It seems that force is far less a problem in prisons than it is in jails or juvenile institutions. "In most cases," write John H. Gagnon and William Simon, "the 'passive' partner drifts into the relationship through falling into debt, being afraid of the environment, and feeling that he requires protection, or because he already has a well-developed commitment to homosexuality that he cannot or does not want to conceal."[14] Kinsey observed that such a developed commitment could be very much the result of experiences in institutions during adolescence; it does seem apparent that inmates most likely to become very involved in sexual affairs are those who had extensive institutionalization during their teen-age years, and those most likely to avoid such involvements are inmates who did not come to prison the first time until they were mature adults.[15]

Sexual activity in prisons for adults "is quite a different phenomenon than homosexual experience in the outside community. . . . Homosexuality in the prison context is partly a parody of heterosexuality, with the very sexual activity suggesting masculine and feminine role components. We now know that this is a basic oversimplification not only of homosexuality in general, but heterosexuality as well. It is, however, in the prison environment where this parody is most likely to occur, for the crucial variable is that many of the men who take part in homosexual performances conceive of themselves, and wish others to conceive of them, as purely heterosexual."[16]

That parody includes not only romance and marriages, but also such outside institutions as the gang-bang: "It goes kinda far in here. We've had situations here where they'd stand in line for a boy. I mean really form a line with the boy in a little cubbyhole of one sort or another. One guy comes out and the boy says, 'Next,' and the next guy comes and takes a crack. This is where it gets to be ridiculous. I can see where a guy can get himself worked up, but that's pretty cold, just standing in line like you're buying tickets to a theater."

There are a number of factors reducing the frequency of sexual activity in a prison. The most obvious is that the individual inmate is almost continually observed by the custody staff and the other inmates. In addition, note Gagnon and Simon, "the man in prison finds himself without the appropriate stimuli which suggest opportunities for sexual activity or situations that are appropriate for such activity. Without the existence of these social cues, the biological imperative of sexual arousal is never even elicited. The absence of females, the sheer sensory monotony of the prison environment, the absence of those social situations that call for sexual responses (being out on the town, going drinking, etc.) serve as effective inhibitors of sexual responsiveness. The most successful aphrodisiacs seem to be an absence of anxiety, the presence of available sexual cues, an adequate diet, and plenty of rest. Of these, only the latter two are commonly in the prison environment and in some cases only the last is.

"The other source of sexual cues is fantasy, those remembered or desired sexual experiences that commonly serve as the basis for masturbation. However, as a result of the social origins of the bulk of the prison population, there is a major taboo against masturbation and a paucity of complex fantasies that would sustain a commitment to sexual experience."[17]

To the same point, Kinsey wrote: "In a prison, there may be opportunity to such outlets as masturbation, nocturnal emission, the homosexual, or a stray experience of some other sort; but the sum total of sexual activity is very much below that found in similar groups outside of an institution. In a short-time prison, the majority of the men do not accept homosexual contacts, and there are a great many who, coming from a social level at which masturbation is taboo and from a social level where nocturnal emissions are at a minimum, may go for long periods of months, or for a year or more, without ejaculation. A few of these men are emotionally disturbed as a result of their lack of outlet; but most of them live comfortably enough, apparently because there is little erotic arousal which needs to be relieved by orgasm. The men in such institutions regularly insist that there is very little if any arousal from conversation, printed pictures, descriptions in literature, or anything short of contact with a sexual partner. Educated persons are commonly misled by the constant discussion of sex for which prisons, armies, factories, and other places of partial restraint are notorious. Academically trained students are too prone to interpret such situations in terms of their own, highly conditioned responses. For the more poorly educated portion of the population, however, there is a minimum of erotic fantasy. . . . In consequence, these prison males do not illustrate sublimation, for they have little or no aroused sexual energy which needs dissipation."[18]

Assuming that Kinsey is right, one might wonder why sexual activity, even on a limited basis, goes on at all in prison. The probable answer is that the sexual affairs and adventures are often enlisted in the service of ends not basically sexual in nature. ". . . it is suggested that what is occurring in the prison situation for both males and females is not a problem of sexual release," write Gagnon and Simon, "but rather the use of sexual relationships in the service of creating a community of relationships for satisfying needs for which the prison fails to provide in any other form. For the male prisoner homosexuality serves as a source of affection, a source of the validation of masculinity, or a source of protection from the problems of institutional life."[19] The problem is that "men get into relationships which have some potential for shaping their future commitments to sexuality; relationships which leave them open to exploitation; and, especially for those who take the passive role, the possibility of distortion of their self-conceptions. Further, there is some tendency for these relationships to create problems of sexual jealousy. When a relationship deteriorates or when a transfer of affection takes place, there is a distinct possibility of violence. The violence that does occur often is extreme, and at this point becomes a serious matter for prison management."[20]

There is a peculiar romanticization of the criminal in this country, one shared alike by thieves like Sam and the free-world population on which he preys. As my friend John Gagnon is fond of observing, the dashing screen romance of Bonnie and Clyde fails to show that those policemen gunned down bled as redly as the two lovers, that the bank clerk whose head exploded on camera may have had a family. That isn't a sentimental observation: a day spent in a urban police station or hospital emergency room will set you straight pretty quickly. Watch the victims, the dead or maimed or dying or just terrified; talk to the young girl just gang-banged by four or five healthy men; watch the secondary victims, the families of the dead clerks or policemen.[21] The romance withers quickly.

Prison is even less adaptable to romantic interpretation than crime: no matter how you slice it, the cake is bitter. The prison population, you should remember, represents the losers, the clumsy, the mistaken. A very few are professionals who made a rare mistake, but they are too few to matter much. Whatever the causes for the presence of most (bad schools, broken homes, early maltreatment by the system when the individual could still have been repaired, greed, genes, germs, whatever), one has to face the fact that the prison dweller is, on the average, not very nice, and the worst part of living in prisons usually is the company of the people with whom you have to live.

III

Sam and some of the consultants will discuss in detail the pros and cons of police brutality, but there is another aspect of the working criminal's relationship with the law enforcement mechanism that is perhaps even more important: the trade, formally called "the negotiated plea of guilty." Deals have always led to more guilty pleas than truncheons, and now that the Supreme Court has pretty much supplied ground rules for police departments who wouldn't act civilized on their own, the deal is more important than ever.

The prosecution of criminal offenses in this country would come to an abrupt halt did not about 90 per cent of all felony convictions result from guilty pleas. Part of that 90 per cent consists of felons burdened by rare consciences, or represented by inefficient lawyers, and that part, which is very small, pleads guilty simply because it wants to or is afraid not to. But almost all offenders who plead guilty do so because they get something in exchange. This ranges from the murderer who pleads guilty to second-degree murder or manslaughter and thereby avoids a likely death penalty or life sentence for his real crime, to the new felon who trades his chances with a jury for the promise of a suspended or very light sentence.

"Maybe the most common crime in America," a New York lawyer told Martin Mayer, 'is the perjury of the defendant who swears before the judge that he hasn't been promised anything in return for his plea of guilty.'"[22] ". . . little or no purpose is served," Mayer writes, "for the accused individual or for the society that has to supply the courts and jurors, when people who are clearly guilty insist on [the right to jury trial]. 'The fact is,' Judge Henry T. Lummus of Massachusetts once wrote, 'that a criminal court can operate only by inducing the great mass of actually guilty defendants to plead guilty, paying in leniency the price for the pleas.' More than six hundred people are arraigned every day in one of the seven significant 'parts' of the Manhattan criminal courts; and there are fewer than a hundred lawyers in the District Attorney's office. If even one percent of these arraignments were actually to proceed to a full-fledged trial, the system would break down instantly. A Midwestern prosecuting attorney told an investigator from the American Bar Foundation that 'All *any* lawyer has to do to get a reduced charge is to request a jury trial.' "[23]

But there are problems created by the trade. The taskforce report on the courts by the President's Crime Commission notes: "The system usually operates in an informal, invisible manner. There is ordinarily no formal recognition that the defendant has been offered an inducement to plead guilty. Although the participants and frequently the judge know that negotiation has taken place, the prosecutor and defendant must ordinarily go through a courtroom ritual in which they deny that the guilty plea is the result of any threat or promise. As a result there is no judicial review of the propriety of the bargain—no check on the amount of pressure put on the defendant to plead guilty. The judge, the public, and sometimes the defendant himself cannot know for certain who got what from whom in exchange for what. The process comes to look less rational, more subject to chance factors, to undue pressures, and sometimes to the hint of corruption. Moreover, the defendant may not get the benefit he bargained for. There is no guarantee that the judge will follow the prosecutor's recommendations for lenient sentence."[24]

The last item seems to be rare: the trade system would collapse if word went out that it was inefficient. But far more important are the excesses resulting from applications of the trade to other stages of prosecution. Narcotics officers, for example, will often file sale charges on a defendant they feel they can convict only of possession because they and the defendant know that sale penalties are so much greater that the defendant will often plead guilty to a reduced charge—of which he may or may not be guilty— rather than risk a jury trial that may send him away for a long time without even chance for parole. Repeaters will plead guilty in exchange for a maximum sentence (as did Sam, who accepted the twelve-year maximum for burglary) rather than risk being filed on as habitual criminals, which usually carries a life sentence.

"The most troublesome problem," says the courts' taskforce report, "is the possibility that an innocent defendant may plead guilty because of the fear he will be sentenced more harshly if he is convicted after trial or that he will be subjected to damaging publicity because of a repugnant charge. The danger of convicting the innocent obviously must be reduced to the lowest possible level, but the fact is that neither trial nor plea bargaining is a perfectly accurate procedure. In both, the innocent face the risk of conviction. The real question is whether the risks are sufficiently greater in the bargaining process to warrant either abandoning it entirely or modifying it drastically. Such improper practices as deliberate and unwarranted overcharging by the prosecutor to improve his bargaining position, threats of very heavy sentence if the defendant insists on a trial, or threats to prosecute relatives and friends of the defendant unless he pleads guilty may, on occasion, create pressures that can prove too great for even the innocent to resist. The existence of mandatory minimum sentences aggravates this problem since they exert a particularly heavy pressure on defendants to relinquish their chance of an acquittal."[25]

One study in Minneapolis "disclosed that in the year 1962, out of 91 cases of burglary, only 1 was originally charged as first degree burglary. It is difficult to believe that the facts supported a first degree burglary charge in only 1 out of 91 cases."[26] The reason for the large number of obvious trades is apparent when one notes the sentences: "First degree burglary carried a minimum sentence of 10 years and second degree 2 years. There was no minimum sentence for third degree burglary."[27]

Sometimes the trade never goes beyond the police station: police, especially in vice cases, will use the threat of a charge to force people to become informers. Without this device, narcotics agents would be pretty much out of business. Unfortunately, the technique is sometimes abused. I think particularly of one young student I know who was stopped on a street one evening and arrested for possession of a small quantity of marijuana; the detectives told him that if he agreed to work for them, they would not press charges. "Hell," he said to me, "they want me to get evidence for them on people I don't even know, and they want me to keep doing that until I graduate." He went to a lawyer instead.

It frequently turns out that the *guilty* criminal who engages in the standard deal is among the few who get a good return from the criminal court and its bargaining process. The innocent are put to great expense and are subject to unwarranted stigmatization and, even worse, unjust conviction. This country has the longest prison sentences in the Western world, and they work so that only the guilty in a position to negotiate stand to profit, and the innocent, especially those without significant resources, stand to lose.

Sam discusses at some length how the trade works for and against a criminal like himself. There is never any question of his guilt—only the potential charge and resulting sentence are at stake.

Several thieves with whom I spoke about the trade felt there is something *morally* wrong about the whole process. Sam points out that the procedure can be used as a weapon when the real evidence is weak and the police or prosecutor decide that getting someone for anything is better than not getting him at all and when the defendant feels that taking a chance on losing a court trial, which always results in a much longer sentence, just isn't worth it. In the past the prosecutor and police would use the trade against the ignorant and the unrepresented, but now that all felony defendants have rights to legal counsel, that is no longer so outrageous an abuse of civil rights. But procedural changes do not protect everyone: in some jurisdictions court-appointed lawyers care so little for their assignments that the defendant is little better off than before.

Whatever changes occur, the inherent irony remains: the process of the trade is covert, so it always exposes the criminal and noncriminal alike to a stage in the operation of the law where the entire set of agents—judge, prosecution, defense—formally lie to one another about conspiracy; it is a stage where, with the cooperation and sometimes the blessing of the defendant, the representatives of law and order formally apply themselves to the perpetration of perjury.

IV

Words may not make the world we perceive, but they surely give us useful handles for aspects of it. Not only do different people in different roles perceive the same situations differently, but they may on occasion use the same words about those situations with entirely different connotations and even denotations. This is especially the case when the group in question is an isolated, deviant, or stigmatized one, which develops such words and word usages both as convenience (to express things the larger society has no need to express) and comfort (to give a sense of groupness that might otherwise be difficult to acquire).

Most career criminals have in their experience sources of three special vocabularies: their profession, their criminal role, their prison service. Of these, the trade supplies the fewest terms and the criminal role the most. There might be a functional necessity here: the trade needs no crystallizing by words, one is a gunman or one is not, one is a safe-cracker or one is not, and the words are specific nouns and verbs; the role is far more problematic, and it has far more argot words, many of which are ambiguous and connotative. The argot words of the role are often drawn from a general vocabulary of outsiders (hippies, Negroes, etc.).

Prison for someone like Sam is a temporary interruption of an expected kind. He easily sheds the prison vocabulary; he can slip in and out of it without difficulty. If he is going to talk about safes at all, he cannot avoid using the technical terms of the safecracking trade, for there are no other words available. The general criminal vocabulary is one he can avoid if he is conscious of a necessity for avoiding it; otherwise he will tend to use it.

Slang is usually far more connotative and far less denotative than ordinary language (hence the multiplicity of meanings or applications of many of the terms), and it is by the connotations that the outsider is usually kept outside. He perceives the denotations easily enough— they can often be inferred from the context—but the connotations are embodied in the milieu that necessitates having an alternate or special set of words in the first place. It is not that members of an in-group plot so their words will be unknown to an outsider, but these words obtain currency specifically because they express a particular aspect of reality not adequately handled by the more quotidian vocabulary. It is the situation that is incomprehensible to the outsider (which is of course what makes him an outsider), not the definition.

An example from the free world might illustrate this most easily. In the 1940s and early 1950s, the word *fay* or *ofay*

(Pig Latin for *foe*) served a New York Negro as a suitable term of identification for a white man, carrying with it a contemptuous connotation, especially for slumming squares and roaming cops. With the increase in interest in jazz after the war and subsequent influx of whites to bars previously all-Negro, the word slipped into more general usage. White musicians and their friends used it for whites who were not hip to Negro music, and blues fans used it to refer to squares and to one another (since that seems to be a group among whom degree of hipness is of special importance). New words—Whitey, gray—assumed the old function. The new words in turn were also picked up by whites, most notably (and most audibly) by so-called "liberals" trying to show how "in" they were. Now one hears "Charley" and "Jolly Green Giant." When those words are picked up and used by whites, the black community will find others, for there will always be at least one part of the meaning the whites—be they sincerely friendly or simply lusting for cool—cannot know: what White means to Black.

Not all prison inmates use the criminal and convict vocabularies, but all seem to know the meanings of the words. Highest currency is among members of the convict society (that portion of the prison population oriented to prison rather than crime). The thief, as Sam points out, is often a bit wary of it. "I don't like to use slang," a fellow prisoner told Alexander Berkman (the anarchist who attempted to assassinate Frick during the Homestead Strike). "It grows on one, and every fly-cop can spot you as a crook. It's necessary in my business to present a fine front and use good English, so I must not get the lingo habit."[28] A midwestern inmate, who told me about his participation in well over a hundred robberies, said, "I don't use slang. You want people to think I'm a crook?"

Prison slang and argot deal with anything of local interest, and sex is high on the frequency list. Donald Clemmer noted that a 1940 compilation of 1,000 slang and argot words from an Illinois penitentiary produced 116 with a sex reference—and over half of these had a homosexual reference.[29] The other major category is composed of words peculiar to specific crafts or roles, such as Sam's safecracking terms.

The italicized words in the quotations from Sam that follow, and in the alphabetized list following them, are all used by Sam in the text of this book. The meanings given are those current in the Texas character and convict vocabularies only. It should be kept in mind that not only do slang and argot words change frequently with time, but they also vary considerably with place. *Shakedown*, for example, in Sam's vocabulary always means search of premises or person by guards or police, but in the North the term means a particular kind of extortion; *made* means a variety of things to characters, but to none of them does it have the meaning it has for the police—recognized. The word list consists of words used by Sam in this book only; it does not attempt to present a large portion of the words current among Texas characters and convicts.

Sam says:

I've noticed while I've been in the penitentiary that we have a lot of slang words that we use here. When I get out and I go back into society, I have a tendency not to use these anymore unless I'm around other ex-convicts. Sometimes when you run into ex-convicts, you use them, but even then you don't use them much. It's a language that's just used here. And not only do the convicts use it, but the officials use it and understand it and talk it too. We call it being *con-wise*. They, just like us convicts, adopt this slang and use it in the normal habitat of working here.

A hoe that we work with, for example, we call an *aggey*. We say *drove up* for time of arrival, no matter how you arrive. And *busted* is a common word here—it means arrested.

But once we get out, these words are more or less forgotten. Especially by me. I go back into a different environment than a lot of people. I was raised in the country till I was set, and so all of my really old friends, my boyhood friends, the ones that will still speak to me and associate with me when I'm out, they're not characters, and around them you can't talk like that.

If you're around old convicts and you happen to run into them crossing the road somewhere, then you all get together for a drink or something and you revert back to it a little bit, but most of the reverting back means you're talking about the penitentiary. The terms that we use down here can't be applied to any other place *but* a penitentiary—they're strictly inmate folklore or whatever you want to call it.

What about the slang of your trade, do you avoid using that?

Depends who you're talking to. There are a lot of those words you have to use just to say what you're talking about; there aren't any other words for some things.

There is one type of bar that's better than any other type of bar for getting into a building. We call it a *jimmy-bar*. Now there's many jimmy-bars, but the part of the country where I come from, the safe men around there call a jimmy-bar a multisided bar that has a nail puller on one end and a bill on the other; the bill turns slightly so you can put it in there and it gives you that leverage. They're very heavy-duty and real strong, and you can rack on them or beat with them or do whatever you want to do.

We don't call a safe a safe, we call a safe a *box*. A *square-door box* is an ordinary one-door box with the dial in the center and the handle usually on the left middle; it opens, looking at the safe, from your left to your right. We also have what we call a *double-door box*. Then you get into your *keysters*. A keyster is, as anybody knows, an ass, and a *keyster stash* is an asshole.[30] Keysters are the asshole of the safe profession because they're so hard to get into. And safe salesmen, they call them keysters too. There are different types. You have a *square-door keyster*, and you have a *round-door keyster*, and you have a *nigger-head keyster*. A nigger-head keyster is a large ball, just a round ball that's set in concrete.

I can't get in them. I have heard of people that could get

in them, but I don't believe it. I had one one time, I had it
on an island. I had a bunch of dynamite and I blowed that
thing. I dug a big hole in the sand and buried it there and
blowed it, and it would go up like a rocket. And finally I
blowed it all the way out in the ocean. And I never did
scratch it. I couldn't get in. I tried to cut them and I can't
get in. That time, I knew I couldn't get in the safe, so I went in
the building and took the safe with me. And I still couldn't
get in. Later on, I had guys tell me, "I heard about that safe
you had, the keyster that you had, and I wish I'd had it; I'd
have got into it and split the profits with you." But I don't
believe it. I don't believe that they can get into them.

Other slang we use: A *jigger* is used by a lot of people. It
means a lookout, someone that you put on the point that
notifies you in case the police are approaching. Not so much
the police, because you're not so much worried about them—
it's the old person out for an evening's stroll or straggling
along in the street, someone just wandering around, they're
the ones who give you the trouble. The police catch very few
people. They always have someone who calls and tells them
somebody's in the building. The chances of them catching
you are outlandish if someone doesn't inform them. So you
don't actually worry about the police—it's just the person
strolling down by the store who hears the noise.

And then there is *punch* or *punching*. That is when you
knock the numbered dial off. There's a pin in there, and that
pin holds the tumblers in position. You knock the pin and
the tumblers fall down and the door will open. One safe in
Harlingen, Texas, a Trans-Texas Airline office: I went in
and out in about four minutes. If a safe is punchable, then
it's very easy. Nowadays they weld a plate in the back where
you can't punch that pin through the metal, and the pin
mushrooms on you and blocks the tumblers.

Peel—that means just what it says. You open them like a
can of sardines without a key. You just get at the corner and
whip it. You need a big cold chisel. You put the cold chisel
up into the first layer of the door. Now a safe door is thick,
but it's not all iron; it's hollow, and inside is asbestos fire-

proofing and cement and other stuff. It has just a small layer of steel—about one-quarter inch—on the outside. That depends on the price of the safe and the year it was made. I think L. C. Hall is the best single-door safe ever made; they were made in Cincinnati, and they stopped making them about fifty or sixty years ago. Every time I run into one it's hell. Anyway, about the safe: if you just get into that first little ridge where that front plate is, then you drive your bar or chisel in there and just pry it loose. Then you get your jimmy-bar in there and you just rip either the weld or the rivets that are in there. Once you get a start, it's just a matter of minutes. It's getting the start that's the problem. I've tried as high as ten hours to get a start on a safe and never did get it.

GLOSSARY

aggey: hoe or other hand-held farm implement.

beef: argument, criminal charge, arrest, fight (*fade the beef,* *q. v.*).

bitch: life sentence as a habitual criminal.

boosting: shoplifting. Sam says, "To me, boosting is what you can pick up with somebody watching you, or as soon as they blink their eyes, you cover something and go on out. But whenever you start carrying out a stereo or something like that, I would consider that just stealing."

boss: prison guard.

box: safe.

bring: force. "I can't be brought" = "I can't be forced to do anything I don't want to do."

buck: inmate sit-down strike.

bust: arrest.

c. c.: concurrent sentence. Refers to multiple sentences served at the same time. A five-year sentence for breaking and entering and a ten-year sentence for theft served c.c. would be ten years total sentence; if not c.c., the sentence would be cumulative, in this instance a total of fifteen years.

can't get there: cannot do something.

card mechanic: a person skilled in deceptive manipulations with playing cards, a card cheat.

carry: bring someone somewhere, be in charge of someone or some group. "The police carried me to the airport" = "The police drove me to the airport." "The sergeant who carried the squad . . ." = "The sergeant in charge of the squad . . ."

character: See Chapter III for Sam's extensive discussion of this term.

Christmas Tree: Tuinal (Lilly brand name for amobarbital sodium and secobarbital sodium).

cock: vagina.

come down: come to prison.

cop out: inform, usually on oneself.

country: In Texas and much of the Southwest this word means area, not a national political entity. The size of the area must be inferred from the context. "We worked the country around San Antonio" = "We burglarized in towns in the San Antonio area," and "This country down here" = Texas, or the entire Southwest.

detainer: a request from federal authorities or law enforcement agencies in counties or states other than the one of conviction for custody of the prisoner immediately on expiration of his sentence or release from jail, usually for prosecution on another charge. Some parole agencies will not grant parole to an inmate who has holds filed on him by other jurisdictions, so some law enforcement agencies use the detainer merely to force an inmate to serve his full sentence somewhere else.

    Since parole is a privilege, not a right, this kind of inequity is not open to any kind of appeal. The filing agency often does not have enough evidence to go to trial or even to get an indictment, and it frequently drops the hold or detainer as soon as the prisoner is released after serving his full sentence. Same as *hold.*

ding: A manuscript by another thief described a ding as "anyone outside the group of good fellows who is too square or too stupid to be accepted. The good fellows haven't any real reason for not liking him; he isn't a fink or a punk. He's just a ding." In the North, the term is *dingbat,* which in hobo slang was a beggar or, as Nels Anderson puts it in *The Hobo,* "the dregs of vagrantdom." [31]

drive up: arrive.

fade the beef: handle the argument, deal with the arrest.

fall: arrest.

fall partner: person with whom one has been arrested. Often the term is used by thieves who have done time to mean anyone with whom one is stealing, even though the two have never been arrested together.

file: to press formal criminal charges against someone.

five-spot: five-year sentence.

flat-time: actual time served in prison, sentence served without parole.

floor keyster: safe (see Sam's discussion above) hidden in the floor.

football: Dilaudid (Knoll Pharmaceutical Company brand name for hydromorphone).

free world: outside prison.

free-world punk: inmate who was acting-out homosexual outside prison.

gear: Sam says: "Characters or people who are more or less in the underworld, they believe that everybody is gear for something. That's because *they* believe that everybody else is. Some people are gear for clothes, some people for girls, some for real weird dates with a gal—they might be gear for any number of things. Maybe airplanes, maybe fishing. I know a millionaire who is gear for dominoes; he'll play dominoes and his secretary comes down there to get his stuff signed right at the domino table—but he's got so much money that it doesn't make any difference anymore. I know a guy that's a big television executive that's a gear for playing pool. He's got three pool tables in his house, and you can go over there any time of day or night if you've got a good pool game and he'll get up and open up the house to let you play just so he can watch you. In other words, a gear is anybody that is geared up for something, which we know—as a character you think—everybody is. But *primarily* a gear is a queer, a homosexual of some kind. It is because somebody goes for something that makes him a gear. You might be a gear for ice cream, but you're geared because you like ice cream more than you should."

gel: Sam says: "Gelatin is dynamite we blow safes with."

get cock: get laid.

girls: homosexuals, especially in prison.

go down: go to prison; perform fellatio or cunnilingus.

good time: reduction of sentence at the beginning on the expectation of good behavior; rather than getting time off for having been a "good convict" (as in the movies), the practice is to take away all or part of the reduction for misconduct.

harness bull: uniformed policeman.

high play: ostentatious spending to impress someone; may be used in verb form—"I high played her . . ."

hog: force someone to do something against his will; tough guy (derives from *tush hog*).

hold: detainer, q. v.

jackleg lawyer: bad or small-town lawyer. The term derives from *jackleg preacher,* one who is self-ordained.

jam-up: first-rate, excellent.

jigger: a lookout posted to watch for police or guards; may be used in verb form—"He jiggered . . ."

Jimmy bar: see Sam's comments above.

job: inmates who have any work assignment other than working the fields as part of the line force. Most job assignments draw *two-for-one* (*q. v.*) time.

john: prostitute's customer.

joint: for Sam, almost always a bar; the term also means paraphernalia for injecting narcotics, a penis, a prison.

Kelsey's nuts: Sam says: "The first time I heard this I was playing basketball at the YMCA in Corpus and a boy on the other team told me, 'You are all as dead as Kelsey's nuts.' It means you're all locked up, all set. Say a guy calls you long distance and says, 'Now I want you to come on up to Chicago, I've got Kelsey's nuts up here,' that means that he's got a safe that's an absolute cinch. All you have to do is walk in and say hello, and it'll give you its money. Kelsey's nuts is absolute, the best in the world, a cinch, a mortal cinch, it's already taken care of."

keyster: see Sam's comments above.

lay-in: doctor's permission for inmate to stay in his cell and not go to work on any particular day. The verb form is "He layed him in . . ."

line: inmate groups working on the various field crops.

loop-scoop: steal quickly.

M.O.: *modus operandi*—police term for a criminal's usual pattern of work.

made: got inside, succeeded. "We made that safe" = "We got inside that safe"; "We made that supermarket" = "We robbed that supermarket"; "I made a meet" = "I kept an appointment"; "I made that girl" = "I had sexual relations with her."

man's man: informer, one who works for the Man.

mark: someone easy to beat, a sucker.

natural punk: free-world homosexual.

old lady: Sam says: "Old lady could be a girl or a woman or a ninety-year-old woman, just whoever you happen to be associated with or living with at the time."

on the square: honestly, truthfully.

peel: see Sam's comments above.

penitentiary punk: catamite or fellator who is heterosexual in the free world, homosexual in prison.

picket: guard tower outside prison buildings; hallway observation cage used by guards to watch inmates.

pull up: stop doing something. When used in reference to a person, it carries the sense of *former, e.g.,* "pulled-up whore" = "woman who used to be a prostitute."

punch: see Sam's comments above.

punk: catamite, usually, but sometimes any covert homosexual.

punk tank: cellblock in which homosexuals and sex offenders are segregated from the rest of the prison population.

put the bitch on you: file charges against a criminal as a habitual criminal.

put your business on the streets: talk too much about personal matters.

queen: free-world homosexual, usually one with exaggerated feminine characteristics.

rapo: rapist; sometimes the term is used for any sex offender.

rapped: convicted, blamed.

redbird: Seconal Sodium (Lilly brand name for secobarbital sodium).

rum: ding, q.v. One thief defined a ding as "a failure, a flop, a total bust."

rumble: encounter with the law, not necessarily one resulting in an arrest; interpersonal difficulty.

score: whatever a particular criminal operation brings: a safe score is what is taken out of one safe, a check score is the total income from checks passed in one operation; obtain

("I scored for a whore"). The term is also used to mean seduce or have intercourse with, but the verb form, at least in Texas character vocabulary, is much rarer than the noun.

scrip: coupons issued to inmates for purchases in the prison commissary; doctors' drug prescriptions.

shakedown: search of the person or a location.

shitter: solitary confinement cells.

shoot her out: train for some profession; a pimp shooting out a girl is getting her into his stable.

snap: realize suddenly.

snitch: (v.) inform, (n.) informer.

sorry: despicable, pitiful.

square: (v.) straighten out, fix, *e.g.,* "I squared the beef by paying off" = "I got them to drop the complaint by paying off." (n.) For a character, it is anyone who is not a character; for a heroin addict, anyone not addicted to heroin and therefore out of the drug subculture. The specific meaning of the noun depends on the role definition of the speaker, but it always means "not one of us, someone without our savvy."

square john: anyone not a character, male or female; a law-abiding person.

stash: hiding place.

stone: an intensifier. "Stone trick" = someone who is very much a sucker (see *trick* below); "stone square" = someone who is very square.

switch: situation with two alternatives such that whichever alternative the actor chooses, he will be harmed or in trouble.

tank: large dormitory room in prison.

tin can: cheap safe made of thin metal.

tool law: law making it a felony to possess or transport burglary tools.

tops: dice spotted so there are no sevens.

trick: Sam says: "A whore considers a trick a man that pays her money. 'Trick' is not flattery; you're not flattering anybody when you're using that word, although you're not slamming them either. A trick is simply somebody that they make their living off of, and they have a certain respect for them, because if he's got enough money to pay a girl what she usually gets, especially if it's a good trick, then he's pretty capable of making money, and you can't knock people like that. But when you use the word for a character who is being a trick, then he is really low, he is way out. If he's going to pay, he's going for his own game. A lot of pimps trick girls, other people's whores, and pay them. But a real character—man, for them to be a trick is way out. For a square john to be a trick, that's all right.

"And you can be a trick for anything: going up against a pair of *tops* (*q. v.*) shooting dice, or letting some idiot beat you for something. Being a trick means getting beat. Actually costing you money. If you let a car salesman make a trick out of you, what happened is that you didn't pay him what the car was worth, you paid him more. A trick is anything that costs you money when it shouldn't. But, as I say, a free-world trick or a square trick, you don't think down on them because that's what they're supposed to be."

trim: (n) female pubic hair; (v) fuck.

turn: sell (stolen goods).

turn a trick: prostitute having sexual relations with a customer.

turn out: to be introduced to or assume a particular role or trade. "Turn out as a whore" = "become a whore"; "penitentiary turnout" = "someone who became a punk while in prison." One may be in the life and turn out as something else, like Sam, who was for years a check writer, then turned out as a safe-cracker.

tush hog: someone who is easily angered; tough guy.

two-for-one: inmates with *jobs* (*q. v.*) and trusties are credited with two days for each day served; if a man has a six-year sentence and spends all of it on a two-for-one job, and is released without parole, he serves actual time of three years. If his crime requires that half the sentence be served before he can be considered for parole, a period of eighteen months on two-for-one brings him to that three-year minimum date. Men in the *line* (*q.v.*) receive straight time, one-for-one.

yellowjacket: Nembutal Sodium (Abbott brand name for sodium pentobarbital).

NOTES

THE CONTEXT

1. *The Professional Thief*, annotated and interpreted by Edwin H. Sutherland (Chicago, 1937), p. vi.

2. Sam reversed what seems to be the usual career pattern: after a number of arrests, safe-crackers frequently turn to checks. As Sam points out, penalties for checks are much lighter than those for burglary, and police don't work as hard catching an individual check writer—there are too many of them around. And safes are less profitable than they once were; few important business transactions put anything but pieces of paper in a firm's safe—cash is rarer than it was. Jack Heard said, after reading the manuscript, that he was convinced that if Sam became a working criminal again, he would go back to checks rather than safes; he felt this was not for the reasons given above only, but also because he sees Sam's obvious con-man orientation as making checks more natural to him. I agree.

3. Some safe-crackers live an otherwise "normal" middle-class life: suburban house, children in good schools, golf on Saturday—the whole program. Jack Heard discussed one such thief with me, a man who had operated for fifteen years without a conviction. The main reason he lasted so long was that he never did associate with anyone who would give police cause to suspect him of anything. His neighbors thought he was a businessman, and in a way I suppose he was. Heard wrote about Sam: "There is no doubt in my mind that this individual has a complete working knowledge of the operation of check writing and safecracking. I think the way he explains his method of operation is basically truthful. He is a full-fledged character. But I have known many safe-crackers and good thieves who did not follow this pattern. . . . When you ask him, 'What do you do with your money?' his answer is direct: 'I party, I spend it on travel.' A business-type safe man will usually live a quiet life on the side, probably have a family or live with his people and put the money away, and will lay low for as long as a year until the heat is off."

4. For a discussion of tripartite inmate society, see John Irwin and Donald Cressey, "Thieves, Convicts and the Inmate Culture," in *The Other Side: Perspectives on Deviance*, ed. by Howard S. Becker (New York, 1964), pp. 225-245. To their trichotomy of thief, noncriminal, and convict, one might add a delinquent category—*i.e.*, those offenders lacking the *élan* of the professionals but having their referents in the free world. At certain times there is a fifth group, the political prisoners (civil rights demonstrators, conscientious objectors, political demonstra-

tors, etc.), who take on an anomalous position in the convict society. For a discussion of roles, argot, etc., see Peter G. Garabedian, "Social Roles in a Correctional Institution," *Journal of Criminal Law, Criminology and Police Science,* 55:3 (September 1964), 338-347. For an excellent discussion of the convict subculture, see John C. Watkins, "The Modification of the Subcultures in a Correctional Institution," *Proceedings of the Ninety-Fourth Annual Congress of Correction of the American Correctional Association* (Washington, D.C., 1964), pp. 161-171. For brief discussions of prisons as folk communities, see my articles, "Prison Folklore," *Journal of American Folklore,* 78:310 (October-December 1965), 317-329; and "Prison Nicknames," *Western Folklore,* XXVI:1 (January 1967), 48-54. For the theory of total institutions as communities, see Erving Goffman, *Asylums* (New York, 1961). See also Donald Clemmer, *The Prison Community* (New York, 1958); Gresham Sykes, *The Society of Captives* (Princeton, 1958); Donald Cressey, ed., *The Prison: Studies in Institutional Organization and Change* (New York, 1961); Hugh J. Klare, *Anatomy of Prison* (Baltimore, 1960); and Daniel Glaser, *The Effectiveness of a Prison and Parole System* (Indianapolis, 1964).

5. (Washington, D.C., 1967), p. 98.

6. Erving Goffman, *Stigma* (Englewood Cliffs, 1963), pp. 23-24.

7. Sutherland's thief wouldn't admit to this: "It is sometimes said that many thieves, especially women, love to steal. Some thieves who have been exhibitionists and have written their life-histories describe stealing as though it were all very thrilling. They do this to make the story dramatic enough to sell to a publisher. What the hell could anyone find to like about stealing, working hard all the time, always being likely to land in the can, paying over to the coppers and the fixer everything he gets? Writers of detective stories who have never stolen a quarter and have never been deprived of their liberty for an hour are the only ones who can perceive any glamor or pleasure in grifting. The eyesight of the professional thief has not been developed sufficiently to see any pleasure in it. A better description of the professional thief is that he seeks money, not thrills"(*Sutherland,* pp. 140-141). Sutherland himself points out that not all thieves agree with his man (p.141n-142n), and I suspect that among moderately and very successful thieves we would find a majority who do find the thrills and dangers at least partially satisfying.

8. Through this section I have drawn, without quotation marks, from two articles of mine: "Who Goes to Prison?" *Atlantic Monthly,* 217:1 (January 1966), 52-57; and "Prison Folklore," pp. 317-325. The discussion of tripartite culture is partially based on the article by John Irwin and Donald Cressey, "Thieves, Convicts and the Inmate Culture," cited in note 4.

9. Irwin and Cressey, p. 233.

10. Irwin and Cressey, p. 236.
11. For a discussion of the Code in an Illinois penitentiary, see Clemmer, pp. 152-164.
12. Goffman, *Asylums: Essays on the Social Situation of Patients and other Inmates,* p. 61.
13. "The notions of 'active' and 'passive' in homosexual relationships are more obscuring of the actual conditions of the behavior than they are enlightening. The psychiatrist Irvin Bieber has suggested the words 'insertor' and 'insertee' be substituted for active and passive, since these latter words assume that role behavior in sexual act has major meaning in psychological personality terms." John H. Gagnon and William Simon, "The Social Meaning of Prison Homosexuality," *Federal Probation,* XXXII:1 (March 1968), p. 25n.
14. Gagnon and Simon, p. 14.
15. "It is obvious that lifetime patterns of sexual behavior are greatly affected by the experiences of adolescence, not only because they are the initial experiences, but because they occur during the age of greatest activity and during the time of the maximum physical capacity of the male. This is the period in which the boy's abilities to make social adjustments, to develop any sort of socio-sexual contact, and to solve the issues of a heterosexual-homosexual balance, are most involved. Since younger boys have not acquired all of the social traditions and taboos on sex, they are more impressionable, more liable to react *de novo* to any and every situation that they meet. If these adolescent years are spent in an institution where there is little or no opportunity for the boy to develop his individuality, where there is essentially no privacy at any time in the day, and where all his companions are other males, his sexual life is very likely to become permanently stamped with the institutional pattern. Long-time confinement for a younger male is much more significant than a similar period of confinement for an older adult." Alfred C. Kinsey, Wardell B. Pomeroy, Clyde E. Martin, *Sexual Behavior in the Human Male* (Philadelphia, 1948), p. 224.
16. Gagnon and Simon, p. 26.
17. Gagnon and Simon, pp. 23-24. They also note that "male prison populations are not random selections from the larger society and do not reflect the usual distributions of the population in terms of education, income, ethnicity, occupation, social class, and general life style. The men who make up the bulk of the imprisoned populations tend to be drawn from deprived sections of the society or from families embedded in what we have now come to call the culture of poverty. As a consequence, the sexual experiences of these men and the meaning that sex has for them differs in significant ways from other portions of the population that are less likely to be imprisoned," p. 24.
18. Kinsey, Pomeroy, and Martin, p. 210. It should be noted that sexual cues are not totally absent, for the queens certainly supply some, and

in almost every prison there is at least one covert artist who spends a portion of his time grinding out eight-page pornographic pamphlets.

19. Gagnon and Simon, p. 28.

20. Gagnon and Simon, p. 27.

21. Or, perhaps watch the national television orgy following a major assassination.

22. Martin Mayer, *The Lawyers* (New York, 1967), p. 158.

23. Mayer, pp. 158-159.

24. Task-Force Report: *The Courts,* The President's Commission on Law Enforcement and Administration of Justice (Washington, D.C., 1967), pp. 9-10.

25. *The Courts,* pp. 11-12.

26. *The Courts,* p. 109.

27. *The Courts,* p. 109n.

28. Alexander Berkman, *Prison Memoirs of an Anarchist* (New York, 1913), p. 199.

29. Clemmer, p. 89.

30. *Keyster stash* is a term used by addicts to refer to narcotics hidden in the rectum to escape detection in a search. In the North, *keyster* is used by some people to mean *any* safe.

31. (Chicago, 1961), p. 101.

1 · The Life

□ □ □

THIS is when we were cracking safes.

I called my lawyer and had him meet me down in the garage of his office building. He came down to the garage and I had a couple of thermos bottles of coffee and we sat there and had a cup of coffee and I told him where we were planning on working. Of course he knew that if we found something along the way, we would probably work it too.

At this time we're giving him $500. Two hundred fifty dollar a week, $500 every two weeks. This $500 was to make any bonds. Fees, if we had to go to court later, that was all extra. The $500 was if we got busted, for him to get there and keep us from getting killed.[1]

You know, they got a law that they can't whip a confession out of you; they won't accept it in court anymore, it has to be given with counsel present. Well, son, when they got confessions in the past, it didn't make any difference how they got them: they were good. They never overruled one in the state of Texas.

But, anyway, that was the purpose of that visit.

We went off on this beef, on this job, made three or four places, and got to running. We checked into a motel, and I called into Corpus and told him where we were working. We looked around and decided that we wanted to get it the next day. We had heard about it, and we had just been putting it off.

It was in Harlingen, Texas; it's a big drugstore, right in town. We went by and looked at it, and it had a regular old wooden housedoor! I mean, you can take anything—you can take a nail or a pocketknife or a pair of nail clips or anything to open it. It's just one of them old spring locks; all you do is barely get something in there and you pull. It's absolutely nothing. I'd rather not have a door.

We saw it and it looked real good. We went in and looked, and the safe was sitting back in the office by itself, so we decided we'd go ahead and make it. And there was a big feed store there we'd heard was good, and we wanted to make that too.

First we went to the feed store and made it, but someone else had made it the night before and there was just a busted safe sitting there.

We went back to the drugstore and made it. Coming out, the police ran up on us. The trunk of the car was open and we were putting the tools and money and dope [2] in the back, and so I just told the chief of police—he was in that police car—"Goodnight, sir." Then we got in our car and we drive off.

That chief lost his job on account of it. He testified at my trial and they busted him to a patrolman.

We headed back to Corpus. We knew that he had got our license number. And we had been in a hurry and didn't change license plates, so we knew there was going to be some heat on the car. He had followed us a little ways, and we knew he got our license and everything. We took off down the highway and we knew he would go back and check that drugstore—it's the only thing of value there. When he did, then we cut and went cross-country, got off the main highway.

We had a real good stealing car that we had bought. A

De Soto. It was a 1957 De Soto and we had brand new tires on it, new engine, everything. It was equipped for that, nothing else. It was kind of a big car and yet it's kind of a small car, and people can't recognize De Sotos. They call them Chevrolets and Fords and Cadillacs and everything, because people just don't know a De Soto. And we got it in this neutral color, an old green color, with black tires, and we had it all fixed up with a police radio in it.

We took off running about 120. We beat the roadblocks back to Corpus. I called there and told these girls—we had a couple of whores there—to clean up the house and get everything out that wasn't bought and paid for, anything that was taken out of a burglary.

You know, we had a lot of little old stuff that we took. I wanted to get it out of there just to be sure. Actually, if they found it, they couldn't make a case on it because it was stuff that all drugstores handle and you could have bought it anywhere. So we got in to the place and I told my fall partner, "Let's go, man, everything's packed."

He said, "I don't want to go. They can't do anything to us."

I said, "They goddamn sure can. If the Rangers get you, they're going to get a confession."

He said, "I can fade 'em." [3] He's supposed to be a hog, you know.

I told him, "Well, I'll tell you what: I can't. Now you do what you want, but I'm leaving. If you want to stay here and fade the beef, as soon as you get picked up, get the people upstairs to let me know and I'll get the lawyers on it and try to make your bond. But don't forget now, when the Rangers get you, they're gonna take you off and hide you. It's liable to be a week before the lawyers can find you."

He said, "Okay."

Down here, the Rangers are all the law. They can just pack you up, put you in a car, carry you from town to town, from city to city, just anywhere they want to carry you, and nobody questions it. [4]

I went and checked into a hotel. This girl I had at my

place, I left her at the apartment too. If they're going to stay, she might as well stay there and answer that phone and make some money.

When I left the house, I took about eight or nine hundred dollars in change we just hadn't gotten time to get rid of. A lot of times, when I first started, I wouldn't even take the change out of a safe, but then you take it out and it's a couple of hundred here, three or four hundred there, and after you make seven or eight safes, you've got a lot of change. So I made a deal down at the bank. I'd send this girl down there, and they thought I was a coin collector, and she could just take it into the bank with no questions asked. At first I let her take it and get more change in return; then after that was over a couple of times, then we told them I had another outlet where I was getting change, and she just put it in the bank and got cash for it. This was just some of that change that had piled up. We was stealing every night, man; we was busting safes *every* night.

I went to the hotel and scored for another whore. I was walking down the hall after I got in there, and as soon as I saw her, I knew she was a whore. So I told her, "Boy, if I wasn't so tired, I'd buy some pussy."

She said, "Would a drink of Scotch wake you up?"

I told her, "Yeah." So she went down and got a bottle, and we got to bullshitting and everything, and about two hours later I had all her money; I had her clothes in my car and everything. She was a hell of a broad; she was a beautiful girl, man.

Anyway, we went on and a friend called me at the hotel the following day and told me the Rangers had busted in and arrested all of them. I got the lawyers working on it, and they couldn't find them. Of course they knew the Rangers had them, but they still couldn't find them.

I had another lawyer I used sometimes. When ————— couldn't get them out or even find them, I went to Roy Scott. He lives in a real nice motel and he's an old bachelor. He's dead now. Got a world of money.[5] I went down to his motel and I asked him what the hell I could do. He told me, "I'm gonna have him in court at nine o'clock in the morning. They promised to produce him at nine."

I said, "Well, how much is the bond going to be? I'm going to go ahead and pay it and get it over with."

He said, "I don't know." It ended up with me giving him $2,500 down. At first he just wanted to make the bond and I'd pay him later on, but I said, "No, I want to leave some of it now so I won't have that big old bill." I only gave him $2,500.

This girl I got at the hotel had $900. I got it from her, made out a deposit slip, and sent it to my bank.

Roy Scott, he told me, "The best thing for you to do is get out of town."

I told him, "Well, all right."

I was going to go to Houston with this girl. She's got an apartment at the A———— Hotel [6] in Houston, and that's a good apartment, a $600- or $700-a-week spot. When I told Roy, he said, "That's the best thing for you to do, go with that girl to Houston. You call me every day and we'll keep in touch." I told him what name I was going to register under in the hotel in Houston and to be sure and call me whenever anything comes up.

I went out to my stash in the country where I had some narcotics and dug me up a big bunch of Dilaudid; then I went back to the hotel and got that girl. We started out of town going to the airport and the police arrested me.

First time in my life I've ever been stopped by a policeman and just arrested! They took me down there on an old warrant that was about forty years outdated. But I thought it was this Harlingen deal, that somebody had cracked, because they had some gals with them and all of them are dope fiends.[7] I figured somebody had cracked.

Well, it was just this old deal. I got them to call this district attorney, and the district attorney said, "Yeah, that case has been dropped." So the police put me in a police car and *carried* me to the airport and put me on the airplane.

While I was on the way to Houston, the Rangers had teletyped Corpus and said to pick me up. Corpus teletyped back and said that the Rangers had made a mistake, that the Sam they had in Corpus was a check man and wouldn't steal anything. So the Rangers thought that maybe they got the wrong one. They went back in and requizzed those other people. They think they've been given a bum steer.

In the meantime I got off the plane in Houston. Well, I've got this broad with me and, like I said, she's a whore. This old boy that arrested me in Corpus, he's the chief of the check detail. He knows me real well, he knows my family real well. So he just put two and two together and figured that where I probably was was with that girl at her hotel.

They arrested me there.

What had happened was, those people signed statements on me down at Palacios, which is where the Rangers had them. When they arrested me, they took me to Ranger head-quarters and carried me on down to Bay City and on down to Palacios. When I got to Palacios, I hadn't told them anything. They had offered me all kinds of deals to sign a statement, and I wouldn't do it.

I remember when they was strumming my head, the sheriff there said, "Cut it out, you can't do that here," and I thought I was off the hook, but then he said, "Cut it out; if you have to do that, take him out in the country and do it."

Man, the last thing in the world I wanted at that moment was that nice country air.

When I finally got there to Palacios, there's all my nar-cotics and the tools and all this stuff just sitting there.

And there's my fall partner.

I walked over to the side where he was. My hunting knife was on the table. I was going to kill him. I was so mad, you know.

When I got right next to him, he said to me, "Don't worry about anything. I didn't sign any statements on anybody but just me and you."

Man, I just slumped. I didn't know what to do.

They whipped this girl that I had, the one that I left at the apartment with them.

There was a boy in the next cell to me. He had nothing to

do with our case; he was there on a deal of his own. He told me his name through the ventilator and he asked me who I was. I told him and he said, "Man, you're in a world of trouble."

I said, "What's the matter?"

"Your fall partner's been signing statements against you all day in Corpus. They're carrying you down there for a lie detector test."

"Yeah," I told him. "I figured that. What about the girl?"

"She your old lady?"

"Yeah."

He said, "Man, she's something else. They worked that girl just unmercifully, and she wouldn't admit she knew you."

Remember, I didn't leave anything at the apartment. I took all my clothes and everything I owned with me when I left, just so they couldn't put me there. And they couldn't, not until those people told them.

Anyway, that gal never did admit that she knew me. A pretty good girl. They whipped her so bad and messed with her so bad that as soon as she got out of jail, her family checked her into a hospital. She came from a pretty wealthy family. She almost died; she had a mental collapse. She was in terrible shape because they mistreated her so bad. A lot of girls can't stand that.[8]

But she did not tell them.

My father was an oilman; he died of a heart attack when he was about thirty-nine. He was moving a drilling rig out of the Valley when he died at McAllen. He was just on the verge of really doing great. Mother kept an interest in the company, and since that time, my uncle, who was my father's partner, has become a multimillionaire. My own family has a little money. We're not wealthy or anything, but they live well, they drive new automobiles, they have nice bank accounts, they take nice vacations, and they give a little to charities. Upper middle class. But still and all, they always have my uncle there with his money and power, and my family is so close that they can feed off his reputation and money. If they want to go to the bank and borrow money, they're so well known that there's never any questions asked or anything.

Why did you turn out?

Why did I turn out stealing? Maybe I couldn't meet their standards. I don't know, I have no idea. I can tell you *how*, though.

My uncle had the largest gambling casino in the state of Louisiana. He owned a grove right across the river from Morris, Texas. One time he had twenty crap tables under one roof. That's not counting the slot machines—he had seven or eight hundred of those. He had a big operation. Well, I started hanging around the pool hall when I was in high school, and I became real good. I got to shooting pool for money, and I could make more money shooting pool than I could working,[9] and yet I could play around, too. I got to hanging around that pool hall, and my mother and them, they snapped to what I was doing. One day my aunt came down to the pool hall with my clothes packed. She says, "You want to be a goddamned gambler, well, I'm going to send you where there's some money." So she put me on an airplane and sent me to my uncle's. I got down there and I started out shilling and I became a crap dealer. About that time I started to get drafted, so I joined the Air Force.

When I got in the Air Force, my family still hadn't given up on me. I could get anything I wanted, like new automobiles and clothes. I could just write and get $500, $600 whenever I wanted to. I stayed in the Air Force about three years, and then I married a square-john girl and had a couple of kids by her, two daughters. We split up in '56, and neither one of us has ever remarried.

Anyway, when I got out of the service, I came back and my uncle gave me a working interest in the company. I don't know, man, I didn't get along with my wife too good, I don't know why. She was real nice—well, not *real* nice-looking, but she was pretty nice-looking. I have a picture of her over there. We just didn't hit it off, so one day I just told her, "That's it." I packed her stuff and sent her home.[10] I told my uncle to take that drilling rig and stick it in his ass, and just walked off.

I started bumming around the country, playing poker and shooting dice, whatever I could find to do, and I got to living real high. At first I was real lucky; everything turned to money. Then I went to Las Vegas and I stayed for about six months, then went on to California and I bummed around out there.

Then I came back and I just got into the check racket.

Every time I'd get low on money, I'd just go and write a check. Especially when I was gambling. I'd hear there's a poker game somewhere and I'd need $500 table stakes, so I'd just go write me a couple of $500 checks somewhere for just that purpose and sign my own name. Then I'd go to the poker game and I'd beat the checks to the bank with the winnings. A few times I didn't beat the checks and I would get called on the carpet about it. And I'd pay them off. People want the money; they don't care about anything else on a check. They just want their money.

So I got to thinking: "Hell, man, Shit. Why should I pay them that $500 back, or even $100, whatever it might be? Why don't I sign somebody else's name, get the money, go play poker with it, and then I make two scores?"

That's the way I got into the check detail, the check racket.

Later on, I did time on checks.

The only reason I did time is because they threw me in an isolation cell and kept me eighteen days without ever getting to a phone or seeing a lawyer or anything and they already had me indicted and damn near convicted before I could ever do anything. If I could have gotten to a phone, I wouldn't have been in jail five minutes and I'd never come to the penitentiary.

Then, when I came down here to prison the first time, I heard so much about safes. When I got out, I was bumming around, gambling around, and finally I got off in a trap where I owed a bunch of money, and I decided I'd put some of what I'd learned in prison and the contacts I'd made there to some use.

You just find somebody that's busting safes if you want

to learn it and you need the money. What happened to me was I was drove up and I needed a lot of money. It got so I didn't have any place to gamble and I didn't have any bank roll to gamble with. I had just gotten out of jail on that two-year deal and I called a friend of mine and told him I needed to find somebody to make some money with. He asked me how I wanted to make it and I told him I didn't give a shit, any way is all right.

He told me about this boy who was in town from Fort Worth and he'd known him a long time, knew one of his uncles, and the boy was all right. So we made a meet and messed around together a couple of weeks I guess. And things still hadn't gotten any better. He loaned me five or six hundred dollars during that time. So whenever he got ready to go, well, I was ready too. I owed him that money and I wanted to pay off.

And I got in a big switch. I wasn't even involved in it, but I got rapped for it and I had to pay the bill. There was a big party at a motel and they filed charges on me. But I was just *at* the party. They knew they'd never get the money any other way than by trapping me. I could have gone to court and beat it, but making bonds and paying those lawyer fees— the lawyer wanted $5,500 to defend me—it just wasn't worth it. It's easier to pay it off and forget about it, mark it up to experience, and the next time I see the people, just take a pistol and get my money back. But I never did see them. It was just one of those deals.

So we started out.

I guess I'm kind of funny. Whenever I start stealing, boy, I dig a hell of a charge out of it. I dig a fantastic charge! [11] At night, whenever we'd go out, if we'd got some places cased out, before we made the first one, I'm scared, I'm scared to death. But after I get in there and make the first one, all my fear leaves and I get maybe too careless. Then I think I'm invincible, and I'd walk up in broad daylight if I wanted to do something.

But he wasn't that way. It took them about sixteen years to ever bust him. And that is a fantastic run of luck those sixteen years. The thing about it is, they *knew* that he was a safe man. They had his M.O., everything, and whenever he'd bust a safe, they'd know. But he's a *lucky* guy.

For instance, we went up to San Marcos, Texas, and they have an aquashow, an underwater thing. We went in and the guy has a tough safe, but he forgot to put the money bag in the safe. He'd carried it into his office and left it there beside the safe and gone out. He'd gotten busy and just left. So when we went in, we didn't have to touch the safe, the money was already out. That's just this guy's luck.

And a supermarket in Beeville. We went in there and I just reached over and flipped it and it was on daylock. We just opened the safe, took the money, and walked out. In there about thirty seconds. But that's this guy's luck, you know.[12]

Then he and I split up. He got hold of this Mexican whore and her old man got after him, so it got down to where it's going to be a killing and he just took the gal and left. Another boy, a kind of friend of both of ours, he cut in and we had been working a threesome for a while, so when Jack left, this other boy, my fall partner, we worked together. We kept going until we got busted on this case. We never implicated Jack in any way, and he continued until about a year and a half ago, when he got filed on in Fort Worth. He had three or four burglary cases up there, a couple of supermarkets I think.

Jack showed me a lot, but you have to remember that when you're learning, you're in a building with the police maybe breathing down your neck and you're up tight and you're trying to get the money, and so you haven't got time for a man to say, "Now you see this tumbler? When you do this, then over here something happens." You haven't got time for all that. You just have to stand there and watch him. You can't talk, it's all too fast. You see what he does and what it looks like; then after you get home, you say, "What did you do here?" And he would draw you some diagrams and you could learn something.

I guess that's about the way I got into it. It seemed like

the most natural thing in the world. It seemed like that's what I'm supposed to be.

I'm sure that deep down I have a fear of failure, and none of my family is a failure.[13]

Safes are good. You know, you can't knock a safe, man. If you can find the place that's got the money, if you've got somebody that can spot it for you, it is *good*. There's no problem making the safe, there's no problem at all. The problem is to find the safe that has the money in it. As far as getting into the safe, anybody can get in. Hell, children get into them all the time; twelve- and thirteen-year-old kids, they bust safes. There's no problem beating a safe, the only problem is finding the one with the money in it.

But with a check, the money is already there, you know it's there, you just have to go in. You don't get as much at a time, but at the end of the day you've got a lot more money.

Something else: they don't get *mad* at you for checks. I've never even been touched; I've never been forced to sign a confession with checks. The police take the attitude that if people are crazy enough to give money for a piece of paper, then they ought to be beat.[14] And they just do not worry about check writers because they are too numerous. Hell, half the housewives, they're always floating bad checks.[15]

You'd be surprised how long it takes them to detect a bad check. First thing they'll do when they see there's something wrong, they'll try to call you and contact you, and they'll try to do everything they can. There's a state law here that they have to call and contact you and give you ten days to pick up the checks before they can file on them. And that gives you all that added time. Something else: if you write a check on one side of town and the bank is on the other, it takes about a week for the check to get to the bank and back. So actually you got a whole week there you can write checks in.

If you're going to write checks on the south side of San Antonio, you'll put them from a north side state bank. And in San Antonio it takes ten days to get from one side of town to the other because it has to go through the federal clearinghouse, so you have all that added time. So whenever I go into San Antonio and I write checks, I go ahead and write checks for about a week, every night for a week. And that makes it real nice.

The biggest score I ever made. I have to think back. A lot of times there were a lot of things involved in a score. Sometimes you get valuable merchandise, diamonds or a coin collection that you have to turn. But I made one $27,000 score in cash. Just the money. Just American money. There was about $700 or $800 in the money sack in the safe, and all the rest was in the pages of the ledger. As I was throwing stuff out of the safe looking, a bill fell out of one of the ledgers. So then I turned it up and held it by the binding and shook it. It looked like it was raining money.

But that was just a little old safe score. I made much bigger scores on checks. We consider a score what a particular proposition brings. If it's a check score, then it's that series of checks from that town. You go in that town, and although you might be there two weeks putting out checks, that's all just one score because it's all one operation. And if you get busted on it, it's all one bust.

Checks are the most lucrative. They're head and shoulders above anything else in the world. After a while though, it's hard to get down anymore. If you're around that part of the country, they look you up every time something comes up.

The police consider a safe burglar a dangerous person because they figure that he is armed and if he gets jumped up on, he's going to hurt somebody. Say the man in the store leaves something there and comes back for it, then—they figure—he's dead. And probably he is. More than likely, with some people. Myself, I'd just hit him in the head or make him go lay down over there. If he came to, it would probably be a godsend, because I could make him open the safe and I wouldn't have to do any work. But the police do consider you dangerous.

Do you carry a gun when you're working?

All the time. The police, they shoot at you without warning. They don't say, "Give up," or something. They just start shooting. And if they're trying to kill you, well hell. I've had some awful good friends who were handcuffed when they died. I'm not going to take that kind of a chance.[16]

Now checks, as I say, they're fabulous. You can go into a store with a pencil and a piece of paper, and that man just *gives* you his money. Just stop and think about it! There's a man behind the counter over there—he might be a college graduate, he might be worth $250,000,000—and you can walk in there with a fountain pen and an old raggedy checkbook and he is going to *give* you his money. He'll give you anything in the store. Anything that you want, he'll give it to you for that piece of paper. It's fantastic. How can they be so stupid?

I read a few years ago that in Dallas they lost $1,740,000 in hot checks in the first three months of the year and it was way *down*. They were proud of it. Safe-crackers wouldn't take that much in Dallas in twenty years.[17] But they were proud of it. Checks are fantastic, you just have no idea. I've used them to buy loads of cattle and sheep and ranches and everything in the world. Just whatever I happen to want to buy, and I turn and sell it and get out of it before they clear the check. I even bought a whorehouse in Mexico once. I sold it back to the guy about four days later, before he had time to clear the check. Got cash for the money. He thought I was taking a loss on the deal, that he really put one over on this gringo.[18]

Checks are the best if you can operate, but now, every time there's a bunch of checks put out in this part of the country, the first thing they do is take my picture over there. They don't never come to your house and roust you and take you down to be identified; all they do is just take your picture. And you can't hardly do it anymore, especially after you're known.

Which do you prefer, checks or safes?

Checks. You ask me why—primarily because there's more money in checks than there is in safes. Of course with safes you're not exposed to anybody and it's more secretive and I guess the chances of detection are a lot less, but there's just not that much money in it.[19]

I was looking in the papers the other day and there were three armed robberies in Houston. One of them was for $46, one of them was for $18, and one of them was for about $150. Hell, that's nothing for a check writer. And there were fifty-eight burglaries committed within the same twenty-four-hour period.[20] And I bet you there was not a burglary that took off over a thousand or at most fifteen hundred dollars. But with checks, hell, that's not any money for a good check man.

When you worked safes, did you always work with a partner?

I did a few by myself, but not very many. It's hard to steal by yourself. I guess you lean on each other for support, for courage and everything else. It's hard by yourself. I know people that claim they steal by themselves, but there's not too many burglars that do. A lot of armed robbers do, but if they're burglarizing, they almost always have a fall partner.

If you're getting ready to punch a safe, you need one man to hold the punch and another to hit the hammer. It's really a two-man operation. After you get it started, only one man can work at a time, but then the other can be a lookout, he can go to a window where he's got a pretty good view of the street. You have to remember that when you're working on a safe and there's always a road or street there, there's going to be people coming up and down. Most of the time when they do catch burglars, it's because somebody heard or saw them and reported it. That's the way it is, and there's nothing you can do about that.

Did you work with a partner when you were writing checks?

Sometimes. Most of the times when I did, we weren't so much out making money as we were out partying. See, damned near everybody that writes checks parties; you don't but seldom see a reserved person that writes checks, they just don't do it. Check writers are usually outgoing and ball-ing and running with the gals and so forth. Some guys will get out and they'll just get to partying, and most of the time they don't start out writing checks without they've already started partying, and then they just go on from there.

Several times I've had goals set where I wanted to make a bunch of money and I've gone out by myself and just worked. Writing checks is better by yourself. For one thing, you have nobody to consult with. Only one person can go up there and get that check cashed, another person is just dead weight; it's not like working on a safe. And then every time you write a check, you're going to have to give him half of it. So it's really not too good.

I have worked with people where we would split the expenses. When we'd get to a shopping center, they'd go their way and I'd go my way and we would meet back at the car. What they made they kept, what I made I kept, and we just shared expenses.

If you're going to have a big swindle where you're going to employ some people to cash checks for you, you're giving them a per cent, which I have done, but that's not actually a fall partner there, you have them working *for* you.

A lot of people use girls to write checks for them, but if I was just going to go out and I had a bunch of checks and I wanted to pass them, I wouldn't want anybody to help me. It slows you down. And I've had some bad experiences working that way.

Maybe if you had an old lady, someone who could drive real well and more or less follow you and pick up the merchandise and money and get it off you to keep you clean in case you did get a bust, well, that would be all right. You're splitting most of your money with them anyway. But as far as going out and getting you some stud and working with him, it wouldn't be any good at all.

How do you feel about working with drug addicts?

You mean stealing with them? It's not too bad if you're stealing close to their home, a place where their connection is.

Some people I know say they don't like to work with ad-

dicts because it's supposed to be easier for police to make them talk.

In Texas they can make *any*body talk. The Rangers can make anybody talk, so it doesn't make any difference. If they're feeling they want a confession, if they think they have to have a confession, they are going to get a confession. It goes without saying that when people sign one that is sending them to the electric chair, that there's something working to get them to sign, doesn't it? I'm not talking about sex killers and people like that, I'm talking about armed robbers, people that have been doing time all their life and they know what it's going to cost them, but they will sign the confession. Hell, you know then that they can get one from anyone.

When you're working, do you put money away in case of a fall?

I do. Most people don't.[21] Most characters, they have something driving them and they go from day to day. They're constantly pulling up. They're constantly stopping stealing. Every time you see one it's "I'm pulling up, man. Fuck all that shit. I'm gonna get a whore and let her make me a living. I'm not going to go back to the penitentiary."[22] So what happens is, they'll go out and they'll make themselves a score and they will live up to every nickel of that money, usually go to the point where they will have to go borrow gas money to go make some more.

I know a boy out of Fort Worth—Jack, the guy who taught me the safe business—this guy is a first-class safe man. I saw him live in the back end of a pool hall on a cot in a little ole room, way in the back of that place, because he didn't want to steal anymore. Of course he only stayed back there about a week, but still in all, something told him not to steal and to stay there, and he stayed there rather than steal. This is a high-rolling safe man, you understand? I'm talking about a son of a bitch who'd go down and buy $300 to $400 worth of records in the afternoon just because he liked them, things like that; he's not a rum. Everybody gets like that and don't want to steal anymore.

You've got to remember: there's a lot of pressure on you. Say you're working the south of Texas, maybe a five- or six-hundred-square-mile area. Say you make five or six joints. Well, they call in the Rangers and everything starts humming and they're working twenty-four hours a day to catch you. They check every car. They don't stop and pick everybody up, but the police start jotting down license numbers of cars driving into and out of these towns, just erratically; anything they see at night they just take it down and call it into headquarters and have it checked out. The heat gets on. You get to thinking, "Well, I've been pretty lucky; I better pull up for a while."

So what most of these guys do is they'll make a score and then they'll stop and they'll spend their money up, they'll live it up, and usually they'll high-play people. See, it costs us three times, four or five times, as much to do anything as it does anybody else because we got to high-play. That's part of the program. You're going to impress somebody else, and you use that money to impress people. Maybe some scaly-leg ole gal who is a waitress in some beer joint. You're liable to sit around there and put $40 in the jukebox. Ridiculous things, just to get her attention and get you some pussy. Whereas all you'd have to do is ask her to begin with. But that's just part of the movement, you know; it's part of the plan, and you just go along with it.[23]

But I'm not too bad about that because I don't go into beer joints very much.

So, they make a score, and then they just live it up, and then they'll go out again. I don't do that. I go out and I say, "Well, I'm going to make $10,000 or $15,000," whatever I want. In my mind I've always got some kind of a business I'm going in. The rest of them is geared up to something else; I'm geared up to getting into business, to buy me a joint.[24] I know the joints are no good because I've owned them and I don't like them; they're too confining and I don't like to have to be there every night, but anyways, I say, "I'm going to get me a joint."

I take off. I take my money as soon as I make it and I send

it to my bank. I don't even carry my money home with me; I've already got envelopes with deposit slips in them and I send everything to my bank. Wherever I am, I just fill it in, drop it in the mail, and I go on about my business. Then, if I'm arrested, I don't have the money with me.

I usually have two bank accounts, one with my name and one with whatever name I happen to come upon, you know, whenever I get ready to open another account. The reason I always have one in my name is in case my car breaks down somewhere out there, I'll have some legitimate identification and my checking account will correspond with that. And you always like to have a little something that you can fall back on. A lot of times I've been out stealing and had to cash a check or had to have the bank wire me some money, and you have to have some identification to get your money. So that's why I always have two bank accounts. I always send my money to the bank.

I have a lot of friends in San Antonio. Sometimes we'll all get in town and we'll all be living there, we'll all have an apartment; maybe we'll be partying and the party will last three or four or five months. Say there's ten or twelve of us in there. Every so often, I'll leave the party and I'll go up the country and make me some money. I don't tell them when I'm leaving or when I'm going to come back. I'll just go out and get in my car and go on up the country, take care of my business, and I'll come on back. And they'll never know that I've been gone, not really. While I'm partying, I'll look around and maybe old John's gone; I won't pay any attention to it—John's done the same thing I've done: he's gone up the country and made him some money. Then he comes back.

You'd be surprised how you will see out-of-state people around the country. One time I was sitting in a little bar in Washington, D.C., and in the course of the night we got to drinking and two or three of them other boys, they'd seen somebody else from Texas who was up there working and they made a few phone calls, and we just had a little reunion.

When we got through, we had sixteen safe-crackers sitting in this little place. It just happened, you know. That's unusual, but at this particular time it happened. We partied for four or five days, had a good time, and then we all went off on our separate ways.

But the point I want to make is that though some of us know each other, we work independent of anybody or anything. The only necessity is money.

A dope fiend's a little different: he'll go up the country and make a drugstore somewhere, or go to the hospital and make a doctor's bag, then come on back to the party.

Colored and Spanish thieves are different in another way. Spanish will not steal by themselves, they have to have a bunch of other people in it with them. The only time that a Mexican—I'm talking generally, now, there are cases where they do something alone—will do anything by himself is if he's going to rob somebody that he knows. If he's going to burglarize the house of a guy he's been working for, something like that. He has to know everything about it, he has to feel at home whenever he does it; otherwise he takes a whole carload with him.

Colored aren't like that. They'll take one or two, or even go by themselves. But their motivation is usually that they're short of money and they're after what they can sell. They'll hang around a neighborhood bar or some place like that in their vicinity and the guy at the bar, he'll have ten or twelve or fifteen of them hanging around there. Somebody, a fence maybe, will tell him, "I need a television set." He'll be at the bar and there will be one of the niggers sitting there who doesn't have any money or owes him a little bar bill, and the man tells him, "I need a television set." That guy goes out and steals the bartender a television set. Or the bartender will say, "I need a new deer rifle." It's the same thing as telling him, "Go steal it." And lawyers will work them the same way.[25]

That boosting is a funny business anyhow. People, they're always talking about fences, fences, fences. I only know one or two.[26] They're hard to find. I've read stories about several of them in the North where they have warehouses full of stuff, but look at the cash money they have to put out. A thief is not going to take credit; he doesn't want any credit. He needs some money. When he drives up there with something, say he's got a little load of cigarettes, he might go up and take $5,000 on account and the rest when he can get it, but that doesn't happen too often. And these people, these fences, they have to be able to turn that stuff to get their money back.

Most boosters have people all over town—in filling stations, stores, bars, places like that—and they try to sell things to them. When the boosters used to come to Corpus— sometimes they'd come in from all over the country— they'd come by and see us guys that owned joints in town. They know you're at least a half character. They'd come up and tell me, "We've got some clothes."

I'd tell them, "Fine. I need some suits." And if they didn't have what I wanted, I'd say, "Whenever you get some 42 longs, bring me some." Of course they only steal the best: Oxxford, Three-G, and so forth. I used to buy my suits for $50 each—suits that usually cost $250 or $295. I'd tell them, "I need a radio for my boat," and they'd go and get it. And I had a hell of a record collection. I'd give them a dollar apiece for those records. A gal can go in a joint and swing out with ten records in nothing but a shopping bag and make herself $10 in a real short time.

In this business you have to have people who will go along with you. Now I have—not bragging, there's not anything to brag about—I have pretty good credit with lawyers. I've had the finest lawyers in the state fight criminal cases for me when I wouldn't have a nickel. They've loaned me money. Say they get me out of jail on bond and I owe them $500 for the bond, beside the fee for fighting the case—I'll tell them, "I'll have your money in a week." Then I'll go out and I'll make the money.

But a colored thief, when he wants to make bond, he contacts the man who owns the bar, and *that* man contacts the lawyer. Then the man at the bar stands good for it. What happens is, the colored boy will take off and steal stuff and give it to the barman, and the barman will keep part of the money and give part of the money to the bondsman. So the colored stud's a lot worse off than I am because he's going to have to pay off two or three times what it's actually worth. Me, I'll go out and steal just money, and I'll pay mine off direct.

And most colored people I know don't steal money, they steal merchandise. It's very few you find who actually steal cash; they always steal the televisions or guns or tires or something like that. They steal hot-water heaters out of new houses before people have moved in, carpets off the floor, and they sell them for almost nothing.

White people don't usually steal anything that there's much work involved in, other than safes. Opening a safe is pretty hard work, but other than that they don't do it. If they have to lug or carry something, they pass it up. They're not going to go out there and get a pickup truck and work all night taking the motor out of some kind of warehouse and put it in the truck and haul it off; they're not going to get dirty and greasy. Negroes will do that; they'll go out and jack up a car and take all the tires off it, things like that. There's no way I would do that.

They work out of a neighborhood bar or a lounge or a barbecue stand or a domino hall, and they're actually working for that one colored stud. Usually, in colored town, you'll have just a few Negroes there that will control all of that town. Anything you want done, you have to go to one of those men.

The Spanish—remember, I'm talking about Texas, I don't know about other places—down here work with the Spanish politicians a lot. Usually he is a bondsman too and a little bit of everything, and when they steal stuff, they usually fence it through him.

In Corpus there's a Mexican bondsman; he's made bonds for me and we get along real well. I went to him not too long before I got busted this time. I had just been in jail and I was broke, so I went to him and told him, "I got to have an automobile. I need it to go steal something." He called the used-car lot, and I went to the lot and the man there said, "Just pick out what you want." I got a real nice automobile, signed my name on the paper, and that was it. No down payment, no nothing; I just went on about my business. In turn, I gave the bondsman $300 or $400 for doing it for me, and besides that, I went back a few days later and made the down payment on the car, and went back a few days after that and paid the rest of it off in cash. But at that time I needed it bad. After I got the car, I had to have money for tools and working expenses, so I went to my lawyer and told him, "I'm broke and I need $500 to get started." He lent me the $500 to get started on; maybe it was $250, I don't remember exactly. Whatever it was I needed, I got.

There's a lot of differences in things around the country. Take jukeboxes. Up East most of that is syndicated, whereas down here it's not, it's all local. In Corpus Christi we have Southern Amusement there, which is sort of a small company; it's owned by some nice guys. The big one is Corpus Christi Amusement. The people who have it now, man, they're fine; good to do business with them. I've done business with them, square-john business when I worked for a wholesale grocery company. When they owe you, they pay you; there's no ifs, ands, or buts, they never ask you any questions; they're good people to do business with. They're good to charities and things like that. They're local and they have nothing to do with the outside elements from New York and Chicago.

Of course those people up there send flyers down that they'd appreciate it if they'd put certain things on the jukeboxes, maybe some dude that they're trying to promote, and the local people go along with it. But by the same token they send down a box of free records to put that guy on with, so they're actually making money by doing it.

A lot of people don't realize—especially from up East—that Texans are thought of pretty highly as badasses. In Chicago they fear Texans. Really, I'm talking about on the

square, because they do. Well, I'll tell you why. They have
more murders and more gangland killings in Fort Worth in
a year than they have in Chicago, and hell, Chicago's four
or five times the size town Fort Worth is.[27] What about San
Antonio? Man, there's never a year goes by there that they
don't have just a gob of them. Houston, what about Houston? Murder capital of the world! What about Dallas? All
your big towns in Texas are like that. Down here we take
care of things pretty rough, whereas up East they don't do
that too much.[28]

And those organized people have tried to come down here.
Hell, you know that they have tried, with this being one of
the most lucrative countries in the world. California and
Texas—there's more money per population than anywhere
else.[29] You know that they are going to come. But they just
can't get these local people; they're just not going to stand
still for it.

I know a guy who is about sixty years old; they came into
his joint and he was sitting on the commode taking a shit.
They came into the restaurant and found out where he was
and they went back there. He told them, "I'll tell you what
I'm going to do. I'm going to give you all a break. I'm going
to go ahead and sit here and finish my shit. Then, when I
come out, if you're not all gone, I'm going to take care of
you. But I'm going to give you all a break." So they just stood
there and he just kept on shitting till he was done. He wiped
his ass, got up, and goddamned near beat them to death. He
ran them right down the middle of Main Street shooting at
their ass.

You know what I mean? You understand, now, he didn't
back off and say, "Well, now, I'm going to take some pre-
cautions here and there." In Texas, people don't act like that,
they don't try to hedge their bet. Whenever there's a play
come up, they just go ahead and take their play right then.
Those people up East, they can't get organized down here.[30]

They'd like to, and in a way I would like to see them do
it, because people like me would be given a spot. If I was
running something, I wouldn't want them coming in, but if

they did come, I'd probably end up with something pretty good. But the rackets, those people in New York or Chicago or the Mafia, they don't like criminals with a prison record anyway; it puts the heat on them. So we're kind of outlawed with them too. But there's very little of it down here anyway.

You're a burglar now; what kind of spot would you have?

I can do other things beside burglarizing. I'm a first-class crap dealer, I'm a pretty good card mechanic, pretty good dice mechanic. And I've always run the joints; I've been associated with a lot of people. I'd find me something to do. Probably start out pretty low, but I'd end up with something pretty good. If nothing else, well, whenever the syndicate comes in and they get to gambling operations. I would take my own money and open me a joint and give them a piece of it. But I would find some way to get in.

You have to remember, this is the only time I've ever messed with safes. Before, I was always a check man. Every time I needed to make some money, I made it with checks. I've gone as high as eight or nine years in the check business without ever getting any kind of a beef. I've had some rumbles, but I've always been able to square the beef where I didn't even go to jail. I'd just say, "You take this money up there and see what you can do with it." Send a lawyer up there with the money. Sometimes I'd spend a little time in jail fighting cases or waiting to get bailed out, but outside of that two-year deal, I always got off pretty good.

Now I'll tell you about the work.

The last set of equipment I had was given to me by a real good safe man in Fort Worth. I had two sets of tools: one set for the safe, the actual box tools, and then a set of roofing tools. For going through a roof you need hatchets and stuff like that. The two sets would run about $350. Not too much. If you have a pneumatic drill, something like that, that's extra. But you don't buy those things; you go steal them.

What they weigh depends on the box you're going after. I had an old army knapsack that rolls out; you hang the stuff on the side. I had one of those and I cut off part of the straps and put my stuff inside and rolled it up. It's a dark color and easy to carry. I could put my tools in there and it would weigh about thirty-five or forty pounds. Not too much that you can't climb with it. Roofing tools weigh a little bit more, and I had those in a larger knapsack.

I didn't fool with nitro because the possession of explosives is a federal offense. If you're driving down the highway and you happen to get a rumble, then not only the state but the federal can file on you too.

Until a few years ago Texas didn't have a tool law. You could drive down and they could catch you with all the burglary tools in the world and they couldn't file on you for having them. But in some states they could, and now they can in Texas too. But you have to have a drill. So if you're going to use a drill, you take two cars and you keep the drill in the other car.

I had boxes built for my tools. Say I was going to Oklahoma City to beat a safe. I'd put my tools on a Greyhound bus and I'd pick them up in Oklahoma City when I got there. That way I'm driving down the country and haven't got a thing in my car, not one thing. And when I get through in Oklahoma City, then I put my stuff on the Greyhound bus and I send it back. I never carried anything far. Sometimes if I was only going 150 miles, especially if I had been working in the area and I knew that the Rangers were looking for me, I would do that.

A well-known safe man like myself, when I go out, they know what kind of car I have.[31] When I drive into a town and if the police see me, they don't arrest me. They notify the Rangers, and they tail me as I go around casing the stores; then they go around setting traps. That's common; I've sat in a Ranger car and listened to them. They know that we know they do that. But the things about it is, we just figure that we're smarter than they are and they don't know what kind of car we're in that night.

I'll tell you what I always try to do whenever I'm going off to do something like that. I always have some kind of square-john girl friend someplace and I say, "How about letting me borrow your car? I'll have it tuned up for you and you can use mine." Then I use *her* car.

I tried to use the airplane for work one time. We were going to rob a little ole bank up in the country. I walked through the doors of the bank and the guy who was with me froze and ran out. He jumped in the car and drove off, leaving me standing inside the bank with a sawed-off shotgun. I turned around and ran around the building. There was a hotel next door. It was a little town up in the hills and there is a river running through the town. Behind the hotel some guy rents canoes, so I just loop-scooped me a canoe and started paddling off down the river. It happened so fast that I just wasn't pursued.

The airport where I had the plane was about sixty miles from there. We were going to drive in the car to a place near the airport, then walk over cross-country and get in the plane and fly off. I finally got to the plane. I flew off, and that's the only time I've ever used it for stealing.

I'll tell you one thing with safes: you have to have your tools and you have to have transportation, and it's better to have your own car that you know well and be able to carry your tools and have some way to get around after you get there. It's all right to fly up, but then you have to rent a car and there's your signature on something.

Something else: you can't ever tell when you're going to make a big score, and you always plan on it. After a big score they're going to call in the FBI and they're going to run everything down. Even though it's not a federal offense, they'll probably try to make it into one by saying you've taken the money across a state line or something. They're going to bring them in. If it's a $200,000 or $300,000 score—which I've never made—I know they'd do that. And a lot of the time you're just scouting anyway, and it sometimes turns out that little towns are better than the large towns. With an airplane you'd have to fly, and you can't rent cars in small towns.

So I've used it strictly for pleasure. I like flying down the coast for fishing and just riding around, or going down to Mexico and getting drunk.

How many places we'd hit a night would depend on how much trouble we had. Anywhere from one to four. I guess those safes would average, good and bad, about $600 each. Some of them you'd get a pretty nice little bit of cash off of, and some of them you don't get a nickel. We went off on a three-day trip one time, and when we got back, we were $50 in the hole. And we were making some safes.

Usually when you're on the road like that, you can't make but one safe a night because you don't know enough about the town. It's hard enough to find one good one, you know. Sometimes we would make one and there just wouldn't be anything in it.

When we were on the road, we didn't take pills or drink or anything—it was strictly business.[32] We'd go to sleep about six in the evening and get up about twelve and go to work. When we'd get through, we'd come back and get cleaned up and lay around the swimming pool until eight or nine o'clock and go to sleep. We actually went at it as a business, no play thing.

You get to be kind of choosy on your safes. I never went into a store to beat a safe when I might not be able to get it open and here I'm takin' all the same chances. Once in a while, though, if I'd go in and find two safes, I'd open the one I could open, and about the other one I'd say, "I'm gonna experiment for thirty minutes." If I could open it in thirty minutes, I'd beat it; if I didn't, I left. And sometimes if it's a real good setup, you can try new things. Say it's a two- or three-story building and you've roofed it and you've come in and it's a big old soundproof place—you know, that you're not going to get run up on—then you can get up there and experiment.

But I was always pretty careful. Every safe I made after Jack split, it was one I knew I could make before I went in. But now, some of them I went in and didn't make. But I thought that I could because I'd made other ones like that.

Like one in Alice, Texas, in a big lumberyard there. Five
people had tried to beat it, and no one's got into it yet. They
keep a bundle of money there. It had $18,000 in it the night
I tried to get in. But it's been whipped over so much and
blowed so much that they've got the mechanism so crazy in
there that now the damned thing's near unbeatable. Nothing's where it should be anymore because they cut holes in
it and they had to plug the holes, and when they did that,
they moved pieces over. It's not a standard safe anymore;
now it's a handmade thing. You can't peel it, you can't punch
it; they've welded deals all around the outside so you can't
get a bite on it with your bar, and it's right in the middle
of town so you can't blow it because you'd wake the whole
neighborhood. You're just stuck with it.

It was a big single-door Mosler, one of the largest single-
doors I've ever seen. We started working on it about ten
o'clock one Sunday night and didn't come out until Monday
morning about five. There was a little extra hardship working there: about every fifteen minutes the police would pull
up in front of the lumberyard office and U-turn there and
go back cruising in the other direction; sometimes they
would pull in there and stop for a few minutes, then continue on up the street. It had a real nice paved drive in front;
they wasn't so much looking in as they were using the driveway. But we had to stay down below the counter, the par-
tition, a lot of the time.

We were in town to make a department store, but I didn't
like it so we ended up at this place. We took it for granted
that there would be cutting torches there in case we needed
them. After we got in there, we found they didn't have anything. They had a display rack up in front of the store, but
it just had small hand tools. We had our own tools for peeling and things like that of course.

We started out working on it, and we worked until daylight the next day. Actually we shouldn't have stayed in
there as long as we did. And we never got in. Up in the
corners of the box where you usually start to peel a box we

couldn't ever get a start because the outer rim of the safe had a little flange that had been welded on, or maybe it had been made like that, I couldn't tell. It came out just about a quarter inch, so that whenever you drove your chisel in and tried to pry it up, the chisel would just get pulled out. And we couldn't get it started. Beside that, the front door of the box was damned near a half inch thick. I've never seen one that thick before, not even on a bank vault.

It got to the point where we actually got mad and flustered. We took a hacksaw off that rack out in front and cut the hinges off this damned thing. And the hinges were monstrous. The safe was over my head, and I'm six-two. Maybe not over my head—but it was over my eye level because I remember that if I wanted to look up on top, I had to get up on my tiptoes. It was about four feet wide and five feet deep. It was the biggest single-door I've ever seen. So we cut the hinges off; we thought by doing that they would slide on those locking bars just enough to where we could maybe slide it over and get a start. No. I kept doing everything I could; I kept thinking.

And I never did get it. It never did give. If it gave a sixteenth of an inch, I could get it, but I never could get a sixteenth of an inch.

After it was all over and I was busted on that Harlingen deal and my partner copped to this one, the Rangers told me that there was $18,000 cash in it beside the checks, and that all those other crews had worked on it and nobody had ever gotten in. They said that almost all of them had the same complaint, that they all thought there would be a cutting torch in there when they went in because it's such a big place, so they'd go in there with nothing but regular old box tools. The reason there wasn't that equipment there, we found out, was that two blocks away they had their pipe yard and that was where they worked on their equipment, so they had that stuff over there. Whenever they needed something done at the lumberyard, a clerk would come over with the welding equipment in a truck.

You said you originally intended to make a department store that night but you didn't like it. What didn't you like about it?

This man was supposed to have cased it out. His wife had worked there, I think. It was one of those jailhouse scores. Every time you get in jail, as soon as they find out you're a safe man, people start telling you about these safes all around the country that have all this money in them that they've seen, and that their uncle or somebody works there.

This happened at a time when I didn't want to get too far away from Corpus because I had a little business going there and I didn't want to be away more than a few hours. I figured we'd just run over there and make that joint. He told me about it and said everything would be all right, and it was only forty miles from Corpus. So we ran over.

The way the back door was explained to me, you could get in it without having to jimmy anything because there was supposed to be just a bar across the back of it and all we had to do was take a long pick or knife and stick it through the door and lift up that bar and walk on in. When we got over there, we drove by the building and it looked real good. You could tell it was a real progressive store. And I had been assured they didn't go to the bank every night; we figured they'd probably have the Friday and Saturday receipts because the banks were closed on Saturday, so it seemed real good. We went out and had supper. After we got through eating, I had my fall partner drop me off and I walked a little ways to where that service door was.

It wasn't anything like we'd been told. It was a double-layer tin-covered door, and I'm sure that it did lock inside with just a bar, but one door overlapped the other so you couldn't slide anything between them. And this was right downtown, and in this town they have door shakers. We would have had to make the entrance in the back there right near where they have a little restaurant. It was summertime and they had benches outside to serve tacos and tamales and hot dogs and hamburgers and stuff to these cotton pickers and lower-class people. So they're sitting right outside and we'd have been about thirty yards from them and they could hear too well.

Right before I got busted, a friend of mine—he's not actually exactly a friend, he's a boy I did time with—had uncles with a bunch of recapping stores, tire companies. Usually a tire company in those towns will also have a recapping plant that services all the stores. I was in Austin one day and picked him up and we went over to San Antonio where they had some of those stores. We were drinking and messing around and he ran out of money, so he went by one of his uncles' stores and wrote a check for $100, which they cashed for him. I got to looking around the store and he kind of gave me a Cook's tour; he showed me the place and we went in back where they had the recapping plant and I looked it over. They had a big old double-door Mosler. I decided that when I was in that part of the country next time, that might be a pretty good score.

So the next time I was around, I rode by there with my fall partner and we parked in the parking lot where we could see the cashier's cage where people paid their bills. We sat there for quite a while and it looked like they were taking in a good bit of cash. That night we went in. It took us about an hour and fifteen minutes to get into the safe, something like that. The entrance to the building was nothing because the big ole recapping plant out in back was just tin and we just pulled up a sheet of that tin and eased through, then pulled it in back of us. We got in there and we got working on that safe and, like I said, it took us about an hour and fifteen minutes to get through it.

We got in the safe and looked around. Usually they'll have a cashbox, and that's the first thing you get. Then you shake the books down later on because a lot of people put money up in the bindings. But there wasn't any cashbox there. We rummaged around in that safe and couldn't find a thing.

Now we had watched these people come out and I didn't see any of them bring anything with them, so I still felt the money was there somewhere in the store. I figured that they had a little floor keyster somewhere. So we started moving things around, trying to find it.

About an hour and a half later I got to this stack of old truck tires in the corner. I pushed them over to look around in back of them, and when I pushed, I heard something jingle.

They had hid the money inside one of these tires; it was strictly luck that we found it.

In fact, that's the best place to put your money; hide it somewhere. If you got it in a safe, then it's not hid, because everybody knows where it is. But if you just hide it someplace, why hell, a man can't never find it. Most of the time I can't be looking all over a place, moving around like that.

But that time we were just lucky. When I moved that tire and heard the jingle, we looked in there, and sure enough, there was a moneybag. There was over two thousand dollars in that bag. There wasn't very much change either; it was mostly bills. Just enough change to hear.

In 1962 we were living in a motel in San Antonio, working out of there. During the day we'd work within about a 150-mile radius out of San Antonio, spotting places we wanted to make that night.

About this time alpaca sweaters were real prominent, so we decided we might as well make a nice clothing store and get a nice sweater. Besides beating the safe, of course. We rode over to Austin to look around, trying to spot what we wanted, and we found a place in one of the new modern buildings without any outside displays. The store itself just had a small sign there with a name, and there weren't any openings for windows or anything. We just roofed it and went in.

The only trouble up there is they have the kids who get drunk and mess around, kids from the college, so there are a lot of patrol cars around Austin, and that is the only real hazard in town. After we went through the roof, then it was relatively simple because all of the walls were solid and you could take your time and turn on all the lights and the air conditioner, and you could work and do just what you wanted to do.

We got in the office and they had one of these older model safes; I've never seen another one exactly like it. It was like a Mosler square-door but all wrong. We peeled the box and there wasn't a lot of money in there, just seven or eight hundred dollars. There were some sheets thrown over the racks where the clothes and suits were, so we took one of those and laid it out on the floor and filled it up with alpaca sweaters. When we left, we just went out the front door (it doesn't make any difference if the alarm goes off; you're on your way then) and took our sweaters with us. They were nice.

Probably the hardest safe I ever made was a finance company in Oklahoma. We were between jobs and were just looking around in west Texas. We'd made a few places in the area. I picked up the paper and I saw where this friend of mine who owns some motels in Oklahoma City was playing in an amateur golf tournament. We weren't doing anything anyways, so we decided to drive up to Oklahoma City to watch him play. We wound up in a motel up there; we called him and that night went out and had supper with him. Next day we watched him play.

My fall partner and I decided that as long as we're up here we might as well make expenses. We got to looking around and we found a finance company. It was isolated pretty good. This was in a district where there are numerous used-car lots, and this old man, he did financing for all the independent lots. I'm sure he had a real good go.

These people were paying by the week or month. I sat and watched these people falling in there and paying this money, making their car payments. As they'd get paid, they would drop by and make their car payment. I looked there for a little while, then we went on down the street and put our glasses on it.

Glasses?

Field glasses. The old man put the money in the safe and just closed up. He was the last one out and we knew that the money was there.

That's the main thing: be sure that the money is there. Otherwise you're taking a chance on getting busted and everything for a dry haul, because you're going to do just as much time for getting nothing as for all the money in the world. You've *got* to establish that there is some money there; otherwise there is just no point in going inside.

Anyway, right before dark we drove right by the building and threw the tools out in some weeds there. That was so we wouldn't have to be carrying them, they would be there waiting for us. Later, about eight thirty or nine o'clock, we went in. It was just dusky; it wasn't real dark, but it was dark enough where things were in shadow and you couldn't see very well.

This damned building, it was one of these new modern places, and the whole front from the top to the floor was glass. The top part was colored glass, the bottom clear. We got in there and rolled out our tools and got everything set to start working on the safe.

And the night lights came on.

This dude, he had night lights all around the building on the outside and they just flooded the area. Inside, all inside was lights, just as bright as daylight. So here we are inside this damned building and we're going to have to go through those lights whatever happens getting out, if we get something or not, so we decided to go ahead and work.

Were there night lights aimed on the safe?

The whole building was illuminated, everything, all over. They didn't have to have one on the safe because it was just as bright as day in there.

Over by the window they had a divan. I crawled over there and I moved the divan a little bit to where from one angle outside you couldn't see the safe. Then we took the other chairs and arranged them, and there was a counter that helped too. We had furniture staggered, so it made a solid block between us and the outside. Then we went on and made the safe.

But we had to make it laying down; we couldn't get up. We had to start on the bottom left-hand corner instead of up at the top because we couldn't stand up and work. We got in, and there was about $6,000 in the safe, which was a real good haul.

Why did you specify preferring the upper left-hand corner as a place to start?

On the upper right side—this is looking at the safe—is where the safe's hinges are; on the left side there aren't any hinges. If you peel to where the hinges are, it's going to stop and it doesn't do you any good, you have to peel it all the way around. But you can get a start in the upper left-hand corner and without having to tear very much get you a start to where you can dig down or reach in there and get hold of the locking bars, or you can just come down the side if you want to. I would say that a hundred per cent of the people that make safes who know that they're going to peel will start at the upper left-hand corner.

So you peel most of the time. Why?

It takes less equipment than almost anything else. Blowing a safe makes a lot of noise and it carries a twenty-five-year sentence for the explosive if you're just caught driving down the road. If you drill, you have to lug that big old drill around with you and they've got tool laws for that. You can punch them—we always try that before we peel—but very few safes punch anymore. I hear people tell me about punching safes here and there, but I've only punched about two. They weld an extra plate on the back and the pin mushrooms.[33] And something else: if it's a real good score, more than likely they're going to have tear gas in it. So it's better if there's any doubt to just go ahead and peel it.

How long would it take you to peel a safe?

Anywhere from ten minutes to never.

Sometimes it's so nice. We were in a little town named San Marcos. They had a little square-door back in a pharmacy. The door going back to where the safe was was only a half door, one of those swinging gate sort of deals; it came halfway down so the pharmacist could look out without having to open the door. I put a big chisel in the top left-hand corner and just tapped it and—I guess the rivets were so old they had calcified, no, crystallized—and it just went *pop-pop-pop-pop-pop-pop* all the way down the side. I hit it once across and that was it. I guess it took maybe three or four minutes to get in the safe.

If you *are* going to use a cutting rig, they have one for $125 now that, my God, boy, it's something else! Hell, you can cut the cement off a keyster; you can do anything you want to. I forget what temperature it gets; it has a new alloy cutting rod, the latest thing out. I was reading in the paper the other day that they're giving demonstrations at the welding shop, so you can go down and take lessons free.

But peeling is best all around. All it takes is two or three chisels and a couple of good mallets and you're in business.

Did you have someone who would spot safes for you?

Sometimes things would just occur. You're in a group of people and you'll be running with a bunch of characters and maybe some of the gals will turn a trick someplace and they'll find out about a score. Maybe they were turning a trick with some guy that owned a furniture store or they just happened up on it.

But information from those kinds of people is pretty unreliable. Most of them, if they see a little money, they think it's a lot of money. They don't know the difference between one-dollar bills and hundred-dollar bills. If they see a couple of bundles of bills in there, they never take the time to look at them and see what they are; all they say is, "There's a bunch of money in there."

As far as using a professional spotter—having someone going out to spot for us and then we give him 25 per cent or something like that—we never did do that. I have heard of that happening, but I don't believe that it's done much in this part of the country.[34]

About the only time I would consider it would be if I knew somebody personally that had a business and figured it would go real good, but because I know him, if something did happen, then I'd be the first one under suspicion. Then I might consider leasing it out to somebody. If the people with the business were friends of mine, I wouldn't do it, but

if I didn't like them or care about them one way or the other
and wanted to make some money, then I would consider putting somebody else on the score. But anybody I put on would
have to be awfully good people or I wouldn't do it.

How much of a cut would you expect?

It's always been 25 per cent. They pay all expenses and
give you 25 per cent. But you might not get that if they
weren't real reliable because you weren't there and have to
believe what they tell you they got. So they would have to be
awfully good people, as I said. And another reason for being
careful: you're as guilty by participating that way as if you
went into the building yourself. Only thing is, it would be
harder to prove.

*You said it was important to know when the money was
inside. How would you find out?*

Any time you see delivery trucks, you can figure that anywhere from $150 to $250 minimum for each of those trucks
is in the building. See, damned near all delivery trucks get in
so late they can't get to the bank, and more than likely the
bookkeeper's gone by then anyway. So they just put the
money in the safe and take care of it the next day. So trucks
are one thing you look for.

Any retail store has to have a certain amount of money to
open up on. A lot of times it's not too much—you'd be surprised how small an amount they can open up on—but as
long as they're handling *hard* money, you're going to get
some.

I said hard money then because there's a problem nowadays with checks. I think I told you one time about making
a feed store in Sinton. We went in and beat it; we went up
through the floor because it was an old warehouse that sits
around two and a half feet up off the ground. The country
down there is so damp—I think that's the reason they build
them like that. Anyway, it had an old plank floor and we
went up through it and beat the safe. The amount of money
we got out of it was extremely nominal—I think it was $250
or $400, something like that. But I guess there was over
$100,000 in checks in there, because not only did he sell

feed, but he was the Phillips 66 distributor. So it often comes to this: there's places with enormous sums of money, but it's not negotiable, it's in checks.

I have heard about guys that went and took the checks anyway and then would peddle them back at a later date. It's so much easier for the company to go ahead and up $400 or $600 to get their checks back than to have to call on the customers and ask them to rewrite their checks and be calling the banks and all. To save their customers and their own bookkeepers all that undue work, they'll just go ahead and buy the checks back. I do know of one gambler that happened to, and he did up the money. I don't like it because you have the tedious proposition of getting your money and getting them the checks.

You told me once that when you made a drugstore, you took not only the money but also the drugs, and some of them you used to get high on. The other stuff: would you sell it to people?

The drugs?

Yes. Are they a valuable part of a drugstore score?

That's one of the main things that makes a drugstore any good at all. Usually a drugstore doesn't have a tremendous amount of money. If you can beat a supermarket, you can figure that you're going to get no less than $2,500, but you're not going to find maybe two drugstores in this country that have $2,500. I don't mean these drugstores that handle everything in the world from books to airplanes, they're not really drugstores anyhow; I'm talking about a regular drugstore. They're not going to have $2,500 in them. But you can make it up in the narcotics. Even if you don't get any money, there is going to be some narcotics there—if he's got a narcotics license, I mean. You'd be surprised that there's some drugstores that don't have narcotics: they'd rather just send their narcotics prescriptions to somebody else and not go through all that bookkeeping and everything, especially an old man that's got his own little ole drugstore.

But anyway, I sold some. I didn't sell nearly as much as I wanted to sell. They estimated when I was on trial in Port

Lavaca, up in Calhoun County—this is after that drugstore I got busted on at Palacios, which is in that county—that the drugs they introduced at my trial were worth $60,000. (The judge overruled it; they couldn't introduce it, he said.) But you have to remember, that was just a portion of what I had. I couldn't find anybody with enough money to buy them and I had made some arrangements a few days before where, if I hadn't gotten busted, I could have sold them all. But at a very cheap price.

When we went into drugstores and were beating the safes, naturally I took the narcotics for the sale value. But the other pills were just for myself to party with. We got Dexamyl and Tuinal, naturally. And also redbirds and yellowjackets— that's Nembutal and Seconal. They're sleeping pills, but that wasn't how we used them.

When I had all those pills, I used to take a redbird and a Tuinal. Or two Tuinals and one redbird. Actually, a Tuinal is a mixture of redbirds and something else. The combination of the two just puts you in a completely hynotic state.

Something else with that: if you'll smoke a little grass while you're taking Tuinal, you'll get a fantastic kick. You don't see purple people, the flowers don't come to life in front of you or anything like that, but still in all it's a hell of a drive.

Now I never did take any pills when I was stealing. I don't know what the sensation would be there. I was always scared to take pills then because they impair your judgment too much.

Once my fall partner took two Tuinals and a redbird when we were going to a steak house. He was in one car and I was in the other. He got there all right and we had our steaks; then on the way back he ran off in a ditch somewhere. I don't know where he went, but then he caught a cab home. It took us four or five days to find the car: he couldn't even remember what part of town he was in when he lost it. And he wasn't drinking, it was just those three capsules.

Almost all gamblers, because of the hours they keep, take pills. That's where I was introduced to them. Mostly they take Benzedrine and Dexamyl. Dexedrine by itself is like Benzedrine—it excites you and makes you nervous. But in a Dexamyl there's enough Miltown to kind of slow you down. They're a good pill, those Dexamyls.

I was raised around gamblers. And I worked as a crap dealer around the country and I've gambled all of my life. And all gamblers take drugs in one form or another. Now I have never seen any that were actually pillheads to where a pill connection would drive them, or any that were narcotics addicts. But almost all I know like to sniff coke—they call it "freezing their nose." The boss gambler in my hometown is constantly on the lookout for some. Now as far as him ever robbing somebody, he doesn't do that, but of course he's got a lot of doctors who gamble with him and they write him a little scrip once in a while. I don't think he cares to have it every night—just once in a while.

Using narcotics as pills, especially if like me you've never shot any dope, you get a pretty good bang out of it. You get a pretty good jolt.

There was this girl once, we were out partying and messing around and she wanted to get high. All my pills were buried out in the country and I had on my real nice clothes and I didn't want to drive that ten miles to where I had the pills buried and dig in the dirt in my nice clothes. So I had some footballs, some Dilaudid. I think it's a full grain. I gave this girl some. She got mad because I broke a football in two; she wanted the whole thing. She thought it was like a Benzedrine tablet; she had no idea what she was taking. I gave it to her and we went to a nice club and were sitting there having a drink. The boy that owns the joint is a good friend of mine and he came over and sat at the table. She told me, "I'd like to go to the rest room."

I told her, "Well, go ahead."

We were sitting right in front of it, so I wasn't paying any attention to her, I was talking with him. I hadn't taken anything because I had a lot of heat on me and the Texas Rangers was looking for me, so I wasn't going to get knocked out under those conditions. She sat there and in a little while interrupted me again and said, "I got to go to the rest room."

I said, "Well, goddamn, go!" Finally, I got up and pulled her chair back and headed her in that direction. I didn't know that it would hit her that hard. She went in there and I don't know how long she was gone but I guess it was a good while. We had three or four drinks and I thought she was off talking to somebody. We had a lot of friends out there and I didn't pay any attention. Finally a while later I snapped that she was still in that rest room, so I got a waitress to go get her. The waitress went in and found her sitting on the commode with her dress pulled up and everything else down, just sitting there. She had gone in there and forgot what she had done; she sat down and just took herself a trip. The waitress brought her back out.

About three hours later we were at another place having a few drinks and it started wearing off a little and she started to come around. The next day she was in hysterics over it; she thought that was the greatest kick she ever had. She was really wild for it then, so I explained to her what it was and I wouldn't give her any more.

Pills are not hard to come by down here, even if you're not stealing them. The Mexican border is so close. You go across the border there and buy you a hundred thousand Dexamyl or whatever you want and they'll deliver them on this side for you. That's not so easy since the new federal drug laws, but you can still connect. Now on marijuana and heroin, that is harder to get. But pills, in Mexico, you can just go into the drugstores over there and buy them. You don't need a connection.

I remember one time a while back when I was in Las Vegas. I was a pretty good winner, about ten or twelve thousand dollars ahead in chips on the table. I said, "Now I'm getting pretty sleepy." I told that to one of the dealers because I *was* sleepy. Hell, it's about six in the morning, I'd been up most of three or four days driving up there and now gambling all night and drinking.

"Would you like a pill, something to wake up you?" he said.

"Yeah."

So the waitress came over and she had a whole box of all assorted pills and she just opened them up and you could take your choice of whatever you liked. Of course those people at the hotel knew me and they knew that no matter what happened I would never say anything about it to anybody that matters. And I could probably have gotten some even if I hadn't wanted to play anymore, but of course they wanted me to play more, they wanted a chance to get their money back. They don't want you to quit.

Then it rocked back and forth for a long time, and the next morning at noon I had a pretty bad run of luck and I lost about half it back and then I cashed out. I ended up about sixty-three hundred ahead. That time.

I believe that when you're high on pills you become more excitable sexually, but you're less able to do anything about it. You'd just rather lay up there and pad and bullshit than really get down, because you haven't much desire for a climax. Maybe because you're already in a climax of a kind when you're high. But when you *can* get a hard-on, then you can go indefinitely. But it's difficult. If you went out with a square-john girl and you're high, you probably never would get any cock because she wouldn't be so inclined to help you, but if you're out with some whore that's high too and she knows and has had experience with pills, then it all kind of goes together. Otherwise you wouldn't be able to do too much good. With some pills I guess you probably could; on marijuana you can. On hard narcotics, not too much.

Pills, especially Dexedrine, it knocked me completely out that way. If I take a Dexedrine or a Benzedrine, I have a desire but it's absolutely a void, I can't do anything about it; I just can't get a hard-on when I'm taking those things. I know a lot of people aren't like that. Now with Tuinal it's not as bad. You can, if you make a decided effort, have intercourse.

Something else: very few narcotic addicts drink, but almost all pillheads drink. I guess one reason is that the kick is so similar, drinking and pills. Most pills are depressive, and so is liquor or beer; the kick is similar and consequently they juice. You very seldom see people sit around someone's house and just take pills: they're all drinking and maybe they'll take a pill too. One thing—when you are taking pills, you can consume an enormous amount of liquor; it raises your tolerance to alcohol, I think.

Tuinal is what I like. Some people call them Christmas Trees. That's the underworld slang for them because they're a kind of a green and kind of a red—not true red and true green, but the green and red they use at Christmastime. If you want to get high and party and want a kick, I think it's the best.

It is a well-being high. You lose a lot of coordination and you lose a lot of ability to reason. To me, it's kind of like getting high drinking. I was always so impressed with Tuinal I didn't mess with anything else much. But it is a weird kick; I've walked into telephone poles and all kinds of crazy things.

I was in a club down there in Corpus in the back room with the boss gambler and we were bullshitting and he had a couple of gals back there and we was just playing. I took a redbird and two Tuinal and I sat there about an hour. Then I started out. His office was in the back and you had to go down one step coming out of it. I fell off the step. I got down to the bar and started heading toward the door and I guess I bumped into six or seven people sitting at the bar. I could see those people there and I said to myself, "Well, I'm gonna give them plenty of room 'cause I don't want to cause a commotion and bump into them." And so I'd get way over to my right, what I thought was my right, and I was still hitting those people. I stopped and looked at those people and said, "What's the matter with you?"

I got outside and stepped off the curb and fell down. I walked across the street, hit a telephone pole, got in my car, and went to this girl's house. I took that road down by the water—it's pretty wide.

When I got to her place, I took some more pills. She wanted to get high, so we sat around and smoked grass and drank Scotch and ate pills. Goddam. And I trimmed her three or four times as I remember and just had a ball. So I can't say they slow you down too much sometimes. Of course now, she was no square-john girl. She wasn't a whore, but she had been married to a notorious pimp and had inherited a bunch of money and they lived real high. She was a swinging gal and she knew the score. So she was a lot of help.

Once I'd been in jail while fighting some cases. They had a bunch of cases filed on me and they were hauling me from jail to jail, trying to get me to confess and go to trial, but I wouldn't go to trial. At that time I had a good bit of money, so I had some real powerful lawyers and they just wouldn't let those people get me in the courtroom. But they wouldn't let me out on bond either; it was kind of a Mexican standoff.

I finally swung a deal and got out on bond. They sent some friends of mine to pick me up; they knew I was getting out. They brought me some clothes and some money, you know, the necessary items. I got out of jail in Austin. I'd been in jail almost two years, and we were going to Houston. We had a real good score lined up in Houston and I think that's one reason these lawyers got me out, because they knew I could make that money.

The boys who picked me up said, "You want to go to Houston and make the money, or you want to go to San Antonio for a couple of days and party?"

Now I'd been in jail for two years, so I said, "Hell, I want to go to San Antonio and party."

We went to San Antonio and checked in a motel, and that night a friend of mine, a gambler in town, gave me two girls, two models that were in a joint there.

One of the girls had a friend who had just come back from Mexico with a thousand redbirds, and she had a bunch. She said, "You want to get high?"

I said, "Yeah."

Now I hadn't had anything to speak of for two years— a little stuff smuggled into jail once in a while, but not much; maybe a few joints of grass too, but not enough to really do anything. When I'm in jail or a lockup like that, I don't care any too much for that stuff. It's when I can go out and party that it makes a difference. I've been in a lot of jails where you could send out and get whiskey, and I never did buy any whiskey because what the hell is the fun in getting drunk up there? I'd rather have some coffee or go to sleep.

But I was out of jail now and these girls were there and one had those redbirds. I took about two or three. The redbirds that come out of Mexico are notoriously weak, and that's why I took so many even after such a long layoff. We were sitting there drinking then. Incidentally, we'd made about $4,000 that evening after we got into San Antonio, so we had a good bit of money.

We decided to go out to a night club that stays open all night. This girl wanted to go and change clothes, which was all right with me. They had just come from a fashion show where they had been modeling and both of them had blue hair; it was all piled up and one had a teeter-totter fixed in her hair and the other had something that looked like a carrousel. Real weird stuff. I gave one of the girls to a friend of mine, and I was taking the one I ended up with over to her house to get her clothes changed. In the meantime I'd taken a couple of more pills—every time she'd take one or two, I'd take one. As I pulled up to the corner of Houston and Travis in San Antonio, there was a place where it looked like there was enough room between the cars for me to drive a big truck in there. I started in and *crash!* I hit right square on both of them. I got out and looked and discovered that there was enough space between them for a motorcycle maybe. The two cars were side by side in the two lanes and I had tried to go down the stripe between the lanes. That's how much my perception was messed up. I backed up and gave them my lawyer's card and told them to get in touch with him about the damages; then off we went.

I drove pretty good then, but boy, I was real careful. We almost got to her house and I started to turn a corner and, hell, I went up on the curb about six feet. There wasn't anything to hit there; I blew out the tire, that's all. I thought I was going around the corner and there I was up on this goddamned sidewalk. As I said, I hadn't had anything for two years, and I know it hits you hard after haven't had any.

She changed clothes and we got the tire fixed and we went on back, but she drove. We went to that night club and partied a while and ate some barbecue; then we decided to go to an all-night café in an amusement park. A couple of gears own it; they dress in drag. One has a girly show in the summertime; she travels the circuit with the carnivals and the other one stays there and runs the joint. Both of them are pretty good people. All the characters go out there at two or three or four o'clock in the morning. They serve steaks but there's no drinking. But the food's real good and you can see everybody in the country. Anybody that's passing through San Antonio always stops there or calls out there. You can go in and find out where almost any Texas character is, where he was last seen, and so I always go out there, naturally.

The girls we had with us, they're of that same bunch and they go out there too. A lot of girls go out there. We went out and we had some coffee. There's a great big monstrous driveway going out and there are old broken-down amusement rides around it, so you can't see the place from the street. There was a Cadillac sitting right at the end of this place and I'm driving out and I looked over at the goddamned car and I said, "I got a lot of room." I said to myself, "I don't want to hit this car. I don't want to hit this car because it's a nice car, an expensive car. This guy probably worked hard for the car or stole hard for the car."

And I went right into it. Straight into that car when I thought I was going by it.

So then they pulled me up and they wouldn't let me drive anymore. That fixed them, but prior to that I'd been bumping into curbs, but nothing serious. Just little stuff. This was a rented car we had, which was one reason they let me go as far as they did.

What do you do with your money?

I party. I spend it on travel. I like to party. A lot of people *like* it; I'm *hooked* on it.

I'm real funny. I am the only safe-cracker or thief I know

of that has a bank account. When I make my money, I don't put it in my pocket, I take it to the bank. I mail it to the bank.

Say I'm going to bust some safes. Now I'll go off and I'll bust safes until I have the amount of money I think I need. Say when I start out I say, "Well, man, I need about $15,000 to get on my feet." That's what I'll say.

So I start out and I'll work and I'll save; I don't spend any money, I don't party, I don't do anything but steal—until I get that amount of money in my bank account, and then I quit; I throw away my tools and I just say, "Now I've forgotten how. I'll never crack another safe."

I'll sit around a few days and say, "Well, now, I've got all this money, I think I'll take a little trip and kind of get my mind off this, and when I get back, I'll be fresh and I'll be ready to do something, go to work, get a job."

And I've had some good jobs offered to me, but I just never take them. I don't know why.

So I'll get off and I'll start partying and it doesn't take me very long to spend that money. But I always spend all of my money at one time; I don't dish a little bit of it out along, I just give it all away at one time.

But getting it, I work real hard.

Safecracking is hard work; it is goddamned hard, man. You don't know. You're cooped up in a little office, you can't turn on an air-conditioning machine because you can't turn the power on, and you're in a little bitty office, and you have got that physical exertion. I tell you, I have seen the floor in an office where I was working so wet with sweat it looked like it rained in there. People don't know how hard you have to work.

I have worked so hard on a safe I have had to lay down and rest before I could get out of the building. You work until you're completely exhausted. You're nervous anyway and that contributes to it. You have no idea. When you come out of a building, you are completely given up. I have come home and slept the clock around, jut absolutely exhausted.

It's hard work. There's climbing fences and roofs and going through those roofs and chipping that cement out and all that. And you're working under a strain and you're looking over your shoulder all the time.

But there's one thing about safes: I think that it actually charges you.

There's only two danger points in burglarizing: your entrance and your exit. Your entrance is the most dangerous, and the reason for that is that if they see you go in, you're inside, and they've got you. But exiting, if they see you coming out, you don't have too much to worry about because you're already on your way. So the entrance is more dangerous than the exit.[35]

After I get inside a building, I consider myself absolutely safe. And you are. When you go in, you get yourself another exit; you know a couple of ways you can get out in case you get run up on or anything, and it is very seldom that they are going to send a force out to a building to surround it, as they say. Something else: that old policeman that drives up there—you know, he wants to live. And whenever he comes up there, he's going to be kind of cautious, and if there's any danger of him getting hurt, nine out of ten of them will let you go. I've had them pull up outside of a building on me, I'd stick my pistol out there and point it up in the air and shoot it, and they'd just get in the car and drive off down the road. Oh yeah, goddamned right! And I would too. Why would you want to run in there and get yourself killed? People don't realize those things, but they do happen.

Now after I get inside, all my fear more or less is gone, as I said. And you concentrate on the safe. Of course you always know what kind of safe it is before you make your entrance. You go in, you've got your tools, and you can estimate what's in the safe. If it's a place that has delivery trucks, you can figure a couple of hundred per truck. That's the average for any kind of business, whether it be a beer truck or a dry-cleaning place.

But still and all: that jewel *might* be the one.

It might be the guy that's beating the income tax, or it might be the guy that's booking all the big football payoff or layoff.

And there is no charge in the world like when you see that smoke. For instance, if you're punching it and you hear that pin hit the back of the safe—*clingggg!*—you know you're home free. If you're peeling it and you see that smoke come out—which is from that fire insulation in there—whenever you pop that door and see that smoke, you know that you've cracked the rivets and it's all yours. And when you pull that safe door open: it is a *charge!*

I think the most safes I ever made was six in one night. But that was four of them in one building, and you just go from safe to safe. But man, it never became less. It's not like fucking, where the first time it's pretty wild, then each time it tapers off; you get part of the same drive, the same action, but it's not like the first. Safes are not like that. Each time it's more so because you figure the odds are more in your favor of it being the big score.

NOTES

THE LIFE

1. Wilson, one of the thieves who read the transcripts of this conversation, wrote, "This may have been true in the beginning, but I personally know this kind of arrangement was short-lived."
2. Sam would occasionally steal barbiturates from drugstores for his own use (he particularly liked Tuinal, a combination of secobarbital sodium [Seconal Sodium] and amobarbital sodium [Amytal Sodium]), but he did not use narcotics. He took them from drugstores because, as he explains below, they often were the most profitable part of a drugstore burglary.
3. Kid: "Many have tried and many have failed."
   Sam talks at some length about police, especially Texas Ranger, brutality, and it needs some discussion. Texas thieves differ on the subject, depending on their line of work and the towns in which they were arrested. Here are comments from a few:
   "Ten years ago it was bad, but now it's getting better, even with the Rangers. There were four Rangers in south Texas who were responsible for most of the brutality; two of them retired, one of them

is dead, and one was transferred, and that is the main reason for the difference."

"Most guys don't get hit just for the hell of it. It's when they give them some lip. You'll find most of them will admit that if you push them."

"When I was in jail, they took a guy and brought him back three days later and I didn't recognize him."

One thief attributed the brutality to the fact that "we're still a frontier kind of country out here, and we handle things quick and even brutal. It's part of the way of life." Another thief in another town made a strikingly similar statement: "This is a frontier state. As far as being up in the world and progressive, possibly we are in professional fields and business and industry. But as far as law enforcement goes, we date back to old times."

The President's Commission on Law Enforcement and Administration of Justice carefully avoided the entire issue of police brutality, but one of its task-force reports did state that "earlier studies . . . found that police brutality was a significant problem. For example, the National Commission on Law Observance and Enforcement (the Wickersham Commission), which reported to President Hoover in 1931, found considerable evidence of police brutality. The President's Commission on Civil Rights, appointed by President Truman, made a similar finding in 1947. And in 1961, the U.S. Civil Rights Commission concluded that police brutality is still a serious problem throughout the United States" (Task-Force Report: *The Police,* Washington, D.C., 1967, p. 181).

Though recent Supreme Court procedural decisions have taken most of the incentive out of the kind of brutality described here (there is no point in getting a confession by torture any longer), it is important to note that those protections matter *only* when the police want to go to court with the person being mistreated. If their intent is to brutalize only, or get information on someone else, there are no more controls than before.

4. Kid wrote, "Yes. He's right."

Another thief went into more detail: "In the last few years I haven't heard too much about the Rangers. Of course they still do some stuff. Like if an old-time character is in trouble someplace and they think that he's been messing with several different counties and towns and stuff like that, they'll go get him. And they'll hide him out. They'll carry him to this jail, and then as soon as they've stayed there a couple of days or even one day, they'll carry him to another. They might take him to some ranch house out in west Texas. They used to have a favorite spot close to Houston called the Windmill. I know you've heard about the Windmill. They used to take you out there and whip you. It's a place out there where they could hold you a couple of days and your lawyers would look for you, and, if your lawyer would get on your trail—say he'd trail you to Richmond or Rosenberg—the minute that he called, then they'd grab you and they'd take you to another jail. And they couldn't catch up with you on a writ that way. And, that way, they'd just whip you, and whip you. And finally get a confession.

"You can't take too much. I used to say, 'Well, they couldn't whip one out of me.' But I've had it whipped out of me, so I'm not gonna say that anymore. You just get to the point where you don't care. You'd rather do some time than take any more of their whipping.

"I'm telling you, I can't see them just slapping somebody and him saying, 'Yes, sir, I'll sign anything.' But I mean when you're *really* whipped. When your eyes are shut and your ears are perforated. Man, in Lufkin they made a believer out of me down there. They liked to beat me to death. They perforated my left eardrum, my groin was swelled up where I couldn't walk, my fingers was swelled. They'd take my fingers and bend them, twist them, stomp on them, and they'd work on these neck muscles here. Did you ever have anybody work on that muscle there awhile? They had my neck where I couldn't even move it. They kicked me in my nuts and everything. All messed up. That was three days and nights of it. Knocked me out. Then as I come to, they'd start again."

5. Notice the tense shift: though Scott is dead, Sam treats him in the present. Note also the apparently gratuitous introduction of the fact of Scott's wealth. It is irrelevant here, until one realizes that in Sam's world there is a Calvinistic equivalence that true worth = professional competence = money. Since one thief rarely has an opportunity to watch another operate and cannot evaluate his style, the operational equivalent becomes how much money one manages to steal, a simple and objective scale. The qualification transfers itself to people in the square world.

6. Kid: "That's a lousy joint."

7. Thieves are divided on the danger of stealing with drug addicts. Some feel that if a man is all right, he won't inform no matter what happens; others feel addicts are bad risks because, once they go into severe withdrawal, police can tempt them by offering a fix. One older thief said, "It depends on what he was first. If he was a character first, then the dope don't make no difference. But if he's a dope fiend first, he's going to get that dope no matter what he has to do or who he's got to do it to."

8. Wilson: "You might doubt the intensity, but not the acts."

9. Kid: "Sam's friends say he's a mullet as a pool player, but *very good* in getting someone he can beat to play him."

10. A man who was fairly close to Sam for a period of several years said, reading this and the preceding paragraph, "Sam is not telling all of his feelings about this 'square-john' girl."

11. Wilson writes here: "Bruce! What's this? I was petrified until the end." The difference between the two is notable: Wilson stole because he needed money; Sam because it was part of a *modus vivendi*.

12. For some odd reason, Sam doesn't consider it *his* luck as well. Perhaps his self-image is such that it is more satisfactory to regard his own scores as dependent on skill rather than serendipity.

13. The same friend who made the comment in note 10 said here, "Very honest for Sam. And I think he's right."

14. Kid: "Hardly."

15. Kid: "Would you believe 1/10 of 1 per cent?"

16. Wilson: "I've myself been rousted while in the middle of at least ten burglaries: *no shots*. P.S. I got away." Another safe burglar said, after reading this section, that he never carried a pistol because he felt that if police suspected he had one, the likelihood of his being shot would be uncomfortably enhanced.

17. To go by recent statistical reports, he remembers wrong. In 1966, according to a letter from Chief Charles Batchelor of the Dallas police department, losses from fraudulent checks reported to the Dallas police department and the Dallas County district attorney totaled $1,108,950; of this, $925,542 was attributed to insufficient funds, and the remainder, $183,408, to forgeries. In the same period, *reported* losses from safe jobs totaled $93,289. Both figures may be deceptive, however. A considerable amount of money taken from safes is never reported—many burglars specialize in the homes and offices of lawyers, doctors, dentists, and other persons who are likely to be salting away cash from the I.R.S., money which, if stolen, cannot be reported as missing. The National Opinion Research Council of the University of Chicago study done for the President's Crime Commission revealed that 74 per cent of individuals victimized by bad checks or swindling did not report the offense to the police, either because they did not want to harm the offender, they felt it was a private matter, or they believed the police could not do anything anyway (Task-Force Report: *Crime and its Impact: An Assessment,* Washington, D.C., 1967, p. 18). Business firms no doubt have a higher reporting rate for bad checks than private individuals, but there is still a portion that goes unreported.

18. Kid: "And I bet he doesn't frequent that place anymore. Mexicans are *very* touchy about being beat."

19. Wilson, himself a safe burglar, writes: "He's right. There *is* more money in checks."

20. In 1966 there were 20,185 burglaries reported in Houston (FBI *Crime in the United States: Uniform Crime Reports* for 1966).

21. Kid: "You bet they don't."

22. Sutherland's thief says something remarkably similar: "Every once in a while some thief will say, after he has had a lot of trouble: 'I am through with this damn racket. I am going to get me a whore and be a pimp. They never get into trouble.' They are generally kidding when they say this, for lots of pimps are in prison, and they generally say it only while they are in prison and are thinking about sex. They do not mean it, for they have a lot of contempt for pimps" (*The Professional Thief,* pp. 181-182).

23. One safe burglar who stole for several years but was never himself part of the character world said, on reading this paragraph, "This is part of the veneer that almost all these types have." He is quite right, but what

I think is more important about this statement is that it reveals how conscious Sam himself is of the veneer. I do not think he is anomalous in that self-consciousness about role. One of the norms of what seems to be character culture is to accept conflicting values, to balance them rather than attempt a reconciliation or selection among them.

24. One old-time Texas robber said of Sam: "Sam for me is a square. He *owned* a joint. I don't know if it was while he was burglarizing, but he had that square job." The man is in part right: Sam's concerns—what he wants to do with his money (or rather, what he says he wants to do with it), his respect for individual entrepreneurship in and out of crime— are very middle-class, very conventional.

25. A Negro booster from Dallas told me about the "proprietor" of the bar out of which he operated: "He'd say to me, 'Hey, look, Joe, I got a neighbor who needs a television. You think you can get me one?' 'Yeah,' I'd say. And in the next couple of days I got him a television or tape recorder or whatever he might want. There was a time when this friend of mine and I, every day this was our job: every day we'd make shopping 'purchases.' We'd drive up to the service entrance and go to work. It was an everyday thing. Where most people work an everyday job and get paid every week, we worked every day and we got paid every day. Sometimes on order, but not all the time. We just worked every day. Say we'd get a bunch of ladies' merchandise, we'd just go to a beauty parlor to get rid of it. You'd be surprised at what we call 'honest citizens,' how they take it. You can just walk in and say, 'How're you ladies doing today? I got something I'm pretty sure you'd like to see.' And you just take it out. They buy it."

26. The fence is perhaps the last of the economic entrepreneurs: as a rule, he is—contrary to the popular image—not a person engaged in a stable operation, but rather someone who adapts to an immediate situation to turn an immediate buck. See Jerome Hall, *Theft, Law, and Society* (Indianapolis, 1952), for a study of fences. Also see J. B. Martin, *My Life in Crime* (New York, 1952).

27. Sam is considerably off the mark here. According to the FBI *Uniform Crime Reports* for 1966, Chicago had 605 homicides in a population of 6,738,000, and Fort Worth had 82 homicides for a population of 639,000; the two cities' homicide rates (per 100,000 population) were, using a slightly different population base, 9.0 and 12.8 respectively.

28 Again, Sam's pride in his state's accomplishments is partially undeserved. Seven states led Texas for homicide rates in 1966: Alaska—12.9 per 100,000 (up to 35 from 16, a rate of 6.3 in 1965, so perhaps anomalous); South Carolina—11.6; Georgia—11.3; Alabama—10.9; Nevada—10.6; Louisiana—9.9; and Mississippi—9.7. Texas, with 9.1, was still comfortably above the over-all U.S. rate of 5.6 per 100,000 population.

Though Sam does overrate some of the cities, Texas does manage to account for five of the twelve leading homicide rates: New Orleans leads with a rate of 14.5; Houston and West Palm Beach are tied with 14.4;

Charlotte (N.C.) and Corpus Christi are tied with 13; Texarkana and Augusta are tied with 12.9; Fort Worth and Fort Lauderdale are tied with 12.8; Atlanta has a rate of 12.5; Birmingham, 12.2; and Dallas, 11.4. Chicago has a rate of 9.0, and San Antonio is almost peaceful with a rate of 8.2 (which is still almost 50 per cent higher than the over-all U.S. rate).

29. Not quite. In *per capita* income, California is third, with $3,457; Connecticut, with $3,690, is first; and Texas is thirty-fifth, with $2,542. But the distribution is skewed, and Texas rates quite a bit higher if we take the *total personal income*, which, in 1966, put California first, with $65,002 million; Texas seventh, with $27,319 million; and at the far end, Wyoming fiftieth, with $874 million (U.S. Department of Commerce, Office of Business Economics, 1967).

30. There is, according to federal investigators, some organized crime in Texas, especially in the larger cities along the Gulf. It is not particularly visible crime, and there is really no way someone like Sam could become familiar enough with its operations to be able to perceive its dimensions.

31. Criminals and police both assume the other knows—and cares—more about them than is ever really the case. It is hardly likely that any working safe man is ever so well known that he will be personally recognized by local police over a wide area, and even less likely that very many of those police agencies and agents will be conscious of what sort of automobile he is using during any particular week. Like drug users, thieves overestimate enormously the amount of time the police spend thinking about them as individuals. The only situation I know in which cars do become well known to police is when the person in question is a suspected narcotics distributor. Since there is a federal law permitting authorities to impound any automobile in which any quantity of narcotics is carried, professionals more and more tend to use rented cars, which minimizes their risk (since often the driver of a car can get off while the car can still be impounded) and keeps police auto registration lists from doing much good.

32. Kid: "I didn't smoke [marijuana] and I didn't drink when I was working. There's no way in the world you can rob somebody or burglarize a bank all doped up. You gonna get killed or you gonna kill somebody."

33. Another safe-cracker said, regarding burglarproof safes: "They weld steel blocks behind them, put soft lead spindles on them and everything else. But when they do, they just get their safe tore completely up. If I walk in and I catch a man's safe door that won't open, I look at it, and if I see that he's got it rigged where it won't punch, well, I'll bring me some gelatin and I'll lift his door off there for him real quick. When you make one burglarproof, it's just more expense on you, because you're going to buy a new one."

34. It doesn't happen often, perhaps, but when it does occur, the effects can be considerable. In one large Texas city there is an investigation currently in progress regarding the activities of a group of lawyers who

are sending burglars to certain homes and offices where they know, from professional contacts, that large sums of money or quantities of jewelry are kept. These set-up jobs tend to be highly efficient, for the sender can give the burglar information on when to go, what to look for, and where to find it.

One of the problems with a 25 per cent arrangement when you don't know what is in the safe is that you can never be sure how much your thief took out. The Bobbsey Twins (the two California robbers mentioned in the introduction) commented to me once that of all their jobs only Safeway holdup takes were accurately reported in the press; everyone else overestimated, presumably to collect more insurance. I doubt that is limited to California victims. If the place robbed were the hiding place for someone with covert income, on the other hand, the press reports—as we have suggested earlier—would be considerably under the actual amount taken out.

35. Not all burglars share this opinion. Wilson said, "I'd a lot rather come in than go out. It's not as scary going in as it is coming out because you never know, there's always the idea that maybe somebody saw you go in. And around Houston you know those police won't come in after you. They lay out and wait for you to come out and then they try to kill you. They're not going to come in after you. They're going to let you come out and then they're gonna shoot you. Or if they can see you when they drive up, then they're liable to shoot you inside or come in after you. But if they can't see you, they're not going to come in."

I asked him, "Do you carry a gun when you work?"

"No. It's a bad thing to get the reputation of carrying a gun. You know you've got your death certificate signed then."

2 · Lawyers, Fixers, and the Police

◻ ◻ ◻

SOMETIMES I think the moral fiber of the police officers in the state of Texas is worse than the criminals.

Take the head of the check department in one town where I operated out of and worked out for a long time. We've had so many dealings that we've become close acquaintances. Not friends, we could never be friends. Once he came out to Las Vegas to pick me up to bring me back to Texas, and while he was there, he and the other officer who came out to pick me up were arrested for rape. Put them in the same tank with me. They had lost all their money and they didn't have any money left, so when we all got out of jail, we went down to the motel and checked in. I got my clothes and everything; then we partied for two or three days. I scored for some grass and some pills and they all got knocked out. I had to drive part of the way back. When we got to El Paso, we stopped and went across the border there and stayed awhile. Of course now, if I thought I was going to get convicted on the case, I would have left them, but I knew that I couldn't get convicted and so that's the reason I came back under such congenial terms.

This same man who was in charge of the check department, I have had him call me numerous times wanting gals for the policemen and wanting to score for some grass or some pills. He'd get to partying and want to stay high. Or when I had my joint, he'd call me up and tell me that the chief wanted a case of liquor because he's going to have a party. And all this is accepted.

And never will they arrest a burglar that has a bunch of merchandise and give it all back. It is just not given back, that is all there is to it. For instance, at my first trial, there was over a thousand dollars cash I had on me at the time of my arrest that was never accounted for. I got beat by a policeman and I'll tell you his name, it's —————————, and I don't care if you do print it. He busted me and I had $1,200 in my pocket and it was never accounted for. They steal everything that they can get ahold of. A harness bull or somebody like that, he probably doesn't get a showdown to get anything, but the rest of them, everything they have in their house, damn near, I bet is stolen. But it can't be traced back, you know; they just take it off a burglar.[1]

I've had times. I'll be driving down the street and they'll pull you over and want to take $50—maybe they want to take a little trip or something. Well, to stay in their good graces and live in that town, it's worth $50 once in a while. So you just give them $50 and go on about your business.

Then I've had a lot of times, I'll be eating in a restaurant and there will be four or five of them over there eating and they'll just send me the bill. Just have the girl hand me their check.

And it's just all part of the game. I mean, you go along with the program so that you will be left alone.

But by the same token, in this same town I can walk down the street at four o'clock in the morning drunk and I don't get arrested. I can drive sixty or seventy miles an hour through a school zone and they'll pull me over and see who I am and let me go. And other little courtesies.

I had California call down on me one time to pick me up for a felony charge out there. And they told them I had been killed in a car wreck. So it's the little things you do.

But, still and all, what they do doesn't make it right.

Because of the new laws[2] there is a kind of law enforcement officer that is going to be forced out. They are going to have to revamp their whole operations. They are going to have to use crime detection where before, in the state of Texas, all they used was violence and coercion and things like that. Now they are going to have to catch you. Before, they might just suspect you, and then they would beat it out of you. There are hundreds of guys in the Texas Department of Corrections doing time for crimes they did not commit. Now there is probably crimes they *have* committed that they haven't been caught for. But I say there are men in here that are doing time, actually, for crimes they did not commit. And I believe it; I know it is a fact. This results from a kind of corruption in the police department.[3]

Did you ever run into any trouble with the tax people?

Hell, yeah. But they're kind of understanding, you know. I've got a good friend that's in the Internal Revenue Service; we've been friends all our lives. I'd talk to him about it and he knows what I do for a living. But how can you squeeze blood out of a turnip? It's impossible. They could come down here and file on everybody in the penitentiary that made over $600 a year, no matter how they made it, but they don't ever do it because think of the money it would cost them, and they'd be forever doing it. They can't get the money, these people here—where in hell are they going to get the money? So the tax people just blow it off. Last time I filed an income tax was when I was on parole. I had to file one because I worked a few days. But I got all my money back. I guess it's been fifteen years. I doubt if I even have a card in the deal now, it's been so long. I think the last time I filed was in 1953, that's when. I don't plan to file again, either.

No, I probably would if I ever squared up or something. I still have my social security card.

Now I've never been involved in a $100,000 score, something that big. Then they might come. But, you know, all you have to do is pay the tax on it and the federal won't prosecute you unless there's a federal offense involved.

When you worked as a check passer or safe-cracker, how did you deal with the police?

Well, you try to have no contact with them.

But it doesn't quite work out that way, does it?

No, not really. When I was busting safes, I hung around a pool hall in Corpus quite a bit, a place that a friend of mine owns. A place to pass the time. It had a nice lounge next door where I'd sit and drink awhile, then go next door and play a little pool. Some of the detectives on the burglary division came in and shot snooker all the time and I'd sit there and gamble with them during the day. And I'd go out at night and burglarize. If there's not a pickup or a warrant out for you, then you had no reason to act any different than you normally would.

I was in a place near Brackenridge Park with Willie the other night, a place that stayed open after hours. It was about two in the morning and a city detective came over and sat with us and I asked him who else was in the place because I noticed some real nice-looking women there alone, which struck me as odd that late. He said that some of them were whores, but they weren't working out of the place, that it was a place where people just went to relax. Then he pointed out a number of policemen and a number of characters sitting down along the bar. And everybody seemed very relaxed and very friendly.

That is *the* exception that way, I think. San Antonio has always been like that. I have stole out of San Antonio and I've lived there. I love to party in San Antonio. If you know the spots to go, it's a swinging town. Man, I dig it, I really do. A lot of times, when I don't have time to go to California or Vegas or something and I want some place to party, I'll go over there for a while. I like it there. Of course I went to military school there and I was born there, but that doesn't make any difference. I still dig the town. I know it real well because I've been in and out of it all my life.

And in that town, the characters and the police department, they had a personal relationship. I've been at parties and the police have been in there, smoking grass, shooting dope, cutting up scores, and turning you on and saying, "Oh, you made such and such a joint over there and I'm still going to bust you one of these days." And most of them bought pussy, you know? It's the only town that I have been in where they were like that.[4] You take a lot of policemen there, they're ex-characters.

Probably the best pool player that ever came out of San Antonio beside Bananas is Li'l Abner. And now he's a terror, a sergeant in one of those precincts. Boy, he's a holy terror. I can't think of his real name.

You asked if there's a feeling of relaxation between the two. Yes, but don't think that they won't strum your head. If they get you down to that police station, if they bust you, I mean if they arrest you in the line of duty, they're no different from anyone else. But still in all, they're very relaxed.

My lawyer, when I got busted that time in San Antonio on that check deal, he made an ass out of the detective that arrested me. Just terrible. The case was thrown out before they ever called the rest of the witnesses. The detective didn't initial any of the evidence. My lawyer said, "How do we know that this is what you picked up? Did you initial it? There's no initial here." He asked him, "Did you have a warrant?"

"No, sir."

"Why did you go out there?"

"Well, they called us in on a raid . . ."

Art just made him look terrible. And reporters were there and we had a bunch of publicity.

So that night I'm in a character joint, kind of a hip place, and so I walked in to pick up this broad. I knew that she was going to be there, but she didn't even know I was going to be out of jail. I walk in, I'm sitting at the bar, it's still kind of early and I'm having a beer and a sandwich, and in he walks. I thought, "Godamighty, man! Boy, my head's going to be sore tomorrow."

He walks up and sits down at the bar and he asks, "How are you doing?"

I say, "Fair." And he just sits there and we had a nice conversation. He paid for my beer and my sandwich!

And he was laughing about how they made an ass out of him on the stand. Of course I had one of the best attorneys in the country there. He said, "Boy, he's an oil burner."

"Yeah," I said. "He's a good lawyer."

And he said, "Hell, he does that all the time." He said, "I'll see you later."

I said, "Well, okay. It's been nice talking to you."

So there was no animosity whatsoever. Now that same guy, if he ever did bust me, well, he's going to take all that out on me. He's got a split personality: one's a party personality, one's a duty personality. They all do. As long as they are not on duty at that particular time, everything's sweet.[5]

You asked me about paying off the cops. It's not really done like that in San Antonio. I know guys that are good to the policemen: they'll buy them a hat once in a while or a new pair of shoes or maybe a shotgun or something like that, or they'll hear that one of them's in trouble and help them out a little. Or maybe they're playing poker and one of them gets busted before he goes home—I might give him a hundred or so. But as far as him coming around each week and getting his money, I don't believe there's much of that. There might be somewhere, but I've never come in contact with it.[6]

I know that at one time San Antonio had a bunch of massage parlors. They're a front for whorehouses. And naturally those people have to pay off somebody because those people have to have some place to operate. They were left completely alone. And when they were to be closed down, the police would telephone and not raid. They'd telephone and say, "That's it; pack your stuff." And that was all there was to it. There wasn't any massive arrests, no campaign, and there was no cases made on them and no charges filed then. They were just on the telephone; they were told, and that was all there was to it.

In Texas it's like other places: the way your payoff comes is where you have an established business of some kind that's illegal. It might be a private club where you have mixed drinks[7] and your payoff maybe is in whiskey. You let them run up a bar tab, or maybe you send them a case of whiskey at home, or it may be that you have to pay off in cash. Other things like that would be a bookie house or some kind of gambling casino, or a whorehouse. It has to be something that is settled and established and where the customers come to you.

But as far as the criminal element goes—and I don't consider a gambler a criminal, I don't think most people do—like burglars, heisters, things like that, in Texas you don't have a payoff. I know for a fact that in Chicago you do. You operate altogether different up North than we do here.

There was a time down here when there were whole towns that were open. Galveston was one. It cost you say $25 a week and another $25 for your old lady if you were running one. And this money was taken off the top of what she earned in the whorehouse. If you were in town by yourself, gambling and partying, you just paid the $25. What that did was this: you didn't *have* to pay the $25, but if you did, it immuned you from all arrest. Say they'd pick you up, you would tell them to call Mr. So-and-so. They'd call Mr. So-and-so, and if he cleared you, if he was one of them that got the $25, they'd just drive around the block and let you off.

But this was when they had the town wide open. This is when they had houses of prostitution with girls hanging out the window naked and all that, waving at you, one house after the other, and they had probably thirty-five, maybe forty gambling joints going there. All kinds of things. The town was wide open. This is the way it was then; now Galveston is a closed town. It's not that way anymore.[8] This was back right after the war.

The difference between the North and the South is something. You take like Chicago. Usually in a district of town there will be somebody there that runs the district. If you're a burglar and you come in from out of town, you scout around, look around for a while, and find out who this man is. It's not hard to find out, anybody can. Hell, all the policemen know this, every whore, every character. All you got to do is run into one. And sure enough, you just go up to him and say, "I just came in from out of state and I need to make some money," and he'll give you an address, tell you what kind of safes you'll meet, and you just go make the safe. Of course he gets his part of it. And God help you if you don't check in with him before you go make it. Don't just go in there and start making safes, because then you've got two people looking for you: you've got the police and you've got this dude who's got the district, he's looking for you too. And I'd rather the police get me.

Have you done that?

We used to. Chicago's full of Texas people. Chicago and St. Louis are the two favorite places they go. Most people go to California or Florida, but the Texas people just migrate to Chicago and St. Louis. One thing, St. Louis is such a good whore town, and Chicago is so good for heisting and things like that.[9]

When you want a lawyer, you don't want a trial lawyer, you want a fixer. You don't care how good he is in a courtroom, you want to fix it; you don't want to go to trial. You're hiring him *not* to go to trial. And if you *have* to go to trial, you're hiring him to get you the least amount of time, you're hiring him so whenever you walk into the courtroom you alre dy know what you're going to get because he's already dealt out what.[10]

If I'm going to trial, actually going in to have one, you know what I like to have? I like to have me a little bitty young lawyer, a fire-burner. You know, one that will go up there and really argue the case. But then I also want a real good old appeal lawyer to get the reversal. And you got some good appeal lawyers in Texas. We got one in Corpus who doesn't ever try a case, all he does is sit there. At Jack Ruby's trial he was there. He doesn't do anything, but he's a research man, he's the best. If you have to go to trial and if you have the money, then you can hire that kind of counsel. Most of these lawyers need fixers because they can't fight their case. They don't know how to fight it. A lot of them haven't tried a case for the last fifteen or twenty years.

Something else: in Texas, if you can stand a jury trial, you beat the case about 80 per cent of the times. But it's hard to fade a jury trial when you've got a record. If you don't have any record, then you can take the stand. It's all right. But if you can't take the stand because if you do they can introduce your record, you've lost half your defense. So in Texas you want a fixer, not a lawyer.

But if you got to go to trial, then you don't want any one of these old fixers that doesn't know how to fight a case. You want a good trial lawyer. And most good trial lawyers are young lawyers that are right out of law school, because at law school they've practiced on this and they're actually better than some of your older lawyers.

Now Percy Foreman in Houston is a wonderful trial lawyer, but he tries cases all the time. The reason for that is he tries capital cases, mostly murder cases and habitual criminal. In other words, they don't have any choice *but* to go to trial, and so he's real good because he's got a lot of practice.

Anybody could be a good trial lawyer if he went to trial often enough. But these lawyers down here, they don't go very often. For a man like Foreman, or any good trial lawyer that's noted as a trial lawyer, the fees are fantastic. Anywhere from $8,000 to $10,000 to fight a case. More sometimes. And you don't have that kind of money. But next to them, you want to get you a young lawyer that's trying to make a reputation for himself. If you're a police character, then usually you've had some pretty good publicity on the case, and if he can get down and win the case, then he'll become known as a character lawyer. And he can make a lot of money.[11]

If you can, get a good criminal lawyer, one that you can trust, and pay him in advance. Just like protection, pay him so much a week and tell him, "I'll give you $150 a week." Or maybe $100 a week or only $25 a week. It just depends on how much stealing you're going to do or whatever else you're going to do.

I had a gambling casino there in Corpus—of course that's all illegal—and I sold mixed drinks there, and that's illegal too. All my legal fees were furnished by the company that had the jukebox concession in my joint, and they made all my bonds. Police used to raid me about every month and take all my customers to jail. I had to make all their bonds. The jukebox company had a man who stayed at the police station to take care of things like that.

And when I used to run whores quite a bit—I had four or five at one time that I ran—I had a lawyer and I paid him $100 a week and he made all their bonds. Of course, when he makes their bonds, all it costs him is the ink out of his pen to sign the bonds; you don't have to put up any cash and you don't have to forfeit any cash, all you do is write your John Henry. So all it is is the inconvenience of having to go down there and to sign your name. What I did, I paid him $100 a week, and I'd probably have to use him once a month. Then if I decided to fight the case, we paid extra for that. But now I wasn't the only one; there was about seven or eight of us that was using the same lawyer. So I'm giving him about $450 a month, and all the rest of them are doing the same thing. So at the end of the year, he's got about $60,000- or $70,000-a-year law practice and it's nontaxable because all that money is cash.

Now that's where I'm different too. Whenever I paid him, half the time I'd make him take a check. Just in case he didn't represent me or didn't do what I wanted him to, I'd take his ass to the grievance committee.[12] The law association has a grievance committee in the state of Texas, and they govern their own. If he fucked me around, then I've got something to take him to.

But it's awful hard anymore to fix these cases. Just about all the old judges in Texas or old district attorneys, people you used to be able to do all that with, they're all gone now. The main thing is to have two kinds of criminal lawyer: the court lawyer and the fixer. You *always* have a fixer. Court lawyer doesn't do you any good because you might get convicted. You got to beat your case *before* you go into court. I have never gone to court in my life and pleaded guilty to a charge if I didn't know what my sentence was going to be beforehand. I would not plead guilty if I didn't know.

Some guys tell me that the judges turn around, they tell them one thing and then do something else. They've never done that to me. They've always done what they said they was going to do.

Most characters are not going to put any money away because there's so much pressure on you when you're stealing that you try to dodge that kind of thing as long as you can. It's like a man with a bad tooth: he'll put off going to a dentist until he just has to go. Same way with a thief. What they'll do is, they'll go out and they'll make some money and they'll party it up until all their money is gone. Not all of them. We're not talking about the big criminal, we're talking about characters that just steal for a living. They just don't have much. Some other guys I know, if they make a big score, they'll buy a little something, maybe a coffee joint, or an apartment house. Things like that. But most of the time, whenever you get down to the real nutcutting of it, if you're in bad trouble, you'd have to see if you can sell your car. You can always sell that. And sometimes you have a little jewelry—you can always give that up. But as far as most characters go, they don't put any money away. Whatever they've got, they've got it in their ass pocket. Some of them, very few of them, will stash some money. I do. But, as I said, very few of us do that.

But about paying off, what we were talking about before: only once in a while can you do it, and the time to pay off is before you ever get arrested. If you got a policeman in town and you're going there—say he's chief of detectives or he's chief investigator for the service department or something like that—then before the case is ever even negotiated, before you've ever even done the crime, if you have given him a new hat or bought him a steak once in a while or taken him fishing or something like that, then you have a better chance. Then you can *talk* to him. The hardest thing about getting a fix in is getting able to talk to the people. If you go up and tell a man, "Look, let's talk this over. I got a thousand dollars, let me go"—if your ties are close enough or your past association is such that you can talk to him like this—he might go for it. But if you're a total stranger, he's going to laugh at you.

Is this the fixer's job?

It depends. Sometimes it's yours.

Say you're in a strange town. Does your lawyer from back home come into this, or do you find a fixer there?

Well, thieves are pretty funny. Most thieves, because every town is different and every state is different, they usually only stay in one state or town, or the surrounding towns that they are known in or growed up in or whored in, and so consequently, what with partying with other characters in those towns, you get acquainted with the lawyers there.

What I have always done if I was in a town and I didn't know anyone—say I just drove into town and got busted— I always contacted my lawyer at home and got him to hire me a lawyer there. Or I would just take any lawyer I could get and just used him as an errand boy until I could find what I wanted. I'd have him call my lawyer in Corpus or have him call the one in San Antonio or someplace I'm well-known. Then you can do what you want to do.

But as far as taking a jackleg lawyer, you don't use them for anything but errand boys. Most of these lawyers in these little towns, they have a little agreement with the chief jailer or someone, and they give him a cut. So if he makes $100 off you, he gives him $20. And most places want you to have a lawyer. If they're investigating, whipping your head, and trying to get confessions out, then after that's all over they want you to have a lawyer. They'll see to it that you have a lawyer sooner or later.

You might wonder how a man in jail could deal with a district attorney. You can, actually, because you have a few things that he wants.

Say they bust you in a building and they've got you dead to rights. They arrest you inside the place, working on the safe. They put you into a jail and you still have some deal-ings. First of all, they give the district attorney so much money a year to operate his office. If you've got a good lawyer or you got one that the district attorney knows will fight, what happens is this: say the maximum he can give you in the state of Texas for burglary is twelve years; all right, I'll take a five-spot and go on down. A five-spot does this for him: on his record, it shows that he *did* get a conviction, and that is all that ever really matters. At the end of the year when he runs for re-election, all he does is amount the con-victions that he has on the record. It clears up the case, it doesn't cost the state any money, and the people that you were stealing from feel satisfied because he sent you to the penitentiary.[13]

But if he tells you, "No, I'm going to give you ten," you tell him you won't take ten. That gives you two alternatives. You could either go to trial with your lawyer and if you get con-victed appeal it, and sign a pauper's oath. Then the state— I guess the county, really—has to put out all that money, they have to type up all those court proceedings, your tran-scripts of your trial, and that's a big job. Then they have to write their briefs for Austin, they have to do all of that. A lot of work for them. Or you can just go up and let him impanel you a jury and plead guilty to the jury. And all the district attorney can do is go up and say, "We caught this man in this house of business working on a safe, and I would recom-mend he gets ten years."

He sits down, and your lawyer gets up and says, "It's true. But this man is hungry, his wife was hungry, his children was hungry, and I don't think it would be justice to put him in a penitentiary for ten years. I think that if he could go to the penitentiary for a couple of years—which he deserves to go—and he gets out, well then he can straighten up."

All right. The jury goes out. They're the ones that set your sentence, and they can set it anywhere from two to twelve, so you still take a pretty good chance of getting a lesser sen-tence than that district attorney was willing to offer you. The district attorney can't tell them if you've been to the penientiary ten times or what you've done before because you didn't get on the stand. And the district attorney knows this. He still, with that jury trial, he still has to impanel the jury, he has to send out subpoenas for the jury, he has to pay the jury. All of that. And if you want to make it harder for him, you can spend four or five days selecting a jury. They got these big court dockets and they want to get these cases off. Because of that and because of what you can do to his budget, most of the time you can deal out so you get just a little bit, then go on down.

The relationship between thieves and lawyers depends on what kind of thief you are. If some guy that works in a filling station or garage gets in a little trouble and his people go down and hire a lawyer, any kind of lawyer's all right, but when a thief gets busted, he has to have a good lawyer. He has to have one that can keep him off that stand, and—the main thing—he has to have one that can keep these police from beating him to death.

Nowadays it's a little bit different and you don't have to contend with beatings,[14] but it used to be that there wasn't but three or four lawyers in the state that the police respected enough where they wouldn't whip you. And if you could get ahold of that lawyer and he could get ahold of them before they whipped you, you wouldn't get whipped. Of course a lot of times before you'd get ahold of him, they'd already done it. Then you have to have a good enough criminal lawyer to get them to throw that confession out, threaten police with filing charges on them, and so forth.

Now a criminal lawyer has to give credit, and the main reason for this is that burglars and armed robbers, if they had any money, they wouldn't be out stealing, they'd be partying. It's as simple as that. If they have money, they're partying, and when they're broke, they start to stealing again. If they get caught while they're stealing, they're broke. Your big-time criminals, they have a lot of money, but they're not getting busted for burglary either.

I don't like to let myself get broke. When I'm busted, I

usually have some money. But I go so strong sometimes, and that's when I get busted.

You take a lot of people, a lot of thieves, they have a hustling gal working for them and she's always in and out of jail. So you have to have a lawyer for her all the time. Usually you use the same lawyer. Where I come from a good lawyer, like the ones I use, if my old lady gets in jail, he doesn't have to go down to sign a bond, he just picks up the phone and tells them to turn her out. He says, "I'll be down in the next few days to sign the bond." And it's all forgotten about. But if you have a mickeymouse lawyer, they make him come down and go through all the formalities, they run the girl through the clinic and all that.

So you more or less establish credit with these lawyers. When my old lady gets busted, I just call him and he gets her out of jail, and the first time I happen by his office I stop and pay him. If I don't have the money, I tell him, "I'll give it to you in a few days." And when I get it, I take it by.

A criminal lawyer has to start out giving credit until he can build up a reputation like Percy Foreman or Fred Semann. They have to give credit because most of us simply don't have the money.

Most of my encounters with lawyers has been in Texas, but I know it has got to be that way everywhere because they couldn't operate if they didn't. For instance, if I am in jail, you can't make a nickel off me if you're my lawyer. You have got to put me on the streets where I can steal something, where I can get ahold of some money. If I want you as my lawyer, hell, I can get the judge to appoint you as my lawyer—it's not hard to do that, you just request it and the judge will do it, and the lawyer doesn't get a nickel that way. But if you can put me on the streets, I might give you $500, $600, $700, $1,000, $1,500, whatever it might take. And you have to remember, when I give you this money, I don't get a receipt for it. I don't want a receipt, all I want is off the hook. If you tell me you can get me off for $25,000, I'll probably go try to rob a bank rather than come to the penitentiary. In other words, if I figure that that amount of money will get me free, then I'm all for it.

The lawyers, they have got to put you on the streets, and they know that when they put you on the streets, that you've got to steal. How can I go out here and get a job for $60 a week and pay a lawyer that kind of a fee?[15]

But a good criminal lawyer, he's worth every nickel of it. You cannot stay on the streets without a good lawyer. They're more essential to you than anything else. And now that the laws are the way they are, boy, they are more necessary than ever, because now he can actually keep you on the streets.

A lot of lawyers can't make it in criminal law because there's not enough thief in them. A good criminal lawyer has to be a good thief. There's no getting around it.[16] Otherwise, he'll have to get in corporation law or something else. But any time you see a successful criminal lawyer, you see a man who'd be a good thief. Because he thinks like a thief, he acts like a thief. And they all party like thieves. They like gals, they like to get a little high, freeze their nose once in a while. Now there might be exceptions, but I'm talking on the general rule.

I have had a judge take me in his chambers and tell me how to steal. Of course he wasn't a big judge, but he *was* a judge. He had the power to set bond on people and turn people loose. I have gone before a judge where his brother was my attorney and where the district attorney's sister was my other lawyer's wife. And we'd all go outside, we'd have some coffee, and wait till the judge got ready. I'd go in and they'd tell me exactly what to say. I'd say that and the judge would dismiss my case. But it cost money, you know; that sort of thing costs money.

There is one lawyer that is doing eighty years down here now. He actually told them where to go, how to get in the building, all those things. It's common underworld knowledge; everybody knows about him. Sam Hoover—he used to be mayor of Pasadena. But those people are few and far between.

Most of them will take jewelry. Any time that you've got a diamond ring or watch, they'll always take that. Especially if it's something for a gal, because they'll give it to some other gal. A lot of lawyers, if you need to get out of jail, you send your old lady up there and trick him two or three times, and you'll get out of jail until you can get some money to pay him with.[17]

Usually, if you're a burglar, then he knows that you're going to go beat somebody's safe somewhere, and if you're a heister, then he knows that you're going to go heist somebody else to get his money.

But I've never seen any of them whose conscience bothers them too bad.

NOTES

LAWYERS, FIXERS, AND THE POLICE

1. This is also the most common complaint of arrested drug users.
2. He means Supreme Court decisions such as *Gideon, Escobedo,* etc.
3. When we squares discuss corruption, we usually mean improper conduct for money or because of political influence. Sam's definition is broader and I think more realistic: brutality in office is as much a corruption of public trust as venality.
4. Wilson: "I have rarely heard of such camaraderie from the characters I know."
5. Jack Heard wrote a long note about this section:
    "What he says about the police is, in some areas, unfortunately true, but I honestly do not believe it is true in the majority of places. There is no question (I've seen it myself; I've handled such cases) that some officers have been overly friendly and have dealt with criminals. There are some towns and cities I know of that, as long as they behaved themselves in the city and as long as they just lived there and were not cracking any safes or cashing any checks or becoming otherwise involved, they were safe. You might call it a safe city. But they had to behave themselves. In some cities it is rumored (and some cases are known) where police departments have had so-called 'goon squads.' If the criminal didn't obey the law according to *their* rules and regulations—I'm

talking about the policemen's law, not the state law—they would go out and take care of him individually. I do not think this is in the majority of places, but it has occurred in the past, and not just in Texas. Sam concentrates on Texas just because he is here. And there are some officers who will deal with criminals in this manner in order to clear up other cases, saying, 'I will let you alone if you'll stool on so-and-so.'

"And about that paragraph where he talks about the place in San Antonio where there were policemen and characters and everybody was very relaxed and very friendly—this is not uncommon nor necessarily immoral or illegal. There is hardly a time that I go to Houston or Dallas or some place like that that I *don't* run across some character I know. If, for the sake of keeping contacts open or getting information, or if the character just likes me and I like him as an individual but not what he stands for, it wouldn't be unusual for me to have a cup of coffee with him. This last week, for example, I was in Houston and I met an ex-convict, a narcotic addict who has straightened up and is doing extremely well. I happen to know his people, too, and they're a nice family. This man got out on parole, served his time. I was staying at a motel there (not a joint) and was in the bar having a bottle of beer and a sandwich. He came in, sat down, and had a bottle of beer with me. This type of thing is not all bad.

"Policemen *must* associate with characters and thieves. So having a cup of coffee or sitting in a bar where a character happened to be wouldn't necessarily mean there was anything unusual or immoral going on. I don't say a policeman should fraternize with them, but if a man is a known thief and he isn't wanted and may be working at a job and the police know this, a decent officer could go in, sit down and talk with this individual and have a cup of coffee and in no way become involved in deals, illegal or otherwise.

"I'm *not* talking about the type of thing he says where the police were smoking grass and cutting up scores and everything."

Sam, because of his position, does not perceive two important elements: (1) a policeman must have some association with criminals, as Jack Heard points out, to maintain adequate channels of information about other criminals; law enforcement would be in a sorry state if characters ever stopped talking about one another to police; and (2) the kind of policeman who will party with him, the kind he sees engaged in illegal acts, is not representative but is the kind he is most likely to seek out himself; he suffers from a kind of tunnel vision and does not realize (or want to admit) that by far the greatest number of the policemen he knows do not engage in such activities.

6. I asked one thief, "Did you ever buy your way out of a charge?"

"Yes, sir. I've bought my way out at times. One time I put three thousand dollars in escrow to a district attorney and got ten years cut off. Of course I couldn't have done that to get out of it, but I did get it cut down. Later, that district attorney got impeached. Not on my deal—it was because he was operating whorehouses in Houston. And another one, I sat right across the table and gave him four hundred dollars in San Antonio for a no-bill, for no indictment.

"If you've got a reputation outside with police officers as being tight-mouthed and tending to your own business and not putting your business on the streets, they'll talk to you pretty much.

"I had a payoff with that man who finally done time out of Houston, a city detective. They know now that every time I was raided I was tipped off first. It used to be, years ago, that he sat with the police car radio and jiggered while I made joints. Heck, I've gone to the border and scored [for heroin] and had him come. I'd call him that I was on my way in and he'd come and take my stuff off me because he knew they were going to try to raid me as soon as I hit the city limits."

7. Many Texas counties are completely dry. In those that are wet, public bars may serve beer only; mixed drinks may be purchased in private clubs only. In Houston the fiction is maintained by having all the big bars incorporated as private clubs, with guest cards easily available. In some towns the fiction isn't even maintained. I remember one night when Sam and I were out in Corpus Christi. One place asked if we were members, we said no; we were given guest cards by the bartender, who then asked what we wanted. In another place, a public bar that wasn't supposed to serve mixed drinks at all, we were refused setups and told that if we wanted cocktails we should order them, at which point we noticed liquor bottles freely displayed behind the bar. Since that place ostensibly didn't serve liquor, we didn't need a guest card—only money.

8. Kid: "Galveston was swinging. Too bad—no more."

9. Kid: "And it's also good for lots and lots of time if you don't have a big bunch of money when you're arrested there."

10. Wilson: "Fixers are becoming passé, but his statement about sentencing is true most of the time."

Sam uses the word "fixer" in a more general way than Wilson or Sutherland's thief, both of whom take it to mean someone who negotiates a payoff with police or prosecutors, a middleman in a bribe. Sam doesn't mean that so much as a skilled negotiator who can talk the prosecutor into a negotiated guilty plea with as small a sentence as possible. If that process requires a bribe, that function is included also.

11. Sam overvalues his colleagues' trade. Most characters, when busted, have no money, as he points out; only some of these have an opportunity to go out and steal enough to pay a lawyer well. Most people arrested on criminal charges are not characters—they are one-time criminals or rums. With not many exceptions, a practice based entirely on criminal cases may be rewarding for one's lust for verbal combat, but not for one's bank account. The great majority of persons arrested on criminal charges do not know how to steal well, and the ones who do do not account for enough arrests to finance very many lawyers.

12. Jack Heard writes here: "He says he was different because he made the lawyer take a check part of the time so he could take it to the bar association. Most character attorneys like that would say, 'Drop dead, get yourself another attorney.' It may have been an agreement whereby the attorney wanted half in cash and half in a check so he would have a record for his income tax. Most sharp character attorneys are as smart as the characters themselves in situations of this type."

13. Martin Mayer quotes "a Midwestern prosecuting attorney [who] told an investigator from the American Bar Foundation that 'All *any* lawyer has to do to get a reduced charge is to request a jury trial.'" *The Lawyers*, p. 159.

14. The Supreme Court decisions and a good lawyer may keep a working thief like Sam from police maltreatment, but there is still little to protect those whom the police have no intention of prosecuting, such as people from whom they want information, or citizens who for one reason or another antagonize them and whom the police wish to punish or harass—depending on the location, civil rights workers, Negroes, students, etc., often so qualify.

15. I once tried to contact a robber I had met in a Missouri prison and found out from friends in St. Louis that he had been picked up on two old detainers by Kansas authorities immediately on his release from Jefferson City. But, I found out, he was not in jail in Kansas. "They got him out on bond. He didn't have any money and those cases are going to be expensive trials. They put him on the streets so he could earn their fees." I naïvely asked how he was earning that amount of money in so short a time. "The way he always does," I was told.

16. Kid: "Not always, but certainly sometimes so." I suspect that not all criminal lawyers would concur. As with police, Sam tends to read lawyers in terms of the few who cater to his very specific needs.

17. He might send women around to his lawyers as a present from time to time, but I doubt that many lawyers good enough to get him out of the kind of trouble he usually finds himself in would find such an arrangement very satisfactory. One lawyer, discussing an incident in which a client tried to send him a girl in the course of a case, said, "I told him, 'Ours is a business relationship. Period.' Why on earth would I want to let him get something on me? I'm representing him because he's paying me to represent him. With the money I make I can get my own women." If Sam is talking here about the kind of third-rate lawyer who handles mechanical affairs for petty criminals, the offer still has little value, for such lawyers always have several prostitutes as clients who are usually more than willing to provide whatever services are required or desired. One lawyer said, after reading this section, "Hell, if he's got a hustler working for him, why would anybody take a trick when, if she's any good at all, she can go out and earn more than it's worth?"

3 · Stealing Is a Full-time Business: Characters, Convicts, and Squares

□ □ □

DOWN HERE in prison, one of these rums, one of these idiots, he's not going to get in my face because he knows that he can't survive and do it. He knows that I'm not going to bull-shit with him, I'm going to hurt him. And so they think about that. That's part of being a character, and they back off. They get in their little ole cliques and their little ole groups and they stay there.

Your rapos, they get ahold of the Bible and they start going to church and they stay there.[1] Your other people, the educated people, they're kind of in and out. If they want to come over and bullshit with us, that's fine. I'll walk around with them and bullshit with them. But you have to under-stand that characters see that other characters have some-thing to smoke, that they have toothpaste, that they have hair oil. We kind of take care of our own, whereas the rest of them don't do it.[2]

Now there's guys down at the penitentiary say they got a world of money, but they're still not characters and they still are taken advantage of. They might be a real badass, but still and all, they are not characters.

A character is a professional thief, I guess you would call

it, whereas the rest of them are on-again, off-again, hooligans-mulligans. Something. They're just not professional. I guess we frown on them as much as a doctor would a chiropractor. It's the same thing. A doctor, he's got his profession, and anything short of that, they figure, is not enough. It's the same thing with us. If you're gonna work, work; if you're going to steal, steal. Stealing is a full-time business, you can't do two things.[3] Just like a pimp: it's hard for a pimp to steal well because you have to do one thing to do it well.

When you say "character," do you mean someone who is actually in the rackets or somebody who acts or operates as if he were?

I mean somebody who makes a living without a legitimate job. Their income is not legitimate. He might be a pimp—he's a character. Of course a dope fiend considers anybody a square who doesn't shoot dope. Don't make no difference to him if you're John Dillinger; if you don't shoot dope, you're a square. They're not really *that* strict, I guess, but in a sense they consider only a narcotic addict a character.

A character is a person who makes his money outside the law. It doesn't matter how. He might be a pool player, which is very rare, because most pool players are squares. But some of them do other things.

Now there is such a thing as a square that could be a safe burglar. He's just one of these old country dings who is a safe burglar. They'd consider him a square. He has to have a few other qualifications. In other words, you have to be a sharp thief. You can't just be a rum. I know some pretty good west Texas safe men that are squares. When they get their money, they go home; they got a wife and a family, and most of them *work* and they bust safes on the side. Those kind of people are kind of hep squares, I guess. But they definitely are not characters because they work, and a character does not work.[4]

A lot of squares have a little bit of character to them, but a lot of squares have no character to them. Take my two best friends. They're in the wholesale grocery business. I grew up with them and both of them have always worked. They never did go to the pool hall very much after school in the afternoon, and they both went into the service instead of staying around the United States and partying. Both of them went to Korea and got into battle; they spent all their time on the line. Both of them went to Japan for a couple of R&R's. But all of their life they have either worked or been in action; when they came back from the service, they both got married and had families to support. They have no character in them.

There's another thing. You have kind of a "hep square" we call them. A hep square is a person that knows a little bit of what's going on. For instance, I've got a friend who owns some drive-in theaters and some drive-in restaurants. This guy's a fantastic golfer. We were out with the guy that owns the newspaper there in Corpus and my friend had already beat him out of $40,000 that year playing golf. This guy, because of the gambling and the traveling around the country and going to Las Vegas playing in the tournament and going out there to shoot skeet, well, he's about a half hep square. Now he likes to smoke a joint of grass once in a while, and something else—he likes to trick the gals. He's got a bunch of good-looking girls working for him. Of course he's got a nice wife; I used to go out with her. But he'll ease off and get one of them gals and go party, go off on a weekend, get high, take a few pills. He's kind of a hip square.

The head sales manager of the Ford Motor Company in ———— is a hep square. He likes to get high and he takes bennies all the time; he's always got a pocketful of bennies. A friend of his on the police department is where he scores for them. He may bust somebody with pills and they're used as evidence; then he gives them to this guy. He's a hep square. He likes to go out at night, go to character joints, have a few drinks, and he can talk shit a little bit.

Of course you've got a lot of people who want to be hip squares; they'd give anything in the world to be a character.[5] I know a guy who just inherited over a million dollars who would give every nickel of it just to be a character. He just wants to be, that's all. That's all he cares about.

There's something romantic to a square john[6] about a character. Hell, whenever you have a trial, people line the streets to look at them as much as they would a movie star or something.[7] It's somebody that's doing something that they don't think that they can do or something that they think they can do, curiosity or something, I don't know what it is. But I know millionaires who are very very successful in their field who would like to be characters, and every time they can get away from their business or their wife, they become characters. They party with you, they run with you, everything.

I know two men, their father was one of the founders of Humble Oil Company, and they don't work or invest in the oil business much anymore. They have an awful good income from their father, which they inherited. They run with characters. Hell, one of them stole a gal from a friend of mine, he got her. And then I know a young boy from Victoria that inherited a gob of money. His father just died the other day, but when his grandmother died, he got $9 million, and this guy would rather be a character than anything else in the world.[8]

But he's a mark, and there's a difference between a square that's running with characters being a mark that they're using and somebody that they like. This guy, I felt sorry for him, but I never liked him. Consequently, although I felt sorry for him, when the money shows, I'm going to make some money. That's the difference between a man you let hang around for what he can do for you and somebody that you like.

A lot of criminal lawyers would like to be characters. In fact, any time that they can get around with some characters, they start partying with them. That's real common. And a lot of doctors like to party with characters.

A character life is mostly a party. I don't think people understand that it's quite like that, but it is. In other words, you don't work.

When you get your money, you usually get it real fast and you have a lot of time to spend it. You can sleep all day if you want to[9] and you can go out and get drunk, get high—you don't have to get up the next morning to go to work. The women that you have around you, their moral standard is the same as yours and so you have a lot of fun and get a lot of cock. And as far as sexual drive, what a lot of people call weird is just normal to them.

On the streets I know hundreds and hundreds of characters, but I don't know their names. Say you're a character and I'm a character and I see you with a character that I know. I have no way of checking your credit rating or anything else, so I judge you by who you associate with. If I know that this person is a good person and not a polecat, not a stool pigeon, not the man's man, then I have to give you credit for being all right.

That's one reason the narcotics addicts have such a hard time in surviving. The police, all they have to do is buy narcotics from one and they've got him, whereas me, even though they might know I'm in town, they still have to catch me. Say you're an addict and we get in pretty good together and I'm an agent. We're shooting dope and everything and I go off and can get all the dope I want, naturally, so you and I are shooting dope. After three or four days I tell you, "Man, my connection has blown town, he's not going to be in for three or four days. Can you score?" Well, you've been shooting dope with me for that time and so we go around and buy it from four, five, six, or seven people. And there you go: I've got you all. That's the reason it's so easy to catch a peddler.

We have to justify people by how they appear to us and who they associate with. Now that fella you asked me about this morning, if I didn't know him, I could sit down with him and in just a few minutes I could probably tell you almost his life story. First of all I'd ask him where he's from, and say he says, "I'm from San Antonio."

I'd say, "Well, do you know Harry T————?"

And he'd say, "Well, no, I've heard of him. But I know his brother."

Then I know that he's a pretty high-rolling thief. But if

he says, "Yeah, I know Harry T———— real well," Then I know he's a booster or a carny or something like that, because that's all Harry is.[10]

I have never had a character tell me a good score, never. I had one tell me about all kinds of scores, and the last time I got out, I made about eight or ten joints that he told me about. Companies, shipping outfits, YMCA's, things where there's supposed to be some money there. Well, there wasn't any money there. Things change. Anyway, I never had a character tell me a good score, but I have had some of them tell me they knew there *wasn't* anything in there or some place had been beat lately. But characters, they stick together more or less, whereas these other people, they don't stick together too well.

Characters and pimps and whores, they're all in a family, kind of like the cat family. They don't all have the same personalities and they don't operate the same way, but still they all operate outside the law and that gives them a common bond.

I don't know what it is about me, but anywhere I go, whores are attracted to me. I can go into a whorehouse and leave with a couple of them. I can go in a bar and end up with two or three of them. Square girls are different, and I don't have nearly the amount of success with them as I do with the hustling girls. I don't know why.

For instance, once I got jumped out of a building out in west Texas; I had been in there working on the safe and so I had some heat on me. A friend of mine got arrested in Galveston and he had a shoot-out with the police and he was connected with me. What happened is, we had been in Houston and he had the old motel room key in the car and he had to tell them I was in Houston. They wanted to know where he got the key because they thought it came out of a burglary. All they had on him was assault and he just told them that he was there with me, but anyway it all got around that I had some heat on me and I knew it. The ex-mayor of Pasadena, he's doing eighty years down here now, he called me long distance and told me I had the heat on me. This boy had tried to retain him as counsel and he showed me the courtesy to call to tell me to lay low for a while.

I went to a little Western resort town named Bandera, Texas, up by San Antonio. There's a lot of legitimate ranches around there, but it's primarily a dude-ranch town in the summertime. They have Western bars and dances and all that stuff. I remember when I'd get out of military school in the summertime and I'd go up there working as a dude wrangler. You got $75 a month, but you had all the fun in the world; it's hard as hell to get a job, but once you do get it, you've got your summer made.

So I went up there and I sat around two or three days. I was messing with some little tourist girls there and having a good time. I had plenty of money and I had a nice room and I'd just swim and eat and party. The law enforcement there was nil—there just absolutely wasn't any—so I had no chance of getting jumped up on. I was registered under an assumed name, and there were no other characters there.

I was sitting at the bar and this guy came in. Up there everybody's very friendly and everybody buys the house a drink and so on. We just got to drinking back and forth. This ex-movie star was there and I had known him for quite some time, partied with him several times, and he just knew my face and not my name, and so when I told him the name that I was using, he just went along with it. Anyway, it's one big party. You go in the joint there and sit at anybody's table; everybody's very friendly. Ask any girl in the house to dance and nobody ever refuses you a dance; it's that type of environment.

I was sitting there, as I said, and this guy was sitting at the stool next to me. We sat there and talked a few minutes.

Now years ago I heard about a boy that had retired. He had made a pretty good score and he retired and they told me he bought a ranch up around Bandera. This boy I didn't know, but I had done some business with another boy that used to run with him. The boy that retired, his name was Speed. I don't even know his real name, just Speed.

So when I looked at him, I thought, "I bet this is Speed." We sat there and it wasn't but a few minutes. We had a couple of drinks, everybody's drinking, talking together, and it's very casual. Everybody's wearing Western clothes.

So he got up and he's standing there getting ready to leave. He asks me, "Where you from?" I told him I was from Odessa. Of course I'm from the other end of the state, from Corpus Christi. And he said, "Well, I'm going to Odessa right now."

I said, "That's good."

He said, "You don't want a ride back home, do you?"

And I told him, "No. I'm gonna be here a few days."

I got to thinking: "Man, this has got to be Speed."

He introduced me to his wife and I spoke to her and we had a drink and he said, "I've got to go." And they left together. They went out and got into a Ranchero, one of those Chevrolet pickup cars. And they left. I dismissed it because I didn't figure I'd ever see either one of them again.

The next afternoon that girl came to my room at the hotel and she knocked on the door and she said, "Won't you buy me a drink?" Well, as I said, this town is so casual that it's not really outlandish. Only thing is, she's a permanent resident and this is a hotel where everybody knows her husband. Or seems to.

I told her, "Well, okay." So we went in there to the bar and it was a madhouse. We kind of separated and we'd get back together and have a drink, just very casual.

I was standing by the jukebox getting ready to play it and she walked up to me and she said, "You're a character."

I said, "What do you mean? That I'm a nut or something?"

She said, "No. You're a character. What are you, a pimp?"

"No, I'm not a pimp," I said. "Are you a whore?"

She said, "I used to be. And I know goddamned well that you're a character."

She couldn't have picked up on slang or anything else because I just don't use that kind of language. She just snapped after an introduction and maybe a four- or five-minute drink when he was getting ready to leave.

I guess to people outside the law there's a certain aspect or a certain look they have.

But as far as the police are concerned, I don't have that look. I told you before, I'd be sitting in a bar and they'd come in and arrest half the people in there and let me go. Never even question me. I don't know why. But to another character it's automatic.

Another time I was sitting in a joint in Houston. I had bought an airplane and it was out at the airport. I got it secondhand and it was delivered there, so I'd driven into Houston and a friend was going to take my car back to San Antonio and I was going to fly the plane back. The name of the place was the Four Palms and the girl came up to the bar and she served me and I thought she was quite attractive. We sat there and we bullshitted for a few minutes, nothing important, and then she waited on the other customers. Then she kind of came back where I was. We sat there and messed around, messed around a bit. The weather came in, as it does in this part of the country, and I did not want to take off, so I figured what the hell, I'll just pick up this girl and go partying. We sat there and I had some more drinks and she's really friendly and everything is fine. So I told her, "What time do you get off? Let's go have something to eat and party awhile."

She told me, "I don't party with characters. I got my fill of them a long time ago."

Now I didn't mention anything out of the way, I'm dressed like a businessman in a dark suit. She must have been a pulled-up whore or something. She knew, without question. She didn't say, "Are you?" She just told me, "You are." To her it was positive, just like I'm a white man. No ifs, ands, or buts about it.

Whenever you walk into a jail, if you're a character, the other men there will recognize it. Most jails let you go in in civilian clothes. Some jails, like Harris County, which is the largest jail in Texas, they put you in dungarees there, but you still keep your shoes. A character's not going around in old beat-up shoes, you know. Not if he's a money-maker, and most characters will have a lot of money, because they're going to steal until they get some. They can tell if you're a character. You can tell in your line of work about someone else, and you can tell if a man comes up and sells you something—you can tell if he's a successful salesman. You can tell by his coat; he may have a suit on and you can tell if it's a good suit or not. It's the same thing with a character. With whites, one thing that usually designates a character from someone else is his shoes. When you come in, naturally, they've stripped you of everything and all you have is your shoes. So you can look at a guy, and if he's got on a $40, $50, $60, $100 pair of shoes, you can consider him a character.

Even in prison it works that way. The first impression you make on inmates here, unless you're known, is by the kind of shoes you got on. Where you come from, Stacy Adams are worn by colored people and way-out people. In this part of the country, especially the big cities of Texas, they're worn by all the thieves. So if you come in with a pair of Stacy Adams shoes on, automatically you're classified as "not a dingbat." You're not down here for beating jukeboxes or something like that. More than likely you're down here for stealing or shooting dope or running a whorehouse. Anyway, something that's productive.

Now a nigger, if he's got some gold on his teeth, then he's probably a character, because you have to have extra money to have gold put on your teeth. You have to have cash in your pocket—colored people call it "cash dollars." You know, they've got cash dollars; that's no check, just cash, you know, the green. So anyway, if you have cash dollars to get the gold put on there, that means they've got extra money, that they've got some good clothes. So when you see a Negro coming in and he's got gold on his teeth, you can almost figure he's some kind of character. Just like with whites, they'll look at your shoes or your ring or your watch. Usually your shoes are most prominent because by the time you get to the penitentiary, the lawyers have your nice diamond ring or diamond watch. When you get here, about the only thing you've got left is your shoes; other than that you're just about blowed. Lawyers, they get all the rest of it.

In your profession you have ways of recognizing the good from the bad, just like we do. It's just something that stands out. It's not something that you can say is one thing, because it's not. It may be just the way he's carrying himself. He's not a guy who goes into a jail and is looking around and is afraid of something. When I go to jail, I been there so many times, I'm not scared. The only thing I'm trying to do is find out who's the best lawyer to call. If a guy comes into a tank or cellblock, the chances are more than likely if he is a character that there will be somebody that knows him. If he is from out of state, there's a difference. He probably won't know anybody, but he won't be there long before somebody'll know him. They'll ease up and they'll ask him two or three questions and then they'll back off and somebody else will ask him some. They feel him out; it doesn't take long.[11] If he is a character, then they take care of him. They give him something to smoke, some clothes to wear until he can get some, some hair oil. Things that in here are luxuries outside are nothing. All these things, if he is a character, will come to him. And when he goes to work like here, out in the fields, they'll take care of him. They'll go tell the boss, "Boss, he's a pretty good ole boy, he just drove up. Give him a chance to harden up, we'll arry him." And they'll let him strike and they'll do his work for him until he can build himself up to where he can do it. Otherwise it'd damn near kill him.

Probably would. Characters don't work on the streets, and when they come down here, they're usually pretty dissipated. And after laying in jail for maybe a year or two, physically they're in pretty bad shape when they drive up. Not always, but most always. And all these things are taken care of as long as he is a character.

Say that a person comes in and he's unknown. They assign him a cell and maybe he's put in with a character. That character in time will be able to get that man moved out.

If nothing else, they will probably end up fighting if it'll help get him moved.

But when he's first put in with this character, there will have to be some kind of association even if the character doesn't want him. You're living in a little small cell with no room to walk around, just the two of you in there; you spend so much time there that you have nobody to talk to but him. This person, he will more than likely be on the fringes of the characters.

In the wing you'll sometimes have as high as 130 or 140 men. You'll have several groups of characters in there. They won't all be in the same group, but you have to respect them. If they need to borrow something, you give it to them. You don't actually loan it to the clique or the group, you're loaning it to an individual out of that group. And when I say the word "clique," I don't mean they have cliqued up and are going to hurt somebody or offer protection or something like that. I'm using the word "clique" as friendship; they just kind of clique up together. When they go to the store to buy food that they all eat, they go together. They kind of take care of each other. If a guy needs something, they see that he has it.

Now the boy that's put in the cell with them will be on the fringe of these cliques. When they eat, they'll ask him to join them until they see how he is, what he is. And always you can get hold of his record. You can find out what's the real scoop behind him. Sometimes it takes a while, but you'd be surprised at the times that the officials let it out. Anyway, through hook or crook, however it might be, it finally gets back. So then you know what his crime is, the conditions of it, and the way he conducts himself. If this man does not fit in, he's eased out. But if he does fit in, he's still not accepted fully for a long time. He has to earn his respect from these men. But by the same token, you can take another guy, a new guy, bring him in and you put him in a cell with a rum, he is liable to be the one who revolts. He is liable to have the rum moved out. Then gradually he will clique in with someone else.

Now you have a lot of guys that are characters and good convicts, good characters, that don't clique up with anyone, that don't join anyone. Myself, I'm a lot like that from time to time. When I first went in the wing, I didn't know but one boy in there. I knew a boy over there that was a damn good character and everybody knew him. We grew up together in the same neighborhood. Consequently, he paved the way for me for everything. Any time I needed anything done, I asked him and he asked the right person and had it done for me. Like I needed some new work clothes, I'd ask him and he'd see that I had some new work clothes. If I needed some information about mailing packages in and out, I went to him. He told everyone in there that I was a character and was stealing a long time but just hadn't been caught and that was why none of them knew me. He left soon after this. We were in the tank together only two or three months. I would have moved into his cell but he had a punk in there and the punk was supporting him and everything.

But I stayed on the fringes. I was well respected. Nobody jumped on me or even thought about it. They helped me in the field when I couldn't make it, and if I needed something, I could borrow it from anybody. But then gradually, of the different character cliques in there, I found one that I liked a little better than the rest of them. I liked those boys better and I just eased in. Then I became real entrenched in this one group. The main boy in this group and I are still real good friends. He's a librarian up there now. He's a good boy.[12]

There's other characters, as soon as they walk in the wing, they'll just clique right up with a group. They'll just go right in with it. I didn't do it because most of the cliques there had two or three guys in them that I just didn't really care for. I mean I didn't dislike them and I knew that they weren't snitches or anything, but I just didn't care much for them. Either they were loudmouthed or boisterous or nasty-mouthed or something like that.

Probably we're more class-conscious here than you are on the streets. Probably much more, because that's all we have.

Out there you have a home, an automobile, and airplanes and bank accounts and clothes. But here we have none of that. We all wear the same clothes except for shoes, and now the state is furnishing us with what they call "low-quarter" shoes. Actually it's a dress shoe, like a plain-toed navy shoe. The only thing we had was our jewelry and our shoes to distinguish us from anyone else.

You know, you can look at a person, the way they carry themselves and the way they act, and know a lot. A guy can walk in the penitentiary and I've never seen him before in my life and I know whether he's a character or not. They just have a look about them of—you know—intelligence.

Now some of your characters are *not* very intelligent. Some of them can't even read or write. Well, this puts them in a class too. But they're accepted because they are good thieves and on the streets they live good.

But crimewise you have a differentiation there too. First of all, you've got your rapos, and you've got your women-beaters and your women-killers and your incests and all of these crimes that are against another person that is more or less unprotected. Those people are looked way down on. Because we know that they will do it to my wife or your wife or our children just like they'd do it to anybody else. And don't ever forget one thing: that characters think a lot of their families because that's about the only thing that they have. They're the people that, whenever we get in jail, they're the ones that send us money to have something to smoke; they're the only ones that you can depend on. So, actually, characters really know what a family means, probably more so than anyone else that never had to call on their family. So they're pretty conscious about their families.

Now, you've got your intelligents, your intelligent people in the penitentiary that are not characters but they're fuck-ups. A lot of these check writers are college graduates. They're not a rum, you can't consider them an idiot or a rum, and you can't consider them a character, so they're just some of the people, you know, they're just part of the people that make up the population of the prison system. They don't have any definite place in a prison system.[13]

Now you take, for instance, your burglars, armed robbers, especially guys that have been down here two or three times or have a good reputation on the streets as a money-maker, and your dope pushers and your first-class pimps, they're usually pretty much all right.

Usually a pimp's a sorry motherfucker. He don't have cods enough to steal and all he wants to do is stand around and whip some gal, you know. But where they really sin and get so many people down on them, that's when you come to the penitentiary they'll go loop-scoop your old lady and get her selling cock and they don't send you any of the money. They play you for a sucker. Well, when you get out, you take care of your business. Most of them are sorry, but some of them aren't. And almost all burglars and almost all characters from time to time have a gal that sells cock. When you're out, you're associating with those kind of girls and they'll say, "Well, I've got a chance to go over and make a hundred," and you tell them, "Hell, go make it." So then, that's pretty easy and you tell her, "Go make some more." It's just one of those things. In other words, if I'm sitting here drinking Scotch day in and day out and you're sitting here next to me, sooner or later you're going to have a drink of Scotch. It's the same thing with them gals and characters: you're around them and they're selling that pussy and sooner or later you're going to get hooked on one of them more or less and that money's going in your pocket. But don't ever think that a character feels like that's a permanent arrangement. He knows that gal's liable to be gone tomorrow. There's no real feeling or anything. They're just there, that's all.

Your real characters are not just people that shoot dope or take pills, but they're the ones that actually get out and use the underworld as a means of livelihood and go at it in a professional way, in a professional manner. That's their primary concern and that's the way that they make their living.

And you'd be surprised at the way the police treat us and these other people. I mean they treat us with a certain amount of respect because they talk shit, you know. Hell, they talk as much character talk as you and I can. And they get their point over and you get your point over to them. Of course sometimes it don't do you too much good. But still in all, with the new laws it might.

A lot of times you might define somebody or a good friend of mine might define somebody as a character and I might not—because I have my own standards and he has his. To him a guy might meet the standards and to me he doesn't. To me, if a man has ever gone on a stand to testify against anybody or signed a statement against anybody or did something wrong, I don't consider him a character. But nowadays it seems like the statute of limitations on that is about six months; then it's all forgotten.[14] But I don't never forget it; I can't help it, it's just the way I am. Everybody has their own conception of what a character really is.

I think a character is somebody that makes his living completely outside the law but yet has some principles about it.

You know, I live good on the streets; people don't realize it. I live in a nice air-conditioned apartment, I drive a nice air-conditioned automobile, I spend my leisure time in Las Vegas or New York City or on the West Coast. Sometimes on the way out there I'm working or on the way back I'm working. When I go out at night, I go to a nice night club and I see good entertainment and I eat real well. I live as good as a president of a bank when I'm on the streets. Sometimes I don't stay out there too long . . . but when I am there, I go first-class. In every way. If I don't have the money to go first-class, I just don't go. But I can't stand to go short, man, it just burns me up.

But that's what I consider a character.

We've got guys like Bulldog, you know him. He's been a thief all his life. Now he's a thief, but I don't think he's a character because he doesn't have enough class. He's just one of the multitude. Whenever he gets ready to rob somebody, he has to have somebody to drive him there because he can't read a road sign, he'd get lost on the way. To me, that's not a character.

A character has to have some kind of polish about him, a little bit. When I'm on the streets, I pride myself on having a little bit of class. But some of them don't.

In your view of the class system in prison, then, the characters are at the top?

Right.

How do the people on bottom feel about the characters?

They're envious—just like the people in the free world would like to be president of a bank.

I'll give you an idea of how it works. My job is prison dentist. One day a week a free-world dentist comes in to do the major work; I do the other stuff the rest of the week. I learned that stuff in here. Now teeth are a prime concern. If a character comes on the farm and he has a hole in his tooth, the hole in his tooth gets filled. I'm different than a lot of dentists here; a lot of them use their job to make their spending money. That has always been done in penitentiaries. But, you see, this is some of my crazy philosophy; I don't believe in it, I don't do it, and that's all there is to it. I'm not scared to do it; I just don't do it because I don't believe in it. But a lot of places, a lot of farms, a character will get his teeth fixed free and it costs somebody else money. That's not just Texas; it's like that everywhere. Here, about the only break I give them is that I fix their teeth first. But that's just a matter of choice, there's no monetary value or anything connected to it. And I do fix the other man's teeth, too. I don't break it down and say "I'm just going to work on a character." I don't do that at all.

And something else: the penitentiary officials, they recognize this; they recognize the class consciousness—I mean the class distinctions—and they operate accordingly. You take all the key positions in a prison: they're either given to the intelligent person I was talking about, like the check writer, somebody like that who got off in a storm, or they're given to characters. But if it's handling other convicts, if it's down to where you're going to tell another convict what to do and dictate his policies to him, they always get a character to do that.[15]

Hell, the penitentiary knows it, man; it's on your record. They realize it the second that you come in. They know that I'm a character. I've never been taken to the captain's office and asked to cop out on somebody or tell him something; he knows that I'm not going to do it. He respects me enough where he doesn't even ask me. So we get along fine. Most of the times, when they give one of these idiots a job, they bring him in and tell him that; well, he didn't even bring me in and talk to me. But he knows it wouldn't have done any good. He knows I would have agreed with him. I'd tell him, "Yes, sir, I sure will," and all that. He knows I'm lying to him. There's no sense in it, so he doesn't even bother; he just blows it off.

But the penitentiary knows that there's characters and that there's idiots and these rums and so forth. And your characters will always be running the penitentiary. They can't hire enough guards, so consequently they're running it.[16]

I have more power on this farm right here than some of the bosses. They can't lay a man in, but I can. All they can do is get out there in that picket and sit there, whereas I set policy and I spend state money; they can't sign an order and get a thousand dollars' worth of supplies, but I can. I can't abuse it, you understand; I have to get it cosigned by someone. But still and all, that boss up there in the picket can't, because most of them can't read or write. The new ones can, but the old ones can't.

Does this character and noncharacter dichotomy apply to Negroes as well as whites?

Certainly. You have colored characters and you've got colored rums. And the same thing applies here as it does there. I don't know enough about them to know how closely you can compare, but I do know that the boys who are building tenders, who are running something, are all pretty good thieves on the street. Of course, as I say, I've never stole with niggers.

Do you ever hear of squares who become characters by this kind of association?

There has to be some, really. You know about Smith. Now Smith was a square. Maybe he's not too good an example because he still thinks a lot like a square. The only time he steals something is when he needs some dope. But when he does need dope, then he becomes a character. Once he gets hooked, then he runs with characters on the streets too.

But I'm sure that a square with some intelligence—not a rum square, I don't believe he'll do it—but you take maybe a used-car salesman type, one that dresses sharp and he's been around the joints and he knows some pretty fast girls, he can do it. I don't know how to explain it except that he has been in action, he's traveled, he has made pretty good money, and he knows a little bit about sports and he likes to bet on sports, things like that. These people in their own field are characters, so whenever they come down, they come right on in. But they have to have a pretty good personality.

You can't take a guy who might have been president of a bank and send him down here, he would probably never become a character, because he never associated with anybody. But people in some work, they're on the fringes of the underworld anyway. You take a used-car salesman: they always overcharge on cars, misrepresent them—they're stealing in a legal way. People like that, they're easily adapted to prison and prison society as far as a character is concerned.

The men who have no criminal record but this one offense, how do they make out with characters, and do they ever turn into characters?

If they committed a crime—say they killed someone in the act of trying to rob them—that makes them a criminal. I think what you want to know is about a wife-killer or someone like that, maybe a used-car salesman who happens to get pissed off at his wife and kills her. He comes down. He'd probably turn into a character.

You don't have to have any outstanding free-world attributes to become a character. You don't have to be able to shoot dope and things like that to come down here and become a character. It's more or less how you handle your personal business while you're here. If you're a snitch on the street and you're a known snitch, when you get here, you've got a bad road to go. You could never become a character. You take a person who comes down here who is a good character and figures that snitching will get him out of the penitentiary soon and turns into what we call a "man's man," then he could never go back in the free world and become a character.

But the crime that you commit on the street that you come down here for, whether it's your first crime or your hundredth crime, that doesn't qualify you to become a character or not become a character. It's just the way that you are.[17]

One guy I know real well, he killed his wife while she was ironing. He'd never become a character. He's a painter by trade and he's going to paint while he's down here. They'll put him to painting water towers or buildings. He'll never become a character in no way because he's too set in his ways. He thinks like a square john and that's just the way he is.

Characters, they don't think like a square john. Values don't mean the same to them. For instance, this man who killed his wife while she was ironing, he would rather kill her than see her out selling pussy. A character, he might kick her ass but he'd never kill her; he'd make her sell pussy. They have different values on things.

Well, you say, how can a guy send his wife or his old lady or whoever he's living with out to sell pussy? It doesn't mean anything if she goes out to *sell* pussy. But if she goes out and screws somebody for nothing, *then* she's sinning.

Or if she goes out and turns a trick with another character for money, she's sinning then too. Why would another character *buy* pussy from your old lady? He's trying to steal her, he's trying to get his story down. He's not buying pussy so much as he's buying time to talk, time to get his story down. And you don't want her to hear any stories. And so if she took off her clothes and she's going to hear a story, well! As soon as he walks in the room, she's going to know that he's a character and she doesn't have any business listening to his story.[18] In other words, she knew that she was doing wrong when she did it and there's no excuse for it. But it's only the way people think, you know.

I was trying to think of other people besides car salesmen. I keep bringing them up because they are so prominent in this part of the country. Some of your biggest gamblers and biggest spenders in this part of the country are used-car dealers or they work for used-car dealers. If you go to a strange town and you got a gal and you need some money, you just put her in a car and she'll go from used-car lot to used-car lot. Just drive up and say, "Anybody want to buy some cock?" And you can make some money. Or if you've got a bunch of pills that you want to get rid of, all you've got to do is go to a used-car lot and get rid of them. Get ten cents apiece for them. If you've got five thousand of them or six thousand, maybe you got them by hook or crook, then you can always get rid of them.

And truck drivers, some of the truck drivers in this part of the country make big money. They don't drive on the road, they drive right in town for the oil refineries and things like that; they make a couple hundred a week. Some of them are awful good tricks and they gamble pretty good. They could easily become a character if they went to the penitentiary. Of course they could easily become a character if they stayed on the streets, too; they don't have to come to the penitentiary to become a character.

How does someone like a bank official who has been convicted of embezzling, one of those people who is completely noncharacter but has been carrying on in a very criminal way and hasn't associated with characters, how does he fit in?

I'll give you two examples. The Premont State Bank, which is in a small town below Corpus, has about a $1,500,-000 capital; it is a small bank. The vice-president actually ran the bank because the county judge, who was the president, lived in another town about twenty-five miles away from there and he never went to the bank. This boy, Archie, didn't have a degree from college but he had banking experience, he had worked in a bank a long time even though he was still a pretty young boy. He got to running around with some friends of mine down there and got to gambling, went to the chicken fights, playing a little poker, shooting a little dice. He got to losing a little money. Well, he got to floating some loans through the bank.

There's a bunch of Mexicans down there that are real wealthy; they own a lot of land and land's worth a lot of money in that area, $600 or $700 an acre. One of them owned a dairy. The bank took care of most of their land transactions, paid their taxes for them and things like that, because most of them couldn't read or write hardly. So Archie said, "How about signing this so I can take care of this tax problem for you?" The guy would sign it and he doesn't even know what he's signing. Archie would type him out a $25,000 loan and he would sell the loan to the National Bank of Commerce in San Antonio and he would get that money. It ended up, with all his deals, that he got about $800,000.

Archie started running around with gamblers and characters and whores around Premont and around Corpus and then he started going out to Las Vegas and a real good friend of mine set him up there. I don't mean he set him up, he provided Archie with the kind of entertainment he liked. But it came to the same thing. So when Archie gambled out there, he gambled in a joint where Sonny Quilt is the pit boss. They beat him pretty good. Beat him for about $50,000 and $50,000 on credit, and about thirty days later he sent them their $50,000. Then he flew back out there with a gal who worked at the bank. She wasn't a whore, but she was a pretty hep gal. He bought her a new Pontiac and things like that. He made two or three trips to Vegas and he blowed a bundle. Then he got to plunging at the VFW hall and places like that where they have gambling. And in that part of Texas they have a lot of games, a lot of poker games.

Finally he got busted on it. The bank examiners came in and he hired a lawyer. The lawyer he hired was a fine lawyer, but he had a lot of clouds on him. He was held at one time for murder and a political slaying. But at that time he was city attorney.

The boy came into my cell in jail and he lied to me. We got to talking there and he told me he'd been out to Las Vegas several times and we talked about it a little bit. We talked about the Premont people and I asked him if he knew Good-town Slim and two other people and he said, "Oh yeah, I know them real well. Play with them all the time."

Then I knew. As soon as he said he knew them real well and that he played with them all the time, I knew he was guilty.

Because they're tough. Some of the best poker players in the United States. They go all over the country playing and they are tough. And he's not smart enough to beat them. You know, they can play him and give half his money back, and he still couldn't get there.

So then, as soon as he said that and I knew, I asked him, "Did you play when you was in Vegas?"

He said, "Oh yeah, I got a real good friend out there."

"Who is that?"

He said, "Sonny Quilt and his brother."

I was raised with them. They started out dealing craps in my uncle's joint and I've used both of them as bust-out men in my joint and I *know* he got beat. There's no question about it. So then he tells me about all this money that he won and that's where he's getting all this money he's spending. And I know he's lying.

He ended up with four years, which is real good.

This guy, he was well respected outside. He came in and he's not respected as a character, but he will become a character because he has all the qualifications for it. I mean that whenever he got to gambling, he started messing with a bunch of whores, and I know he's smoking a little grass. He bought him an airplane, he bought a boat, he knew he was going to get busted and he bought him a ranch in Mexico.

All these things. Incidentally—he had to give the ranch back. But he bought him a nice home, his wife had a new car, and the gal he was keeping had a car; he had some real nice jewelery, he was well dressed. What I mean is, he liked the fast life and he will ease into it. Now he is a natural mark and he will be a mark for a long time. But he will change, and when he does, he'll become a character. When he gets to prison, he's going to lose all his money gambling, they're going to talk him out of everything he has, but in time he'll change, and then he'll become a character.

Why are you so sure of that?

He's smart enough that he finally will snap. Now he's blowed over half a million dollars, and you would say, "No, it looks like the guy would have snapped already if he's going to ever." But you have to remember that the people who got that money from him are professionals, they're the type of people that beat the smarts. Anybody can beat a dumb man, but it takes a smart person to beat a smart man, and he would never have become vice-president of that bank if he hadn't been smart. Although he didn't have a college education, he's a pretty hip guy. And he was young, about thirty or thirty-five. He had a wife and three children. He was a northern boy; he'd come down here from somewhere in the North, I'm not sure where exactly. He likes the fast life and he will turn into a character. He went to the federal.

I don't know too much about the federal, but I have heard a lot of stories about it, and I know that it can't be too different from anyplace else. Characters, or professionals, whatever you want to call them, they're about the same throughout the country. They stay pretty much together. Archie, with the banking background that he has, he'll have a good job in the penitentiary. And so they're going to be wanting things from him and consequently he'll drift in and he'll end up being a character.

How typical do you think he is? What about embezzlers in general?

I have known one that knocked out all the money of the Corpus Christi Hardware Company. He was gay, and of course he was never accepted. I know another one that was gay that knocked out the city treasury of Hearne, Texas, and he was never accepted.

But now here's a case in point. Two weeks after Archie left for the penitentiary, this other man was taken to trial there in Corpus. He had embezzled $12,000 over a long period of time. He used it to supplement his income. He was chief or head cashier of a large Corpus Christi bank. They're not paid a great deal of money, but they are given a lot of authority and a lot of prestige. This man lived in a house that my family used to live in. It's in a nice section of town; the house isn't too expensive but only two blocks away there are $150,000 homes. He had a daughter and a son, they were in high school. To supplement the income for people like this, the bank sometimes gives them a kind of little franchise. He was given the franchise to the bank parking lot. The bank charged him so much a year rent on the land and he in turn leased places in the bank parking lot, not only to the bank employees, but also to other people that worked in the surrounding office buildings.

Someway, he was taking money out of the accounts of people in the bank and depositing them into the parking lot account, and then he would take that money out. He was about a twenty-five-year employee, and in all that time, in all those years, he only stole $12,000 or $12,500, a nominal sum. Make it $14,000. But he did it over a long period of time and he never did make a killing or anything. When they busted him, he pleaded not guilty and finally he changed his plea to guilty. He was given a five-year sentence with an eight-year federal probation. He's got five years in the penitentiary and eight years on the streets on parole or probation.

This guy was quite old to be busted; he had two children in high school. I'd say he was fifty to fifty-five, maybe. I can't judge age very well.

The boy from Premont, after he changed his plea to guilty and he came in, I said, "I thought you told me you didn't take that money."

"Well," he said, "you know how it is."

I told him, "Well, hell, four years is not bad, man, not for all the fun you had." And he kind of laughed about that. With him it's "What the hell, I just got caught and I'm going to do my four years and I'll be back out." But the other man, at his age I imagine he'd have a pretty hard time getting another start. He told me that a man offered him a job as an accountant at a pretty good salary, so he'll probably have that when he gets out. I don't know, he might have just said that. But he was real bitter.

In fact, he was so bitter that he told me how to rob a bank. It's actually very simple. The night deposit bank there only holds so much money and it gets full on the weekends. What they do is go by and open the night deposit door and take the money out of it and set it on the floor beside the night deposit box. They'll come down the following day—like if a Friday's a holiday, they'll have all the receipts for Friday, so Friday night or early Saturday morning they'll come down and take that money out and put it on the floor. Then either this guy who told me about it or the man who was at the commercial check-out counter or the cashier's cage would come down and take that money and put it in the vault. Not in the key-ster in the vault, but just in the main vault. But the vault would only work one time each day, so they had to set the clock, usually for about three o'clock. The rest of the time that money was just sitting on the floor. One deposit was from a big department store and usually it had about $80,000 in cash. The only thing between you and that money is a glass door, which is nothing. You can jimmy a glass door in a minute.

When he told me all this, I said, "Man, that's ridiculous."

He said, "If you don't believe me, just walk up to the glass door and look in there. You can see it sitting on the floor."

I told him, "Man, that's funny."

And he said, "You forget one thing: it doesn't belong to the bank."

I said, "Who does it belong to?"

"The federal government. They're insured by the federal government. So long as they have some kind of locked door between the money and the outside, then their insurance is in effect and they have nothing to lose."

And it's just like he told me.

The only reason I'm telling you about this bank is they built a new bank and they have got a new system now. Before I could get there and talk to them about it, they built a brand-new bank and everything is different. But even now at this particular bank they open up one cage every morning with $400,000 cash and there's not any alarm in the bank or any connection with the police department.

And something else: I didn't know it then, but the guard at the bank has been instructed to never draw his gun on bank property. The reason for this is if you rob that bank and the guard pulls his gun out and shoots at you and misses but hits a customer or somebody else, the bank has a lawsuit. But the money's not theirs anyway, so it doesn't make any difference, so why should they take a chance on having a lawsuit or a big stink over something that's not theirs anyway? If he wants to follow you out off the bank property, then he stops being a bank employee and becomes a deputy sheriff, and then he is acting on behalf of the county and can carry out whatever duties he wants to. But as long as he is on the bank property, the only thing that he is there for is to keep out undesirables, drunks, or stop little arguments or help people park, or if their car won't start, he's supposed to call and get them a wrecker or take a battery charger out there to get their car moving, or even help them with flats. He is there as more of a bouncer than anything else, though.

Anyhow, the guy who told me about this bank, he's real bitter, and he's an older man. He'll go to the penitentiary and he'll just sit down in the corner somewhere and do his time; then when he gets out, he'll work in a grocery store or something else, but he'll never change. Actually, he doesn't think that he really stole from that bank; he thinks that they underpaid him and that he was just taking enough to get along on. They shook his house down and they couldn't find anything extravagant there. The FBI ran a check on him and they know he wasn't betting on the horses or gambling anyplace else. He was actually using this money to supplement his income to where he could live and his family could live as a middle-class family. And that's all he *was* doing.

Here are two embezzlers: one of them steals $800,000 and he gets less time than the one who steals only $12,000.

I don't think there's any question but that you should steal big.

I know one thing: you go out and write $75,000 worth of checks and you write $1,000 worth of checks and you'll get in a lot more trouble with the $1,000 than with the $75,000. This is because they want some of their money back and because they have more respect for you.[19] Any criminal law-yer will tell you: the bigger the crime, the easier it is to get off or get you less time. I don't really know why, it seems like it would be the other way. And I'm not talking that you'll have some of the money left for him and his trial expenses either, but it just seems easier.

You take a lot of guys that when they come down the first or second time to the penitentiary, they come down with a good reputation from the streets and they're good characters, they're good convicts, they don't mess with anybody's busi-ness, they're not snitches, they have a lot of friends, they get along with everyone. Sometimes they'll do a small bit, a cou-ple of small bits, maybe three-year sentences; they'll come down and in twenty-one months they're out. Well, when they get out maybe after a couple of times, they turn into pure creeps or pure rums. They stop taking care of themselves and everything. And when they come back to the peniten-tiary, it's the same thing. Instead of coming back and asso-ciating with their old friends, they clique with the rums, the truck drivers, the wife beaters, the child deserters, the rapos, and things like that. They kind of drift off from all the peo-ple they've ever known or associated with or buddied up with while they were in the penitentiary. These guys also stop taking care of themselves in their personal appearance. You can stand in the hall and watch them go to chow at noon, for instance, when they're all working. You'll see some guys go along in a nice clean white T-shirt; their pants might be black and muddy, their shoes might be black and muddy, but they'll have on a nice clean T-shirt and their hair will be combed and their hands will be washed when they go to chow. If you look at them from the waist up, they don't look like they've been out there in that field digging dirt all day. Whereas your rum, why he'll just put his shirt right back on, his hair won't be combed and his nails will be dirty, and he'll just be slopping along down the hall. I don't know why it is, but some guys when they come back, they get like that. I'm telling you this because you should know that if a guy's a good character or a good convict, there's no guarantee he'll stay that way.

There's something else funny that happens to some people: they come down here and their age seems to fix at what it was when they come in. I'll tell you why.

Down here you have no contact. Because of television we have more contact now with the free world than we did at any other time. All the new cars that come out, we see them; clothes, women, homes, things like that, we see. We're all brought up to date in a lot of ways with television, but you still don't have the physical contact with things outside. Television has made a big difference; things used to be really bad because you'd go outside and the whole thing was weird to you, but even so, it doesn't solve the problem.

We have one boy on this farm now, he got seventy years for armed robbery and he came down when he was seventeen years old. Now he actually thinks like a seventeen-year-old boy. For instance, he's always wanting to run somebody a foot race. Who in the hell wants to run a foot race? I don't, but he does. He wants to relate to things that happened when he was in high school or anything prior to that. When he talks about a girl or woman, he's talking about some little young girl that came over and told him another girl wanted a date with him. It's strictly all juvenile, though he has grown in other respects. But years ago, when they didn't have television down here, he just stopped, and he never has picked back up, so now he's like a seventeen-year-old kid. There's

other men who have been down here twenty, twenty-five
years who came down when they were youngsters, and they
remain at that age.

But you take a man who was thirty or thirty-five years old
when he came down here and has had some responsibility—
supported a family, for instance—that man is not inclined
to stay the age that he was when he came down. But a kid
that has never had any real experience in the world doesn't
know anything, whereas the older man has had these experiences on the streets, and so when he gets down here, he
doesn't just stop. His life kind of goes on and he does age.
But he still doesn't age as much as he would in the free
world.

And something else: I don't think they age as much in
appearance as they do in the free world. Down here I see
guys all the time that are sixty or seventy-five who look like
forty to forty-five. Physically they stay younger. The reason
for that is in this penitentiary we have adequate food, you
get plenty of sleep, and you can't become dissipated. There's
nothing to become dissipated with. Actually, you lead a good,
healthy, clean, normal life. Only thing is there's no sex or
anything like that. But as far as being overworked, some of
the men down here have to work pretty hard but they end
up with jobs like I have where after a while you don't have
to work hard anymore. And even the work in the fields, it's
not like it was in the old days when they had all that brutality and you worked sunup to sundown; anybody can make
it once he's had a few days to get himself broken in.

*You just said "there's no sex or anything like that." That's
not quite true, is it?*

Depends on who you're talking about. For some people
there's more involvement in here than they had outside.

I've been locked up for three flat years next month and
I've never had any desire for a punk. And I'm one of the
few people that has access to them. Any time I want a punk,
I just go in and tell that boss, "Let me have So-and-so." I
could be working on their teeth, he wouldn't know, and I'd
bring them up here. You know how long you've sat in here

many times with nobody coming in. I can lock that door, and I'm the only one that has a key to it. I could just lock that door and have a ball. But I don't care anything about it.

But, man, some of these guys go wild over these boys. I've seen killings over them. I saw a guy steal damn near all the money in the commissary and give it to a punk. He was working in the commissary and the punk came up to eat and he'd just give him anything in the world, and he *knew* he was going to get caught. And this guy was getting ready to go home when he started all this. He couldn't help himself. If he could have stayed straight sixty days, he'd have gone home.

Is there any difference in the amount of sexual activity of characters, squares, and dings?

I would have to say that the characters mess with the punks more than anybody else. In the first place, they're about the only ones that can get access to them. The rums, they don't ever have a job where they can do anything; characters are about the only ones who have jobs where they can get access to the punks. Usually the girls are pretty restricted, so it takes a pretty good go to get the punk out.

Now there's only a few natural punks in there that are free-world; the rest of them are penitentiary turnouts. Nobody messes with them. A free-world gal,[20] she's not going to mess with one of them rums anyway. If you're not a character, you know, she's pretty goddamned choosy down here, and she's not going to mess with one of those idiots. If she wanted to do that, she's got a bunch of them in the tank with her[21] that are going both ways, and she doesn't mess with them. So they're pretty independent, you know.

But I do think that characters are more inclined to mess with punks than other people. They've had more dealings with them, they've been to the penitentiary more times, they've been to jail more times. The rest of these people, they probably really don't know what's happening.

I'll tell you something: I did an entire hitch in the penitentiary and actually didn't know what was going on. I mean I knew that they fucked them in the ass and all that, but

I didn't know that they would get as *involved*. I thought they would just go up there and stick a dick in the ass and get their nuts off and walk off.

Let me tell you a story. A boy just went home, a good friend of mine, named Charlie. Charlie got hung up on this kid. Charlie was doing twenty-five years. He had one of the best jobs on the farm. He was in charge of the laboratory, making teeth, drawing two-for-one, getting ready to go home. He got caught taking that punk down one day. It cost him his job, his good time; they put him in the shitter. Well, they raised Charlie on that farm over there; he came down when he was a kid and he grew up on the farm. The major made him his camp boy. That's a good job—two-for-one—almost a cinch to make parole when he comes up. What does he do? He takes that punk and puts him in the camp room with him. Goddam! The same punk. Finally they broke him; they put him in the shitter again and took all his good time, which had been restored, away again. He's got a mother who is about to die and he's trying to get out so he can see his mother before she dies. They put him back in the line and the major called him out one day and told him, "Charlie, would you promise me, if I give you another chance, that you will never mess with that boy again?"

And Charlie told him, "I can't do it." He said, "I love that boy." And all he had to do was just straighten up to get out.

You know how he got out of the penitentiary? The punk was discharged and Charlie straightened up and now he's going home on parole. But if that punk was still here, Charlie would still be fucking that punk.

What happens to people like that when they get outside?

You know, as soon as they get outside, they don't mess with guys anymore, they start messing with chicks and they don't think anything about it.[22] My fall partner was a notorious punkfucker in the penitentiary and he got out and he just converted right over to girls with no problem whatsoever. I don't think he ever got involved with one as deeply as Charlie, though. Man, we've had people down here commit suicide over them old punks. And punks commit suicide over them guys and try to commit suicide, and there's stabbings and killings and everything like that.

Who are the people most likely to become penitentiary turnouts?

It's hard to explain. In the first place, they have to be weak. In a penitentiary, the strong live off the weak. The strong are more or less going to survive better than the weak. They don't necessarily have to be strong physically, but mentally they do.

Physically it's something else. There's a lot of them that are hogged for it. They grab them and throw them down and either threaten or put a knife on them. Hogged—same as bullied.

I'll give you an instance from this farm. You can take two colored guys and both of them are physically capable of handling any situation. They will be put in a wing down here and they'll fall in love and they will turn each other out. And when they get caught, the boss will usually shift one to separate them and put the other one in the punk tank. They'll put him in there and he's just as happy as he was; he doesn't feel like it's a slander or a degrading situation, he don't give a goddamn. He likes it in there.

Whereas me, I wouldn't go in. I'd just stand outside the wing. They'd have to take me to the shitter or transfer me or do something with me, but I wouldn't go in. You know, in the penitentiary they can hog you for a lot of things and they can make you do a lot of things, but there's a lot of things they can't make you do. And that's one thing I wouldn't do. I wouldn't go in.

I don't know why, but the other colored inmates don't think any less of them either. Instead of looking down on them or laughing at them or sneering at them, they start sending them cigarettes. But that is the colored population.

With the whites, a punk is a punk and they have more of a tendency to live off the punks, whereas the colored punks live off the studs. Some guys will send punks a little stuff on a white farm, or a lot of them will, but there is more sent from the punk tank to the stud tank than there is on the colored farm. On a colored farm it's all one way, it all goes to the punk tank.[23]

I know a white boy, a dope fiend out of Houston, he's about thirty years old now. He got in jail and he wasn't a punk, he was just a little old dope fiend. Gordon had a good-looking old lady; she was a real money-maker. This broad got to messing around a little bit with a boy out of Houston when Gordon was in jail one time. Gordon sent word from jail that he was going to take care of him when he got out. Gordon got on out of jail, but the other boy got in jail about the same time, so nothing ever transpired between them and Gordon got back with his wife. A while later, he got put in jail again and he was put in the same tank with that other boy. The boy that was messing with Gordon's wife was in there with about fifteen or twenty guys and they really messed over Gordon. They made him eat a shit sandwich and a bunch of things like that and they started fucking him. And they turned him out.

Now Gordon was a real good boy and he made parole and then got busted and he's back on a parole violation now. I know that he doesn't like getting punked, but it's gone so far now that he's scared to say anything about it. And he is not in the punk tank, he's in the tank with everybody else. And the officials don't know about this. He's not a free-world punk, he's a penitentiary punk.[24]

We classify them two ways: penitentiary punk and free-world punk. If they came down as a gear, they're not looked down on as much as one who got weak and was turned out while he was here; that is the difference.

A punk here, you can screw him in the ass or get him to suck your dick. Now some of them won't suck your dick, they'll buck on that, but they'll take it in the ass. A queen will do everything and a punk will just take it in the ass. But down here some of the punks will do everything, too. It depends on the individual. A free-world gal—in other words, a free-world queer—they're thought a lot more of than one who was just hogged down here.

In the punk tanks, the way the system works down here, they will take a person that on the street, say, has committed some kind of rape, maybe on a little girl or an underaged girl, maybe his sex drive was actually for an older woman but he couldn't find one that day. They take and put him in the punk tank too, and those people are usually the easiest to turn out. They're all easy to turn out.

But you take a free-world gal, a free-world punk—when she's living in the punk tank, she won't have anything to do with the penitentiary turnouts. There's a lot of friction between the two. They hate the penitentiary punk and they talk about him something terrible. They could probably get sexually satisfied if they wanted to associate with them, because when there's one hundred men living in one big room, you can't stop everything. But the free-world gals, they look down on a penitentiary punk, they know that they're weak. Free-world punks don't think they're weak themselves, they think that they're normal and everybody else is not, but they know a penitentiary punk is weak or he wouldn't have been hogged or done something that he didn't want to do. I know a lot of the penitentiary turnouts and I've never seen a strong person yet turned out as one. I know some free-world gals that are physical bulls, bad people who will kill you in a minute, but all the ones that I've ever seen turned out in the penitentiary were weak. Some of them have money, but a lot of them don't and they will sometimes turn out for money and charge for it just like a whore would. But the majority of them too are weak. They got to be weak to sell it.[25]

You have to remember that in this penitentiary the only thing a man is paid is two sacks of Bull Durham; they get that once a week. Everything else you have to buy.

They have two barbers in each wing and they give all the men shaves and haircuts. Toothpaste and things like that they have to buy. We give each man a toothbrush. If he doesn't have any toothpaste, he can get salt tablets and mash them up.

But there's a good bit of money in the system.[26] A man can wash clothes for it or clean up somebody's cell; usually you can manage. If a guy wants to hustle, he can end up with a little something.

Down here, if a person gets a dollar a week, he can live pretty good. Even less than that. If he's got seventy-five cents a week, he could smoke all week, buy all the Bugler he needs, have toothpaste and hair oil, things like that. It's not like in the streets. It doesn't take a great amount of money. If you can just hustle a little bit, you can live real well.

A lot of men in the penitentiary get disability from the government. Sometimes people clique up and take care of each other. The boy who works here with me, he doesn't draw, so I buy all the hair oil and toothpaste, shaving supplies and shoe polish, and things like that for us.

But some of the people, the weak ones who don't know anybody, the illiterate, they're just in bad shape, that's all.

NOTES

STEALING IS A FULL-TIME BUSINESS

1. The belief that sex offenders tend to become excessively involved in prison religious affairs is shared by many inmates and a number of prison administrators in most of the state institutions I have visited. Several sex offenders whom I have interviewed seem to have come from inordinately repressive and religious homes, but it is hard to tell when their prison behavior is a natural reversion and when it is simply an attempt to curry official favor. In an anatomy of prison character types, the authors of the *Convict ms.* wrote: "There is the Bibleback, a particularly disgusting type of sycophant, who attends all the religious functions, wails the loudest, sings, prays, and performs all the external functions required to become known as a Christian. He is an out-and-out hypocrite, and is generally despised both by the officials and the inmates. The vast majority of these individuals are sex deviates."

2. Wilson: "It's not that way with most characters. That's the way *he* believes it is because that's what he done. See, when he shared with somebody it meant it put him one rung above them because he was

dropping them by giving them something. It made him look big in their eyes and that's how he wanted to live."

3. Wilson: "I believe a character is a dyed-in-the-wool burglar, a thief, someone that's making his living solely on others, on society itself."

4. The center of respectability is a shifting point: one thief who knew Sam well in prison said he considered *Sam* a square, not because of any personality defect, but because at *one* time Sam had owned and operated some bars, which is both legitimate and stationary. For this man, the contamination of having worked is never voided.

Jack Heard wrote here: "He is expressing his pride in himself and his profession: 'If you're gonna work, work; if you're going to steal, steal . . . you can't do two things.' I think it is also an expression of pride of his status in the community. Note where he's talking about dings, 'country dings,' and means the safe burglar who is not a character, the ones that get money and go home to their families, men who work and bust safes on the side. He says those people are 'hep squares,' but not characters because characters do not work. This is the type I told you about when I said that not all good safe men are characters. I knew one in San Antonio who is one of the best. He is one of the best thieves I have ever met, yet when he traveled, he traveled as a businessman; he stayed in a good hotel, but in a salesman-type room pricewise; he dressed neatly, stayed out of the joints and didn't run with characters. But when he was in prison (the reason I know this is I was in on the arrest and investigation of the case he last served time on), he would be what your man described as a 'country ding.' But the respect for him and his ability was not questioned: everybody knew of this man somehow and they all respected him because of his ability as a safe-cracker. He was not a character and never has been and I doubt he ever will be. He had a good family, good home, his kids went to school and were divorced from his operation. I have to disagree with Sam on this: a man doesn't have to be a character to be a good thief or safe-cracker. It's just that some of them are smarter than the others, some of them are better businessmen at this sort of venture."

A Negro thief, who considered himself a character, put it this way: "As far as the inmates are concerned, to be a character is a privilege. There are squares in all types of life, even in the field of characters. There are square characters and there are hip characters, and if you are considered a hip character, then you are way on top of the list. You are admired, respected.

"A square character is one who knows nothing but maybe robbing, maybe burglarizing, and it isn't on a large scale—they break into a joint one time and take something and they're hit. He has no fore-thought about how to protect himself. Square character and hip character, this is like being professional and nonprofessional. When you are a hip character, you're one who doesn't stoop to small deals like knocking a fellow in the head or snatching a purse. You have a trade. You are a pickpocket, an extra-good pickpocket, or maybe you're top pimp, maybe you're what we call a 'drag man,' the term to use for 'pigeon dropping,' when you and your friend are able to stop an individual outside of a bank and convince him some kind of way to hand his life-savings to you. This is the highest form of character that you can have—to be able to use intellectual means rather than physical violence to obtain money."

5. Sam sometimes confuses categories. Kid points out: "Sam's definition of character is broad. This type in modern idiom would be a *swinger*, but not a *thief*, which is for me essential." Though Sam several times says a character is a person who makes his living outside the law, he often confuses the life style with the occupational role that produces it. There is no reason at all for his businessmen friends who like to get high and party to want to steal.

6. And, obviously, to a character.

7. They are also mesmerized with the same morbid interest by serious car wrecks, burning buildings, and assassinations.

8. Sam's constant references to millionaires here need two glosses. First, as I said in the introduction, money makes you real in this character world, and it doesn't really matter how you acquired it. Someone like Sam would, I suspect, think more (or at least more often) about a fool worth a million or two than he would a broke genius of noble soul and splendid virtue. Second, the topic is very Texan; it is not limited to characters. Outsiders often joke about Texas millionaires, but residents seem to take the matter very seriously, seriously enough to plug it into conversations frequently. I remember one weekend in the course of which I saw Sam, spent a night with some friends in San Antonio, an afternoon with some faculty people at the university in Austin, and played in a poker game with a judge, a banker, an agronomist, and a fairly high ranking state official. In *all* the conversations, the topic of millionaires came up, either as something to be discussed itself or when people were tagged as one, much like a Homeric epithet—it had no necessary immediate relevance, but was part of the person's name in many circumstances.

9. John Gagnon commented to me once, "Did you ever notice how career criminals of this type *sleep* a great deal? Their life is episodic, going from job to job, party to party, and there is nothing connected with their role to do in between, so they sleep."

10. Sutherland's thief says: "Language is not in itself a sufficient means of determining whether a person is trustworthy, for some people in the underworld are stool pigeons and some outsiders learn some of their language. Another method is by finding out what people the stranger knows. If he belongs to the underworld, he will know some of the important people in the underworld of Chicago, Baltimore, Kansas City, or some other city. It will not take long until a profes-

sional thief will find mutual acquaintances if the stranger really is a professional. What he knows about these mutual acquaintances will show whether he is trustworthy. If he knows someone in the local community, it is possible to ask this one about the stranger." Sutherland, *The Professional Thief*, p. 20.

11. When I asked Wilson if he made it a practice to determine if strangers in jail were characters, he said, "Certainly. You have to. You look and ask what he's in for. Usually somebody knows. And usually somebody knows him. I don't care where you're from or where you appear in the jail, somebody comes in there and somebody else is going to know him. If nobody knows him he's automatically an outcast anyway, so he just goes down to the row."

The *Convict ms.* said: "If he is a good fellow of another penitentiary, he will relocate here as a good fellow. A fink in another prison will become a fink here. There seems always to be on hand in every group someone who knows something about every newcomer that arrives, even the out-of-state convicts. A con's history haunts him till the very end, and prevents the child-molester from Sing Sing from arriving here and commanding the respect due, say, an out-of-state hijacker."

12. One inmate wrote here: "I know who he's talking about. This guy is doing life for traces in a fit [minute quantity of narcotics detected in a hypodermic syringe] !!! Can you believe that? It's so."

13. Several thieves agreed with Sam's description of the prison social structure; one of them wrote, "From the character viewpoint he is very accurate." From the *non*character viewpoint the structure might seem the same, but the weights assigned the different roles tend to vary considerably. There are even some important variations within the context as Sam presents it. Since Sam had money, it was never important to him as a status symbol, but it was to many of the others. Wilson said, "If a man's got money he's in. Whether he's a character or not, the characters accept him because he has money and there's always something they want in jail or something they need."

"*Say he's tight with his money?*"

"He's out. And usually they'll find some way to jump on him, start a fight with him."

"*To get his money?*"

"To get his money or just get even with him for not spending some of it."

14. Jack Heard said, "I have found that as many or more characters give information. They generally want something in return. They will give information if it is of any benefit to them, and they will do it as fast as anyone else will, as fast as any convict or inmate."

15. What he doesn't perceive is that the prison administrations are operating not on the basis of class recognition but rather on the basis of recognition of abilities: the character is the manipulator, the one who (along with the people Sam calls the "intelligents") is capable of doing

good work, the one with enough prison experience to know how to do it well enough to get along without disrupting the orderly processes of the system. There is every reason why he *should* get the good job, especially because (and I suspect Sam might be loath to admit this) he really earns it. Warden Sidney Lanier, of the Ramsey Unit, Texas Department of Corrections, said, "It just wouldn't be fair *not* to give them the jobs."

16. He mistakes administrative willingness to assign earned privileges and options for actually "running." Inmates do not make policy decisions; they do not control prison conditions. The more qualified inmates are put in the positions of responsibility they earn, not just to keep the prison going but because it is good for them. In certain prisons I've visited in other states, but not in Texas, the kind of running Sam describes does exist. In those places the only real rule is "Don't go over the wall." They tend to be rather hellish on inmates, for they become totalitarian states with status predicated on physical power. Sam, as accustomed as he is to having a quiet go in prison, wouldn't tolerate one of those places very well.

17. Here we might distinguish between prison and free-world status. Sam is using "character" in the free-world sense, meaning someone with most of the characteristics described above. It is of course quite important to your prison status that you come in for a "respectable" crime. As we have seen if an inmate has scored for considerable quantities of money at various points in his career, he is generally accepted no matter what his outside social life looked like. To be excluded by the inmate power structure he has to antagonize the inmates somehow; the rum, on the other hand, begins by being excluded and can only gain acceptance by manifesting whatever the particular prison defines as inmate virtues, a process that is usually unsuccessful and, when it does succeed, takes a considerable amount of time.

18. The only time a character would buy time from a local prostitute, as Sam is pointing out here, is if he were trying to convince her to work for him.

19. The former point holds, not the latter. Authorities will deal for a piece of the $75,000 back, but if the total amount is only $1000 or so, there is little to be gained by negotiating; they would just as soon prosecute and be credited with a conviction.

20. *Free-world gal* or *gals*, in this context, are men who were acting-out homosexuals on the streets, especially those who affect gross feminine characteristics. These have considerably more status in prison than do the *penitentiary turnouts*. Sam doesn't mean that *nobody* at all bothers with the penitentiary turnouts; he means that no one he considers of any importance does. And in that he is wrong.

21. Homosexuals, both free-world and penitentiary turnouts, and sex offenders are kept in a separate cellblock.

22. A Missouri inmate put it this way: "A guy doesn't think down inside

of him that he's just a strong out-and-out homosexual. He recognizes and says that now circumstances made it necessary to do this. I have no women, what was I supposed to do? It seems that masturbation has a lot of appeal to the young, in the youthful days, but there's a strong sex urge wanting to go someplace. It's a temporary thing, though. You know: When you can't get wine, get whiskey."

23. One inmate wrote here: "I don't know why, but Negroes are fantastically concerned with punks. From what I hear, this might be different in other parts of the country." Though there have been some general studies of sexual behavior in prisons (most of them are descriptions rather than studies), I know of none that tried to distinguish on the basis of racial, ethnic, or socioeconomic backgrounds of the inmates involved. Sam's impression, however, is shared by many inmates—Negro and white—and prison administrators in the South.

24. A recent article on this topic says, of the role Sam calls the penitentiary turnout, "Once an inmate has fallen into this role it is extremely difficult to shift out of it, and, if a current relationship breaks up, there will be pressure to form a new one. Even in reincarceration there will be a memory of his role from prior institutionalization and there will be pressure to continue" (Gagnon and Simon, "The Social Meaning of Prison Homosexuality," p. 26). This is usually, but not always, the case. When there is a shift, it seems to be not toward a neutral position but rather to the opposite extreme. An Indiana inmate described someone he knew in such a situation: "There's one guy down in the Tag Plant who's supposed to be a real badass of a stud. I did time with him in El Reno and he was the queen of El Reno. *The* Queen. I mean a flat stone queen. Why his reputation hasn't followed him, I'll never know. I'll never spread anything around. First place, I'm not interested in the guy. Second place, there's no sense hurting people."

25. Wilson: "This is a good rundown on punks."

26. There is no cash in the prison, but there is scrip inmates use for commissary purchases. This scrip cannot be transferred, so the unit of economic transactions among inmates, as in most prisons, becomes the pack of cigarettes.

4 · Money-making Women

□ □ □

You TAKE a whorehouse that you can operate, one that you can tell people, "It's there," where you can let them come and you don't have to stop them at the door to decide who you can and who you can't let in—I mean a place where you have an arrangement so you can open your door and just run it— it's nothing to make $100,000 a month. They make fantastic money, you have no idea. I'm talking about a wide-open place, a big one that's got maybe fifteen to twenty girls. Smaller ones, where you've got five or six girls, they maybe make $20,000 a month.

I'll tell you why. Drinks are usually $1 or $2 apiece, and the girls get a little something out of that, usually about 25 per cent. Of course they're not drinking any liquor any-way. In this part of the country a lot of your trade comes from seamen; they're in town for a short period of time, and when they come in that joint, they're going to spend every-thing that they've got in their pocket, they're going to get rid of it. For the sex the house gets 40 per cent and the girls get 60 per cent, but the house gets all the drinks, save the part the girls get for the drinks they hustle, and all the jukebox and all the gambling. Most of them have gambling.

At the end of a month you'd have your $40,000, and out of that you have to pay upkeep of the property, you have to give the country officials some, you have other expenses, so actually you don't end up with all that money yourself. But you do end up with a good bit.

What the girls get depends on where they're working, though the price is pretty standard throughout the state. We have got what we call a circuit in Texas. All of these towns throughout Texas have usually a couple of motels or hotels that run girls all the time. In Corpus we have three or four places. There's one hotel that's been there for fifty years. They've had girls there for fifty years. And new motels are the same way. In San Antonio there's places if you go on up to Wichita Falls, there's places, and if you go to Odessa, there's places.

At the hotel, if it's a straight date it's usually $10, and a French date, a blow job, is $20. All night it's whatever the girl can get. They usually start out at $150 or so, and a man usually can get them down to $100 or $75. Of course an all-night date is not very long because the guy usually flakes out and the girl leaves for a while. She might come back the next morning and get the business straight one more time; then she's through with it. So she might have two or three other dates while that all-night date is going on.

But that is in a walk-in joint, a place where you go in. Your call girls are a little bit different. Call services usually charge a little bit more. Usually if a girl is going to a man's apartment or office and they're regular customers that call all the time, they might work out some kind of special deal, say give them a half-and-half date for $25. That's a blow job for a while, then trick them. Most of the time they're regular customers and that's what you call a book. You'll have their names in there, and every so often when they don't call you, you call them and keep current.

Now massage parlors or health clubs, those girls first make the men get a massage and they charge them I think $5 for that, and for whatever else they want they have a set price for it, about the same as the hotels.

In the better hotels, where the girl is taking a chance on a bust, such as the ———— in Houston, where they have good security services, the girls there always get $35 and $40 on a straight date—that's if a bellhop wants to call them and they go in. In a lot of first-class hotels you can buy pussy that's cheap, but in one where the security is real sharp, the girl gets more money because she's taking a bigger chance of arrest.

In bars and places like that, a girl gets whatever she can get. The prices I told you are the minimum, not the maximum. It depends on how good-looking a girl is and how much conversation she has. Actually, it's more conversation than anything else. You take a gal that can really talk, they can make more money than the best-looking girl in the world. I'd like to have about a forty-five-year-old gal in about an eighteen-year-old's body. You could retire. She'd have enough sense to do it for you.

Most of the guys who are your tricks, traveling people and so forth, conversation means a lot to them. Hell, they're lonesome. You get a gal that's really sharp like that and they can just make money.

I had a girl in Corpus once like that. I had had a little ole whorehouse and it got closed down, so I took that girl down to a motel and I was working with her. She got the john down there and the bellhop came and got her and he gave her $200 for tricking him. She was a pretty smart old gal; she had been around for quite some time and I had had her running this whorehouse.

She was about twenty-nine years old, not too good-looking, but she had a lot of sense. A lot of these young girls, they'll just jump up, put on their clothes, and run on out. But she sat around there for a little while and had a drink with him. So he asked her if she'd go swimming. She said that she would, and he gave her $200 to go swimming with him. She came back to the room and got her bathing suit on and they went out there and stayed for about two hours and had a few drinks; then he asked her to go eat with him. She did. She went off and ate and she got another $200 for that, and they rode around and looked at some of the property there in Corpus, kind of toured the town, rode up and down along the water, went for one of those little hour boat rides along the bay front. When they got back to the hotel, he was ready to trick again, so he gave her another $200 for that. Then she came back to the room, and she'd made $800 where a young what-they-call "racehorse," she'd have run in there, got her $20, and have been back in fifteen minutes. So that's the difference.

Most of these whores think that they've got to hurry up, but its the ones that take a little bit more time that make the real good scores.

This guy called her back the next day, and she didn't make anything like she made the first time. I think it was about $100. But still and all, he was about a $900 or $1,000 customer. And if he ever came back to Corpus, they'd get together again.

These whores have one other kind of trick: your weirdos. If you get a girl that digs it, that actually likes weird tricks, then that is where your big money is.

For instance, there's an old woman in Corpus, really quite wealthy, her husband died and she digs gals. She's always good for $400 or $500 any time that you can get her down. But she has a daughter and a son and they always have a nurse there, and it's hard for her to get rid of all three of them long enough for you to get in there and visit with this gal. But from time to time, if you happen to be on her phone list, you'll get a call that they're all out and you can go in.

And a lot of criminal lawyers are real weirdos. Lot of them are real good tricks. They like to eat pussy or something like that, and some of them are real good spenders. And of course you've always got the sadists.

You take a guy that thinks anything of his gal, he's not going to let her go off into one of those switches. In the first place, they usually whip them so bad that they can't work for a couple of months after that and you lose more money in the long run than you would be taking it straight. But the weird tricks is where the big money is and, truthfully, most whores dig it.

A lot of them turn weird tricks and they'll come home and they don't say anything about it. Say you've got a new gal and she's tricking one of your old customers, one from the previous old lady, and you know what kind of trick he is and you just don't say anything and she just don't say anything, then you know. Some gals won't admit it and others brag about it.

You told me once that there was a big difference in what a good whore would make in St. Louis and down here.

Yes. For instance, down here in Corpus they have a place that's been established for thirty-five or forty years. They've always had girls. They have a regular clientele. And they're so strict that they don't take any chances on new business getting hold of a girl. If you haven't been a customer of theirs in the past, it is hard to get in; only way you can is if you ask one of their old customers to bring you. Now there is very little chance of arrest in a place like that. A girl there, she can clear anywhere from $300 to $450 a week. Very seldom will she make over $450 a week unless there's a big party or somebody gets real drunk and just gives her a bunch of money. But as far as earning a bunch of money, that's all she can earn down here. But you take St. Louis, which is a real good town, that girl can make a thousand, fifteen hundred a week without much problem. And the chances of her running into a big sport out there are a lot greater than they are in Texas. You don't have much more chance of being arrested there than down here.

The only thing is, you're taking the girl across the state line, and that's a federal charge. So you have to be real sure of who you take. A lot of guys will go ahead and marry their old lady and then take her out there rather than be living with some broad and then go.

The same thing applies to Louisiana. Louisiana's always had whorehouses and they always will. You take Appaloosa, all over that country there, they all have whorehouses.

They're usually out in the country somewhere. One of those Frenchmen will own one in one town, usually his cousin will own it in the next one, and his brother will own it in the next one. And it's just kind of a big clique.

Coloreds would probably call me a trick. When I do go down to colored town, I go down to see them dance and sing and have some drinks and I usually end up spending a bunch of money. But I don't consider myself a trick because when I go down there, I go down to spend money and enjoy myself. Of course I wouldn't pay them to screw one of their gals because that *would* make me a trick, you understand?

Oh, man, something else about this. This is a throwback. In the States, if a character is going to screw a gal and pay for it, he's a way stone trick. People, if they find out about it, they lose respect for him and everything else.[1] A character is supposed to have enough con about him to get all the free cock he wants, and a really good character always got a bunch of gals hanging around. Girls are no problem. But a character can go to Mexico and pay money and screw whores for months and months and nothing's said about it because it's expected of him. In Texas especially, when you get out of jail, you're supposed to make you some money and go to Mexico and have you a party. It's the accepted thing, it's all right if you do it over there. But if there's a Spanish girl here and you bought some cock on this side of the border, oh, man, it's way out. But as long as you're on the other side of the border, it's all right.

There's a throwback there. Years ago we could go down there and buy us a big bottle of pills and just sit them on the table and get high all day. Buy you a pound of grass and just put it there on the table, roll a smoke any time you want one. Now it's not that open and you can't do it. So that's the throwback. And the girls are there and naturally you can't talk Mexican and they can't talk English, so the only way that you can get some cock is to buy it. Of course they end up giving it to you for love and you pay about four prices for it. If you don't buy it, it really costs you more.

Do most whores you know have a pimp?

Yes, most do. You know, you take a whore that doesn't have a pimp, she won't make any money.

Why?

What does she want money for? They always find somebody to take care of them. If they don't have a pimp, they're just not going to work. A whore gives all her money to a pimp. Hell, she *belongs* to him. She gives all her money; she'd *better* give him all her money.

Why?

It's just like when I was a square john and my wife worked and whenever she got paid she brought me her check. The pimp and the whore have a man-and-wife relationship there, although they may not be legally man and wife.

Even though the prostitute knows the pimp has seven or eight other women working for him?

Well, sure! And that makes them work harder, because they want to be Number One. They want to make more money than everybody else does. Some girls are not going to go for that and some girls are.

You take most prostitutes, when they first turn out, they are extremely dumb. They come from real slum families, and that pimp, he's driving a big car and wearing nice clothes and spending a little money on them. It's not hard to turn one of those girls out. A few years later, they finally snap, they become educated. But by that time they're so hooked in on the process that they don't care anymore. Then later on, when they get a little older, they'll have broke pimps and they'll go with somebody else, and somebody'll shoot them out. But they always give him all their money. Almost always, anyway.

Of course after they give him their money, they usually party it up and spend it on each other. A lot of them have dope habits and naturally the pimp goes and scores for the dope that they shoot. And it's just like any man-wife relationship: the man is always dominant, or should be, and she'd be just like a square, she just brings her paycheck home and gives it to him. If she needs a dress, they don't go to the store and buy it, they get it from a booster. Well, he's the one who contacts the booster to get it for her. He has to have the money to pay the rent and things. Another thing is—the gal, if she has a bunch of money and gets busted, she loses all the money, too, so there's no sense in her carrying any money. Now I know guys that had gals for years and years and years, and they'd give them money. The girl's got $50 or $60 in her wallet in case she sees something she wanted to buy, but theoretically that money belongs to him.

Everybody's always asking, "Why should a whore give somebody their money?" I can't see that it's any real problem. He's the one who convinces her that she should go sell pussy and to give him the money. After a while she's not going to sell pussy unless she's convinced all the way. And so then, after she's convinced, then there's no problem, she just automatically does it. Then after she's been indoctrinated, if she goes with another pimp, well, she expects it, she expects the same kind of relationship. And if he doesn't get all her money, she'll think he's weak and she'll start talking about him and end up going with somebody else.

But man, that's a tough way to make a living—with one of them whores. Goddam!

NOTES

MONEY-MAKING WOMEN

1. Doc: "Paying for pussy is next to snitching for a character."

5 · The Check Business

□ □ □

THERE'S a world of people that are check writers. Probably more than anything else. You take a good armed robber, he can't see it; there's no way that he can understand how you can do it. Or even a burglar or somebody like that.

The only reason I stopped writing checks was because I had so much heat on me. They put out pamphlets, a little circular with my picture on it: "Let's help this man stay out of the penitentiary: don't cash his checks."

There's probably more money in checks than anything else. There's probably more money made by thieves and lost by merchants in checks than anything.

Something else; they don't get *mad* at you. The police, the law enforcement officers, they don't get mad about bad checks. If they catch you, fine; but they're not really going out of their way. Corpus Christi, for instance, has a population of about 200,000 and they have a check detail of *one* man. He handles all the checks. Now this man is all the protection they have. He can't be in all those stores at one time, and most of his time is spent processing cases and getting them ready for trial, so actually he's very seldom out of his office.

And the descriptions that people give are so varied that it's hard to bust a check man unless you bust him right in the place.

Here's another example of how many checks a city has. Houston has a population in the metropolitan area of a million or a million and a half. I went to Houston and over a two- or three-month period put out about two hundred checks, anywhere from $10 to $100 in value. This was off and on—every time I'd drive through, I'd put out twenty or thirty of them. Well, I was getting ready to come to the penitentiary and I didn't want them to be able to make me on those check cases in Houston, so I wanted to get them cleared up. I had my lawyer check on it and they couldn't even *find* the checks. They had so many checks—hot and forged—that mine had just gotten lost in the shuffle and I couldn't even clear them up because they couldn't find them.

One time I got busted on a certain payroll check and they notified all the rest of the towns that if they had any of those checks to please notify them back. I had them all over the state, but there wasn't but two or three counties that notified them. Hell, Dallas, where I'd done most of my business on those checks, didn't even do it; they failed.

It's real hard to convict you unless the person can get up on the stand and say, "I knew him, the defendant, prior to that, and that's the reason I recognize him." If they can get up and make a positive identification like that, then they have some grounds.

Now if it's an automobile or a big check, if really some major transaction took place, well naturally they're going to remember. But just a pure job of cashing checks with people coming and going and going and going all the time, they can't hardly convict you. If they want to spend a lot of money, they can. But they have to get handwriting experts, and if you have any money, you can rebut everything they say. If ever a handwriting expert says, "Yes, that's his writing," you can find one that says, "No, it's not." He's just like a psychiatrist—it depends on who's paying his money. At any murder trial of any significance where there's any money

involved or the defendant has money, they always have conflicting medical testimony. It's the same thing with checks:
if you have a little money, you can find you an expert that
will testify for you. A lie detector is out, they can't use it as
evidence, so actually, they have nothing to go on. All they
do is just have a piece of paper there. It's hard.

They do get convictions though. I'll tell you what happens
most of the time, what happens in *Texas*; other places I don't
know about. Say you go off on a check spree. Most check
writers are high rollers. Man, they live high and they just
spend that money just as fast as they can get ahold of it.[1]
Well, they'll go off on a spree, and they'll go to San Antonio
and get drunk and they'll put out a bunch of checks. Then
they'll just spend up that money. Then they'll go to Austin
and they'll do the same thing there, just party around the
country, maybe have a couple of gals with them. So they get
busted. All of these places put holds on them. What they'll
do is, they'll go ahead and take a two- or three-year sentence
and get all these other places to go along with it, either to
drop the charges or give you two or three years and run it
all c.c., at one time, and that way you get rid of the whole
thing at once. In the event that you could beat the cases, you
would probably stay in jail longer trying to beat them all
than you would coming on down here and doing a year flat.
It's almost impossible to get out on bond on checks if they
want to keep you in jail.

Once I was in Corpus and they transferred me to San
Antonio. I tried to get out on bond. What they did was, they
set a $5,000 bond on each check. A $5,000 bond is not an
excess, but when you've got three hundred or four hundred
checks out, it's a lot of money, it's impossible to make. And
that's the way they can keep you in jail on checks. On other
charges sometimes they can't do that, but on check charges
they can file each of them on you and they can hold you in
jail. Then you have to go from jail to jail beating those cases,
and it takes a lot of money to do all that court fighting. So
you just get you one lawyer, give him $300 or $400, and all
he has to do is get on the telephone and call these other

counties and they all go along with it, they always do. They have so many check charges that they don't want to be messing with them, so they just call around and get them all cleared up at one time, and you get a two-year sentence or a three-year sentence and you come on down here and you do it in fourteen or sixteen months and you're out.

I had some checks out in San Antonio; I got drunk and wrote the damned things under my own name, so they picked me up on them. All I did was I paid off the checks and they turned me loose. I went down to the bank and got a $1,000 cashier's check and went back up and gave it to them. They dropped all the charges.

If it's under your own name, can't you claim you thought you had the money in your account?

In the state of Texas, a check is a promissory note and you guarantee with that promissory note that the money will be in the bank upon request, and so whenever that check, that promissory note, is handed to the teller, then he has to give the money. But there is also a law that states that the check must be put in normal business procedure or transaction. In other words, it's actually against the law for them to get the check and get suspicious and jump in a car and run down and cash it. It has to go through the same process as all the rest of the checks that they have in the cash register.

But then someone like me, who is occasionally overdrawing his checking account . . .

. . . will get put in jail. Now they have a law in Texas—though I've seen them convict people without it—that they have to notify you and give you ten days to make good on the check.

One thing about checks to show you the volume of them: In San Antonio they have two departments of the district attorney's office; they have one for everything but checks and they have one for checks. The lady who is in charge of the check department has a force of about ten or twelve people, and the district attorney and his assistants are about five people. So it takes twice the number of people just to handle the checks that it does to handle all the rest of the district attorney's duties, whatever they might be. That's how many checks are put out. And they are swamped.[2]

There are two kinds of checks: personal, and business or payroll check. Personal checks, you can make larger scores with them as far as the one check is concerned, but your payroll checks can be cashed in a group.

Some towns are good check towns and some aren't, and the word gets around about what towns are good. Houston, Texas, is one of the hardest towns to put checks out in. Everything there is screwed down.

When you put out payroll checks, most of them are put out in supermarkets, places that have check-cashing stands in the establishment. There's a time element there: you want to put out the checks at the quickest and easiest place so you can put out a volume. So you have to find stores and chains that will take the checks in a hurry with just a little bit of identification without stalling you around. You don't want to go in a store that takes you twenty minutes to cash a check. Even though you get the money, there's too much time involved there. I always operate from the time that the banks close till the banks open, in case they do call to check on it.

In Houston, if you go in there with a company check that you've had printed up in Mexico or San Diego, they'll have a sample check there with the correct signature on it, and the color of your check has to correspond with theirs or they won't take your check, no matter if the company is a good company and they call the bank and the bank says they have an account on that company. They still won't cash your checks until they have been authorized by the company. Weingarten's food stores, for example, they check the checks out and they have an approved list and you have to be on that list.

I was in California and I needed some money. At this time I would never have thought about busting a safe. That was too vulgar. I didn't do anything but checks. I went in and opened a bank account. I take that back; first thing I did was rent an office. Then I rented the office equipment—you know, desk, filing cabinet, had a phone put in—and after this was all done, I went to the bank and opened an account and I used the office address. The bank will give you the checks or you can call any office supply company and order them. They'll make up four or five sample headings for you and send them over and you take what you want. Or you can send a sample of what you want.

I *never* had a plain check printed. I always like some kind of design or a picture of a building, something to give it a little added personal touch. Anybody can have just a printed check, but if there's some kind of picture on it, the gal in that checking stand will bet her life that it's good. It can be anything, just something that will catch their eye.

As soon as I got my checks, I went to the bank, and I had some blank checks from around the country, so I deposited about $35,000 worth of phony checks. The reason for this is for show, not to draw against that money, because those checks are not any good until they have been cleared. And you have not actually committed any felony until they have been cleared. So the only thing you want to do is just put up a front, so that you can go out in the daytime and start writing checks. In the event that they call the bank, this girl will say, "Yes, we do have an account." And they say, "Well, it's for such-and-such an amount," and she'll say, "I'm sure it will be all right." She's got it right there where you deposited $35,000, and she has no reason to doubt your word. And it just becomes a routine deal with them. If they get to calling in too much, you might have a little static, but still, they can't arrest you because you might be on the square.

In this part of the country you have large shopping centers. Sometimes they'll have a big clothing store and a grocery store and a liquor and a shoe store, and places like that. Sometimes in one place, then, you can put out two or three checks.

But the easiest place is a grocery store with a check-cashing counter. You can go right up there, get your money, put your money in your pocket, and walk right out without buying anything. But if you're in a clothing store, then you have to shop a little bit and you have to make a purchase big enough to where he will take a chance on cashing the check to make the sale.

I like to go downtown. You can go in and buy an evening shirt for $35 or two evening shirts for $70 and you can get your money in a hurry. At the shopping centers you get a $5 shirt, a couple of alligator belts or something like that, and run up a $25 bundle of merchandise. As soon as you get away from that store, you've got to throw that merchandise away in case the police stop you. Then they can't prove that you've been in the store except through the check, and then it's just their words against yours.

You ought to be able to pick up about $10,000 over the weekend. That is, if everything goes real good.[3] A lot of people save the merchandise when they go off cashing checks and they sell it, and that's extra. But you won't make that much every time. I'm talking about if everything goes just jam-up and you've got real good checks.

For instance, if you're in the Fort Worth area and you have Chance-Vought checks, everybody will take them. In Fort Worth, if you've got a Swift Company check, you wouldn't even have to have any identification; just sign your name and they'll take it, and you can take them to banks or anywhere. Of course if you've got your old lady working and you make you a big check and her a little one—maybe you make yours for $240 and hers for $137.50—then when you go, you're both cashing checks and you can go pretty good. Something else: while you're in the grocery stores cashing a big check, you just send her to the liquor store to cash the smaller one. And a girl can cash a check.

Now personal checks, you can use them in a lot of ways. You can use it to obtain money with or you can use it to obtain merchandise to resell. Like you want to buy a load of cattle—well, you can. In Texas, all auctions are free and independent of each other, so I can go in and buy any time I want to. Legitimate people do this; they figure that the price of cattle in Fort Worth is going to be six cents a pound higher than San Antonio, so they'll buy a load of cattle in San Antonio, truck it to Fort Worth, and sell it. Now, they've got to go ahead and sell even though the market drops and take their loss because it costs them more than that to hold the cattle over and feed them. It costs you so much in the feed lot. So what you can do is, you can just go into San Antonio and go to the auction there and buy you a load of cattle. You don't care what they cost or what they're going to sell for in Fort Worth. There is always a bunch of truckers there, so hire you a trucker, carry them on up to Fort Worth, put them in the ring and sell them, and take whatever you can get. The auctioneer is gonna ask as much as he can for them because that's where he gets paid. Then just give the trucker a check, take the check you got from the auction down to the bank and cash it, and go on your way.[4]

You can use checks to swindle a lot of other ways, besides just getting money. For instance, antique stores are good. You can go in one antique store and buy some antiques and give him a check for them, carry them right down to some other antique store or haul them across the state or wherever you want to take them. You can resell that stuff. And anything like that that's a collector's item. You can go into a coin shop and buy some rare coins with checks and then sell them, and the same with stamps. And anything that's negotiable. Without any trouble whatsoever.

You can use a check in swindling like that or you can use it to make money. Say you're in a town and you're going to put out personal checks, you're just going to go in and buy a little merchandise, cash a check, and maybe get $50 or $60 more than the merchandise with the check. I found that the best way to do it is to write out the check *before* you go into a store. Never try, if you're a man, to cash a check in a men's clothing store; it's the hardest place in the world to get a check cashed. Always go to a *ladies'* clothing store, preferably a maternity shop. You can go into a maternity shop and say, "You know my wife is Mrs. So-and-so, a little dark-headed girl." The woman says, "Oh, yes, how is she getting along?" They think they've known you all their life. If you've got the check made out for $75, you can go in and buy a blouse or something and say, "Well, you know, I do like that, I figure I will take it. I made this out for a little more, I planned on spending a little bit more, but I'll get her something else." And you just hand her the check and it's already made out and they will take it. Otherwise you're standing there and you start to write out the check, they might not take it but for a few dollars more than the purchase value. You say, "Well, that's the only check I have with me." They go for it if the check is already made out.

Personal checks can also be cashed in grocery stores or anyplace else. As far as the value in swindling somebody, there's much more than that in a company check. As far as making money, you make the most volume with payroll checks.

Payroll checks sound like a lot of work.

They're a lot more work, but there's a lot more value received.

There's a lot of ways of getting personal checks. It's easy. All you have to do is just go by the bank and say, "Let me have a book of checks," and just put them in your check folder. You can get you a check folder too. You take it and twist it around and beat it up a little bit and tear a few checks out, write in your amount where you have a real nice balance, and you can go in a store and when you pull it open and tear that check out or write a check, then they see that you've got a $1,200 balance, or $1,800 balance, whatever it might be. Little things like that impress people.

I know myself, if I see a guy drive up in a Cadillac, wearing a nice suit of clothes and a nice ring, I just take it for granted that he has money. That's all you can go by is appearance.

Say that you just drop in a town and you're busted and you want to make a little money on checks. Well, you've got to hump and pump just going from store to store to make over $400 or $500 a day. You can make that, but it's pretty hard and you have to know the town pretty well. That's *personal* checks. Shopping centers are best: you can go and put a check in each and every store.

Almost all stores now have insurance and they take checks a lot more. In Denver, I know, you can write a check in any bar. I've never put out any checks in Denver, but I know that you can. In New York City—the last time I went out there on my vacation—it's the easiest thing in the world to cash a check, a Texas check in New York. I've wrote them at "21," the Latin Quarter, at hotels, at clothing stores. Everybody will take a check. Did you know that? Now I don't know about cashing a New York check there, but if you're out of state, boy, they'll take a check in a minute. This actually surprised me.

There's so many facets of passing hot checks that it's really hard to define. First of all, in the state of Texas the laws control some of the ways that you might want to do it. You can write a personal check for any amount up to fifty dollars and it's a misdemeanor charge, but you have to have your own name on it; you can't use another name. This is what you call a misdemeanor check. Now anything over $50 with your own name on it constitutes a felony. All right. Next you have forgery, and a forged check in the state of Texas carries seven years. But if you pass it, it carries an additional five years. If you write it and someone else cashes it, you would get seven years and they would get five. If you forge it and you pass it yourself, you can get up to twelve years on it, or they turn them c.c. so you get just the maximum of seven.

Things have changed some since I've been down here. I don't know just what's happened, but I've been hearing things. I know that Fort Worth has one of the best detection agencies knocking off bad checks faster than anyone else I've ever seen. I don't know how they do it, no one else knows, but they get in any hour of the day or night. Evidently they have someone at the bank or banks, but it seems like whatever bank you write the check on they can in a matter of a few minutes trace it down and see if there's an account or not.

Another safeguard that a lot of them are using is getting the Better Business Bureau to put them on their check-cashing list. The Bureau would notify all the chain stores such as Safeways and A&P supermarkets, where the working-class people cash all their checks. A lot of those places would turn down a good company check if they weren't on this list. They would take the name of this company and notify them they weren't cashing any checks until they had been approved by the Better Business Bureau. Naturally if a man's in legitimate business, he'd just go ahead and comply with it. This is to prevent phony companies.

The way you make your most money in checks is with your company check, if you know the town and know where to get the checks cashed, where the shopping centers are, things like that. If you're in a strange town, sometimes they're hard to find. But if you're in a town you know reasonably well and you know where all the big stores are, you figure you can cash a check about every twenty to forty minutes. Sometimes you'll go into a center and put out three or four checks, but then you have to go to another place and you have the traffic problem. With company checks you can't start cashing them until the banks are closed, so there is a time limit there that makes difficulties. Most banks are closed on Saturdays, which means you can work all day Sautrday and all day Sunday. Sunday, you know, all of your big stores are closed, but all of your big chain drugstores are open, and there's quite a few other places you can cash them. I found out that on Sunday—especially around resort areas where they have boat companies and things like that—you can run in there and cash checks real easy. You can buy a propeller for your motor or something for your boat, you know.

You have to know how much money you want to make from an operation. For instance, if you're ready to go out and make you a bunch of money, and say you want to buy you a new car or take a good vacation or go to the races, then you'd probably go into town and get a bunch of good payroll checks and just go to work.

On the payroll checks, if I was going into a town, I would have an oil company, Gulf Oil or Atlantic Refining or something like that, something that everybody knows, some national or state-wide company. And I would have the checks made out two different ways. I would have maybe fifty to sixty checks to each set of identification, that's best. Then, if you get heat put on you on one, you switch to another name.

You want to be sure to put out the checks on the date that the company pays. You'd be standing in line cashing checks on the same day as people with the same company check you have. You want to be sure they're good checks[5] and also you want to check before you start that they haven't changed cashiers, they don't have a different signature on them. What you do is take off and pass all these company checks all day Saturday. You can start it Friday night; most people get paid on Friday night. What you want is two different amounts on the checks. You want one where it's a good payroll check, say $210 or $217, whatever it might be; then you want a small check for expenses, say $67.50 or something like that. A lot of places, small places, they're open Sunday or late at night; they don't have enough money to cash the payroll checks, although they'd like to, but they just don't have the money. So what you do is go into these little drive-ins and auto-supply stores and get a set of spark plugs or something like that, and you use a small check. It's better than making nothing. If you're going to let a girl put out the checks, make like you're man and wife; you have to arrange to where a secretary or an assembly-line worker would get that amount.

What I would do is I would go out in the daytime. All day Saturday I would make all the supermarkets and things like that. Then Saturday night I put out the small checks, and do that all day Sunday. On an operation like that, running from Friday night until when the bank opens Monday morning, you should be able to make $8,500 or $10,000. That's working alone.

If you want to keep the merchandise, you can probably make a little bit more. In grocery stores or drugstores you can buy Sheaffer fountain pens, some kind of camera or Timex watch or a Ronson lighter, and all of this stuff is easily turned, you can get rid of it in a hurry.

A lot of guys will set up a phony company. They'll just come into a town and they'll rent an office—like I told you before, but there are some variations. You can rent an office for about $60 or $65, and put in a phone and go down to the bank and actually start an account; put in $1,500 or $2,000, whatever you want, and start an account. The bank in turn will print your checks for you and you can go into any hock-shop and buy you a check protector, one of those machines that imprints the amount on the check. And go in there too and buy you a typewriter if you don't have one. With checks made from the bank you're in business. Just get you some gal to answer the phone, and if somebody calls, she can say something. Then you're actually in business.

Fortunately, you can siphon all that money out of the bank account before you ever start passing on it. Just leave enough in there to cover one check. Say you make checks for $295.95 or something like that. Leave about $400 in the bank and take all the rest of it out. Then if they call in and say, "I have a check here for such-and-such an amount, is there enough money to cover it?" the bank is only allowed to say yes or no, they can't tell them, "Well, I've had thirty-five other phone calls." They're not supposed to. There's been cases where they have, but legally they're not supposed to.

So you can run in and on a situation like that really do good.

Now, if you don't have any checks and you need some, probably the best place now to get them is in Juárez, Mexico. Any of their printing shops over there will print them for you. All you have to have is a blank that you want copied. That's easy enough to obtain. You can go around to any beer joint. Say if you want a Swift Packing House check, just go to a bar around the warehouse there where the Swift Company is in Fort Worth, just hang around there on payday, and sooner or later somebody'll start coming in to the bar

with some checks, and usually in those places they run out
of money quickly, so you say, "Well, here, I'll help you, I'll
cash this for you." Just give it to him so he can endorse it;
then take it with you to Mexico and get you some more made
up. Then bring the good check on back and get your money
back on it.

A few years ago there was a real good printer in San
Diego, California. He worked on a flat fee of $500. He could
get up more checks than you could pass, plus furnish you
with identification like air travel cards, American Express,
all of that, a complete set of identification, and the checks
for $500. He's doing time in Leavenworth now. They got him
for some phony money. He was an ex-forger and I guess he
got too slow. At one time, though, you could call him and
tell him what you wanted, he'd have a blank check there,
and by the time you got there, it was all made out—Humble
Oil Company checks, Coca-Cola, Falstaff, he could take care
of it. He worked out of a tattoo-parlor-and-penny-arcade situation, and he had his printing shop in the back.

That's the two best ways of getting your checks.

I know a lot of people that burglarize places, get the
checks, sit right there in the office, and make them out, or
get their check protector and typewriter and take them home
and make the checks out. But the only hazard with this is
that in the event somebody comes in, they'll see that the
checks and all this stuff is gone and they'll see they've been
burglarized and so they'll put out the alarm. Now I know
some people, they sneak-thief them. They'll go around and
stand around these offices in the daytime or they'll burglarize
them at night, and they'll just take ten or twelve sheets from
the back of the book or maybe out of the middle of the book.
That way they're not detected. Then they can feel fairly safe;
they know it'll be a few days before the company knows the
checks are gone.

After you get the checks and get them all ready, then it's
really a matter of experience. When you go into a store, you
sometimes meet with some objections—they'll have some
sign up there saying they don't cash checks maybe, but that
doesn't make any difference.

You learn after a while that there are some stores that will not cash a check, and the reason for this is it's a big national chain store and they have a rule all over the country that they just do not cash checks. They will accept a check for the amount of the purchase, but they won't cash a payroll check. They'll refer you to a supermarket that's close at hand or something like that and say, "Would you mind cashing it over there?"

There's also an insurance policy that a lot of stores have— like Joski's in San Antonio; they'll let you give a check for $5 above the amount as long as you have a valid driver's license. Above that amount, the store stands to lose it. If you buy a $150 suit, you can write out a check for $155 with no problem at all, but if you try to write it for $160, you'll run into static. But this is just one of the peculiarities of certain stores.

About the easiest place to cash a check, especially a company check, are the supermarkets, because they're ready to cash them. They have their check-cashing booths and they want you to come in; they expect you to come in and cash a check. They always have a lot of money on hand.

There was a time they hired very obscure people to work in there—young girls, anything that didn't cost them much money. Now, they have a different policy and they hire a little higher grade of personnel and they send them to school. Almost every district attorney's office in Texas in a large town has some kind of a training program to help the merchants; they'll have some assistant district attorney that goes out and makes a spiel to them and shows them this, that, or the other thing.

They claim that if a person is overly nervous when they're writing, well, you can knock them off. But a good check man, you can't tell. You get to believing that it's all right to cash those checks and you're not nervous.

It's kind of hard to explain how to cash a check because I guess it's really a knack. Each time you cash a check it's different. You're dealing with a different individual but you have to, more or less, inject some kind of personal feeling there. They'll look and say, "You live at this address?" And you tell them, "Yes, ma'am, right next to Dr. Smith, you know, the one that is over here in the Medical Building." Something like that. Anything to give them a little personal feeling so they feel that you are all right.

Now, as I say, supermarkets are in the business to cash checks and that's that employee's job, and consequently they're looking for an excuse to cash your check. They *want* to cash that check.

In those stores the clerks wear name plates and this is really a boon. This lets you come into personal contact because you can call their name. They wear the name plate so much they forget they even have them. Even in here, our names are on our shirts and I know that, but I have people call me by name and I say, "Well I don't know them," and then snap as to how they know it.

You scout around the store and find the manager and you can go up the cash register and say to the cashier and say, "Well, Mr. Jones okayed this," and you're standing there by the checking counter and you see the manager in the back somewhere, so just wave at him. This gives whoever's cashing the check an impression that you know each other. And he's in there to please his customer, so he's going to wave back automatically. Any time you can inject any little personal thing like that into it, it makes it real good.

One trouble that you have in cashing checks is that you acquire so much merchandise; one good thing about supermarkets is you don't have to buy anything. You can push that cart up there with all those groceries on it and then just push it down an aisle and leave it, just walk on out. A lot of people just go in and cash checks at supermarkets and don't even buy anything and don't intend to buy anything. The supermarkets expect this; it's a service that they perform.

Now downtown, if you cash your checks in the downtown stores, you have the problem of getting rid of the merchandise that you buy. You have to pick your stores. Some stores are bad for a man and good for a woman. A men's clothing store, for instance, it's hard for a man to cash a check in one of them, but it's ultra-easy in a women's clothing store because they figure, "Well now, why would he buy this? The check has got to be good, he wouldn't come in and buy something that's useless to him." But as you go through, you end up with these packages. So you can find a car that's parked, with the windows down, and just throw it in, or find litter receptacles and you just stuff them full. But you have to be careful no one sees you, because they'll report you. And also I know people that have gotten busted simply because they come out of a supermarket and see a car out there in the parking lot and they'll have a bag of groceries and they'll set it in there, and the people call the police. They don't think it's anything wrong, but they don't want to be accused of stealing anyone's groceries. They feel someone who had a car similar to theirs made a mistake, and they'll call a policeman and he'll know. Hell go into the store, they'll get a description of the guy who gave the check, and they'll notify all the rest of the stores in town. Then they'll notify other chain stores. You have to be awful careful in things like that.

When you cash checks, there's certain things you want to look for, things you don't want to mess with. One is, in a lot of big stores they have a suction tube and they'll push your check in a little metal container and they'll send it up to the office and then it's come back down with your receipt and your change. They have a central casher up there, they don't have any money on the floor. This is bad. Up there they can check all they want to on that check and you don't know what they're doing. But if you're downstairs and this woman is ready to make all those phone calls, you just tell her, "Well! I've never been so embarrassed in my life." And you reach over and just get your check back. And also you can put your hype on her, stop her from making the phone call. But if it goes up to the office, it goes up there dry, without any conversation, without anything. And you just can't tell. A man is liable to snatch you up while you're standing there waiting for your change. So you never go into one of those stores; you just completely disregard them.

And something else: If you want to cash a check, what you can do is you can go into all of these clothing shops or maternity shops or gift or flower shops, places like that, place your order, and tell them, "Well, I will be back at 4:30 or 5 or 5:30." All the time that the bank is open you can make arrangements, just go around and order all this stuff. When the bank does close, you can run in there and don't even have to have a company check, all you have to do is make out a personal check. Say you order a $12 bouquet of roses—you can walk in with a check for $75 or $80 with no trouble at all, because they've already got it boxed up and they've already got it wrapped up. Bookstores are good too. You can ask them to gift wrap all the stuff at each one of these stores, so when you run in to get it, they've already spent this money on ribbon and time and they're not going to turn a check down. They'll just snatch it up and it's real easy. Sometimes you can make more money by doing that than you can by cashing $250 and $300 payroll checks.

When you run in, you get all this stuff. A lot of people take it and keep it or get someone else to return it for a refund. I don't. I just drive down the road and I throw it away. I'll go by a vacant lot and toss it out. I don't want to be stopped with it in my car because that would give them some kind of evidence against me. The only thing they can get me for is personal identification, and with a good lawyer that is real hard to prove.

In certain towns, such as Fort Worth, as I said before, they have a real sharp system and you have to watch them real close. You could run in there and you could pass two or three checks, and when you go in the next store and that lady looks at you, even before you start to cash a check, it burns you down, you know that there's something wrong.

See, after you've written checks for a while, I think your biggest safety factor is an instinct; I don't know what you call it. But you can walk in, and even after you get your money, you can tell whether that lady is convinced that that check is good. Just the way that they put it in the drawer or look at you. If they're suspicious, you can tell. And if they are, you just suspend operations and go somewhere else. Go to another town.

You take most check writers, most of them are party boys. What they'll do is they'll just go out and they'll make a score and they'll put out a bunch of checks and then they'll start partying. A lot of them are gamblers, and as long as they're winning, as long as they stay in money, they don't write checks.

We went to San Antonio, two boys and myself, right after I got out of jail in Austin, and we made about $15,000 there in a day and a half. And we got raided and busted for it. We got busted for vice, not checks. Want to know how it came about?

We had a real nice rented suite at this little motel, a little private rented cabin out by the pool. And a boy gave me a couple of gals. This other boy made all of my bonds for me, so I gave him one of the gals and I kept one, and we were all partying. The third boy didn't have a girl. That night he didn't even try to get a girl because he's a gambler. But the next day, when the party really starts, he's ready for a girl, so I called some people I knew there and had a gal sent out to him. The telephone operator listened in on the conversation and she called their private detective that handles about five or six motels out there. In turn he calls the vice squad and they raided us for vice. So they came in; it was just one of those things.

The friend of mine that went off to get some stuff, when he left, he didn't have any money, so I took my money out of my pocket—I had a rubber band around it—and I just gave him all of it. Consequently I didn't have a nickel in my pocket. Well, the motel people run in and all they're wanting is the money for the room, and they want us to leave. The girls are all just sitting there in their panties, that's all they've got on, and they grab something and hold it up in front of them. I don't have any money on me, but we've got plenty of money in the other room. But if I take them to where we got the money, they're going to snap to what we're doing because we got check protectors and typewriters and all these checks in there.

The manager finally just got out of hand. We owed him about $160 and they're worried about their money. So they got to prowling. They went in to straighten a picture. This detective said, "This picture's kind of crooked." He's employed not by the city but by the motel and I guess he wanted to see if there's any damage done to the picture. He kind of moved it and had money fall out for what seemed like thirty minutes. We'd just stuffed a bunch of money behind that picture.

Then they got to looking around because they became highly suspicious. They pulled the curtains, and there they have the little hooks on the traveling rod of the curtain. Well, I had money with rubber bands around it and I had it hooked to those hooks in the back of the curtain. So there are just packages of money all in there.

You got to remember: when you write checks, you get a lot of $1 bills, a lot of $5 bills. And you take several thousand dollars' worth of $1 bills and $5 bills, man, it's a wad of money, it looks like a million dollars. And you have a hard time getting rid of it, holding it, keeping it, without its being suspicious.

They got to looking around in suitcases and they found all the equipment and so they took us down. I finally beat my charge at the preliminary hearing, but it cost me all my money to get out. So I didn't end up making any money out of it.

Let me ask you a question: do you like cashing bum checks?

I like the money.

Do you like doing it, though?

No, it's kind of nerve-racking really. You have to be on your toes so much of the time. It's kind of like selling, you have to keep smiling all the time. You know, you have to sell as much as anything else. After a while your face gets tired.

It's all right, really, if everything is going real good. The money drives you. People don't understand check writers I don't think.

Say you're a check writer and you're in San Antonio and you've got a good-looking date that night and you're going to go out and party and everything and, man, you don't have any money. And you look over and see a store just sitting there. It's just sitting there and all you have to do to get yourself either $50 or $75 it to walk in there and get it. You don't have to have a gun, you don't have to have anything but a ball-point pen and you can walk right into that store and you can get your $50 or $75. Now it's just a hell of a temptation. What would you do? Would you call the girl and tell her, "I'm sorry, I'm a grown man, I just don't have any money to take you out tonight?" No, you're just going to go in there and knock you off $50 or $60. Whatever you need. It's so easy. People don't understand.

It is *so* easy. And that's what makes check writers so hard to break. You just can't hardly break a check writer. You just can't do it. I've got a friend who's been down here about seven or eight times. He doesn't ever stay out more than fifteen or twenty days. Most of the time he doesn't even get home. He gets out of here, gets to partying a little bit; first thing he needs is some money. And of course, he's not too cool. He'll start writing checks wherever he is and he's busted before he ever gets home.

You ask me is this fun. I don't know. I guess it is in a way. No one has a wardrobe and things like a check writer. I used to have fantastic wardrobes and I would drive into a motel or hotel and run up a $400, $500 motel bill, and rather than pay the bill, I'd just go off and maybe leave $3,000 worth of clothes. The clothes didn't cost me anything, I can get some more, and I'd just rather leave the clothes in there than pay the $500 because the clothes aren't worth that much to me.

Check writers have all the conveniences or all the niceties of life because they buy them with checks.

I'll tell you another way you can swindle them. I know a hotel in Houston, I went in and I put down a swindle. I met the assistant manager and had him make appointments for me with people in town. I said I was making arrangements for a company there, that we were enlarging and moving in. When I met him, there was a Dun and Bradstreet on his desk. No, on a little side table. I said, "Let me see how I'm rated." And I just flipped the pages over like I was looking for

my company. And said, "Well, here I am. It hasn't changed."
I closed the book and I suppose he thinks I'm in Dun and
Bradstreet. We go on and on. In turn he introduced me to
real estate people and office supply people and all this, and
so when I got ready to leave, I dropped by and ordered equipment, rented offices, and ran ads in the paper for interview
dates for employees at this hotel. Oh, he was just so damned
cooperative. It was pitiful, man. He had all these people in
town wining me and dining me. And of course I was making
all these fictitious phone calls into the hotel, and leaving
messages for myself.

When I got ready to leave the hotel, I got about $500 there,
and then I drove to the places where they were going to
supply the furniture and I got them for $1,500, and each
person that he introduced me to I got them—even though
they didn't have any money themselves, I would get them
to okay the check at their bank and the bank would cash it
for me. It was very profitable.

A check is a very powerful thing, man. Because people,
they use them all the time. Very few people have money anymore.

One thing you have to be real careful of, especially with
supermarkets, and that is your getaway. You have to plan it
just as if you were planning to heist the store. You have to
be careful, because if there is any suspicion or the person
becomes suspicious, you're not always going to know it. But
as I say, nine out of ten times you'll know if the person's
suspicious. If they are, as you're leaving the store and you're
out in the parking lot getting in your car, they'll invariably
take your license number. And, of course, you should have
four or five sets of plates and change them during the day
even if you don't have any heat on them, just as a precaution.
You've got to plan it, just as you would if you were heisting
the store and you were trying to get away after a heist.

If you use a common car, like a Chevrolet, a Plymouth, or
a Ford, something like that, well, they're always good. If you
rent a car, you want to be sure you're not renting it in your
own name on account of the license plates, but you can go

in with the same identification that you're cashing the checks
with and rent a car under that name; then it doesn't make
any difference. Of course you'll want to be awful careful of
anything you touch, but usually a good rental company will
wipe away all the prints themselves because they'll clean the
car up real good before they rerent it.

To illustrate another point in checks, how they're respected: you can go into any bank in the state of Texas and
if you open an account for anything over $500 in cash, they'll
notify Internal Revenue or they'll notify the local police or
someone and they'll have you checked out. If you go in with'
four, five, six thousand dollars, you'd better be legitimate.
But you can go in with $175,000 in checks and open an
account and they'll accept them just as fast as anything.

I'll tell you in God's honest truth, I've had more trouble
cashing good checks and good payroll checks than I have
bum ones. My grandmother had an insurance policy on me.
Paid twenty years on it and I ended up and there's $750 I got
coming after that twenty years. Every week that man would
come and get her nickels and dimes and write it in that little
book. All those years. Every time she'd go out of town, she'd
have to make arrangements for the people next door to pay
that man when he came by. It was one of those old-timey
policies. Well, I had that $750 check and I was in the service
then, so I needed the money. I went down to the bank, and
do you know that they wouldn't even give me a hundred
towards it or anything? And this was on a national life
insurance company. I finally had to deposit the check and
then they notified me when that check cleared; then I was
allowed to write on it.

But that same bank, I beat them silly one time. It's just
one of those things. I went in that same bank years ago and
got a check okayed by the assistant manager and so I went
over to the counter there where you make your deposit slips
out and I put a piece of tracing paper over it and traced his
okay. I went in there a few months later with a $2,700 check
with his okay on it, with what looked like his okay. I went
over and talked to him for a few minutes and showed him

something from out of my wallet. Then I turned and wheeled over to the cashier and just pushed that check through the window, and the man pushed me my money. Of course I hadn't shown that manager the check, I showed him something else, I can't remember what it was, an address or something that I inquired about. And wham! I got my money.

What I mean is, they're easy to beat if you want to beat them, but if you just want to do business with them, they're hard to do business with.

Cashing checks is a real art. Not everybody can cash *good* checks. My stepfather and my mother, they were in Houston at the Shamrock Hotel and he couldn't get a check cashed. He had credit cards, he had everything in the world to cash a check with, but he could not get a check cashed. We have some friends who are permanent residents of the hotel and they called him and they okayed the check and he got it cashed.

But at the same hotel I went up and cashed all the checks I wanted at the cashier's desk without any questions at all.

After you've cashed checks for a long time, you can anticipate anything that they're going to ask you. You can cut all the corners, you can make everything simple for them, where a lot of people can't.

For instance, if you're going to cash a check in a store, you go up and you never fill in the name of the store; just write out the check and say, "You can stamp this, can't you?" Just anything to make them go ahead and get that stamped. Then it's theirs, see, it's not yours anymore. I've never had one of them stamp it and push it back to me. Once in a while they'll push it back to you before they stamp it, but you can push it right on back to them again. You can't back down, because if you do, as soon as you walk out the store, they're liable to call the police. You have got to stay there until you make them take it. It's not always that you can, but ninety-nine times out of a hundred you can. Either that or tear that one up and write another for a smaller amount. A lot of times you can even have big bills in your pockets, hundred-dollar bills or something, and they don't like to cash hundred-dollar bills in a small store, they'd rather go ahead and give you $30 or $40 of their money.

There's all kinds of little secrets. In grocery stores or a little neighborhood supermarket, if I'm going to cash a check, I'll get me a cart and I'll push it around until I have spotted the manager. When you spot him, stay kind of close and shop until you hear somebody call him by his name. Then, as you go by, say, "I want to see you in a minute, Dick. I want to get a check cashed." Don't give him a chance to answer, just walk right on and do your shopping. And next time you see him, kind of mess around until he gets by one of the cash registers there. "Yeah, Dick, let me go ahead and cash this check now while you're up here." And you go ahead and write your check. By the time you call his name two or three times and have smiled at him or waved at him two or three times, he's a pure mark. If I called you Bruce Jackson two or three times, you'd think I knew you. Even if you didn't recognize me, you'd think, "Well, I met him somewhere." If you're in business and these people come in every day shopping, you've got to assume that I'm a customer, a regular customer. There are all kinds of little bitty gimmicks.

But there've been times when I've been hot, when they've been really looking for me and I couldn't go to the grocery stores to cash checks.

In San Antonio all the banks got together with all of the retailers and they decided that they would stop all the hot checks in town. What they did was get all the counter checks, all the blank checks that were out. Before, you know, if you go into a store, they're liable to have fifteen pads of blank checks, one for each bank in town, and they ask you which bank's check you want; then they give you a blank check and you fill it out. What they did, then, is made a more or less gentlemenly agreement with all of the stores there that they would not cash any checks above the amount of purchase, and they put out one blank check or counter check for the banks' uses. It was made by one printing company and it was furnished to all of the stores. On the left-hand corner

they'd have a list of little boxes and the name of the bank
beside it and you just marked off the bank that you wanted
the check to go to and the amount; on the blank is a statement that it would be accepted for the amount of purchase
only. They know that for a check writer that's not good
enough; he don't want the merchandise, he wants the money.
Still, if you had a bank account, a legitimate account, you
could go into your bank and get personal checks. They would
either put your name on some of them or they'd just give you
a blank and you'd put them in your checkbook as always.
After they took out all of the checks from the stores, they
figured if you had a blank check that you automatically had
a legitimate account. And so you didn't have to have any
identification, just the account. Only trouble was finding the
checks.

You could walk around parking lots and find checkbooks
in front seats of a car or up in the sun visor, because they
have no value in themselves and so people just don't protect
them. Now naturally they wouldn't put their wallet up there,
but their blank checks they feel have no value, so they're very
easy to come by. I say they're easy to come by; they're *hard*
to come by unless you know where to look.

I came into San Antonio after I'd been out to the chicken
fights and gone bust, and I had to have some money. I didn't
know about this change, so the first place I go into, wham,
they put that new check thing on me. So I just backed off
and looked at it and everything and signed it, got the carton
of cigarettes, whatever it was. And I got to thinking. I knew
automatically what the play was. I talked to the cashier and
I asked her, "Now what is this?" and she told me everything.
"Well," I says, "I always have my own checkbook, I just forgot it today," and passed it off like that.

I'm walking back to the car and I'm looking in the optical
company window, and they had a rack there with a whole
bunch of these checks that no one had bothered to pick up or
even notify them about. So I went in and got to talking with
the girl, and finally another customer walked in, and when
he did, I just picked up the whole rack of blank checks and

walked out with them. So from then on, I just had more checks than I knew what to do with. I'd write those checks out and just walk into a store with no identification, nothing, and they'd snatch them up. They knew in their own mind that I had to have an account to get that check, so if I had that account, I was bound to have money in it, or even if it *was* hot that I'd make it good. So it was just no problem.

It probably stopped a lot of check writers until they snapped how to get around it. It wouldn't take you long to snap, anybody in the business, but for the banks' purpose at the time, I guess to them it looked foolproof. They just forgot the human element, that they would have to stop giving out all checks even at the bank for that to be any good.

A case in point about how easy it is to cash checks, how powerful they are: The nicest women's store in San Antonio is right next to the Gunter Hotel. This store is exclusive, nothing but the best. If you want to buy a $25,000 fur coat, I'm sure that they have one, or if you want to buy a $150,000 necklace, I'm sure they have that too. But on the bottom floor they have a little corner, a little men's shop, and they sell nothing but sport coats and shirts and ties, cuff links, things like that. Just little accessories. But all their prices are way out. A little plain cotton shirt is $30, short-sleeved, no brand name, just the name of the store.

Well, I went in there and I wrote a couple of checks, three I think it was. One was in the men's store, where I bought some shirts. I went upstairs and dropped some more. On a personal check it's real easy if you have whatever you buy mailed out, so I just stopped in the department and picked up something that maybe cost $50, wrote a check for $150 or $200, whatever I thought I would get away with, told them I'm going to do some shopping in another part of the store and I only wanted to write one check. "I'd like this mailed." You pay the insurance and they think, "Hell, we still got the merchandise." And so they go ahead and just give you the rest of that money. I put out three or four checks in the store, I can't remember what it was. I went back the next day—it was so good—and I put out two or three more.

Of course you have to remember that I have a real good appearance in these stores. I sometimes have on a $100, $150 pair of alligator shoes, an Oxxford suit—hell, I look the part. It's not hard. I had a little education. And the more belligerent you are, the quicker a place like that will cash a check. You have to make them think they owe it to you.

Then along came the weekend and I was partying a little bit, so by Monday I'm broke. I'm living in a hotel right across the street from the store, so I waited until the bank closed Monday and I went back in. I felt kind of funny when I saw one of the girls who was behind the counter looking at me. I thought, "I don't know, maybe I insulted her or something."

I stopped in her department. I went through my spiel and wrote out my check and the girl looked at me and she said, "The credit manager said he'd like you to come up and cash your checks up there."

Well, I was on about the third floor and I knew that if I started out, they would just nab me, so I went on up. I had nothing to lose. He was sitting there and I said, "You wanted to see me?"

He said, "Who are you?"

I told him whatever name I was using, and I was real indignant about the whole thing. Told him, "I'd appreciate it if you'd hurry."

We talked there for a few minutes and he told me, "We were notified by your bank that your checks weren't any good. We called the bank. We noticed we had an awful lot of your checks here and we called the bank and they told me that your checks weren't any good. That you don't have an account with them."

I told him, "Well, is that all they told you?"

He said, "Yeah."

"Were you notified by my bank that I'm in divorce proceedings?"

"No."

"I'm in the process of getting a divorce, and since she's trying to get every goddamned thing off of me, that's what I told them to tell. This is the only place I've got any money

that she doesn't know about. Tell me, then did you send the
check in for collection?"

"No."

I said, "I wrote the check; why didn't you send it in for
collection?"

He said, "Well, we thought that since we had so many of
your checks that we should check on it."

I said, "Are you in the habit of doing that?"

"Well, in rare cases."

"I've been doing business here a long time for me to be
a rare case," I said. "Did you go back through your files and
find out how much money I've spent here over the years?"

"No."

"All my family has charge accounts here. Whenever we
come into San Antonio, we always shop here." And so it went
on and on. So he went for my spiel and I told him, "How
about this check, are you going to cash it?"

He looked up at me and he smiled and he said, "You know,
I know you're lying, but I'm going to cash it anyway."

And this is the credit manager of the finest store in San
Antonio. He went on through this spiel and took it like I was
really something, but then, at the last minute, he snapped,
but he had gone so far then that he had to go the rest of the
way.

As I was saying, then, they just can't turn them down.
More than likely he had insurance to cover most of it, and
they figure on losing a certain per cent every year to hot
checks anyway. Of course, I hit him pretty hard.

You know, at one time there were as high as forty joints
in Corpus that had gambling units staying open all night,
and we always had the Island, and before that, Galveston
and Houston, they've always had gambling. In gambling
casinos and other places that operate outside the law, especially in this part of the country, the only way that they can
make any money is they have to take checks. When people
get ready to go out at night, they don't think, or it never
enters their mind, that they're going to lose all their money.

When they leave their house, they're sober and so they're pretty conservative, but after they get a little drunk or once they start losing, well, all of this is passé, and they will lose almost what you let them lose. So most of the gambling casinos in this part of the country take checks.

With a pretty good front, a little conversation, and a little cash to start with, there isn't much problem. If you go into one of the places and you say, "I want to cash a check for $250," and they cash it and you start to leave, you're not going to get to leave because they are going to know that there's something wrong.

What you do with checks there is get yourself a free roll at them. Say you go in and you lose maybe $100 or so. Then you say, "Well, I'd like to cash a check." If you have any kind of identification at all, they'll always take a check. Maybe you'll write one for $100. If you lose that, then they'll be ready for you to write a bigger check. What you're doing is taking that free roll. If the dice spring out and you get hot and you make some money, well, naturally, it's free; and if you've lost, you haven't lost anything.

Of course when you get ready to cash this out, one way to keep any suspicion from you is to pick up your check along with your winnings, taking cash for the rest of it. But even then, in several places, they've told me they've already processed my check and they went ahead and gave me cash. Maybe if they get the idea that you're a high roller, they want the check so they can check on you and more or less put you in their files as to whether your credit will be good from then on. If they know you're all right, then in the future they'll advance you credit. This is the better-class gambling houses, not those boot-and-shoe places.

These are characters you're burning with these checks?
They're gamblers.
Don't they get pretty annoyed?
Well, they don't have any kind of a police force. They're operating outside the law.
But if you're both operating in the same town and they

find out who you really are, mightn't they try to do something?

I'm talking about this country, I don't know about up East. Down here, the gamblers are more afraid of you than you are of them because they think, "I better leave that old character thing alone; one of these nights he'll come in here and rob me or tear up my joint."

They operate outside the law, as I said, but they are all operating with the law's permission, naturally. If you was to get caught robbing one of them or get caught tearing up the joint or beating the safe, I'm sure the police would give you some time. In fact, I know they would.

But don't the gamblers have collectors, enforcers?

Not in this part of the country. About the only enforcement they have is an off-duty policeman working as a bouncer or something like that. But as far as having strong-arm men— they don't.

In these places if you're a square, a businessman from somewhere and you've gone bust and then gone into them for some money, what they will do, since you're set in the community, they get on that phone and start worrying you, calling your house or calling your wife or calling your boss or your business associates, somebody, until they finally make you pay. But how in the hell are they going to call on a character? They feel like, "Well, we just got beat." And it really just goes at that.

How did you get busted for checks?

I had some girls writing checks. We started out in California and we came all the way back. When we got to Fort Worth, we worked it out real good. All the way on the trip I'd make them throw away all this trash that they'd buy, and they knew that this was the last town and we're splitting after we've worked it. I always made them travel in a separate car and I'd always go on ahead; they had never seen my car and they didn't know my real name. They had seen me, but that doesn't make too much difference. In the event that they got busted in one of these towns, there's no way they can connect me. I'd pick points all over town at these different towns and I'd make them bring me the money. They'd come out of these stores and I'd be standing on the street corners and then they'd give me the money. Everything worked out real good and we came all the way back.

When we got to Fort Worth, they know that they're getting ready to get their part of the money and they're about to go back to California. So they got together and decided, "We'll go to some real good stores and we'll buy some real good clothes. We'll put them on 'will call' and with these checks we'll make the bigger part of the payment." That way, after we split and they get their money, they can go back around and pay the rest of it in cash and get their clothes and they'll have a nice wardrobe to take back to California.

I busted loose from them, and gave them their money. Everything is fine; I'm staying in a hotel downtown, they're staying out in a motel. I had a date over in Dallas with an airline hostess so I checked out of the hotel. As I started for the car, I walked by a barbershop and said, "Maybe I need a haircut, and if I don't get it now, I probably won't get it." It was on a weekend. I ran into the barbershop real quick and I got a haircut and a shampoo and a massage and a manicure and I had my shoes shined. This took about an hour, an hour and fifteen minutes. It was just enough damned time for them idiots to come back to downtown Fort Worth. And they're down there already picking up these clothes. Stores have already snapped that these checks are no good, so the first place the girls go into, they start watching them. The gals don't snap to it. The police don't pick them up, they just follow them. I walked out of the damned barbershop and they was on the other side of the street and they started screaming and yelling and then they came trotting up there and got my arms full of these damned clothes and got me loop-scooped. And that's what got me busted.

It was just pure chance. We came all the way across the country, man. Everywhere.

I got all those holds dropped on me in all those states

except here. Just by using lawyers. And here I just ended up with a two-year sentence. First I got two years' probation, and then I got it violated. So actually, in the true sense of the word, I got cut loose, just scot-free.

How long had you been working as a check man?

Hell, for years and years and years. I can't remember. I can remember in high school, this is when I first turned out.

What I'd do in high school—how I learned the ins and outs of it. What I'd do is, I would write a check on my bank, then if I couldn't get the money to cover the check, couldn't bum it from my mother or something, then I'd just go someplace else and deposit it in there and get money for that check, and then I'd go somewhere else and get another check and cash it and put the money in my account to cover the first check.

Kiting it?

Yeah. Or then I'd go in and just put in a $150 fictitious check and they would, because they knew my family, just keep on cashing checks for me on this $150. And by the time this came back, I'd have won enough in a football game or playing poker or something to cover it. So I just started into it pretty innocently, you know.

Of course at that time, whenever I needed money, it would be $6 or $4 or maybe $10, you know, going off to a football game; $25 would be the most I'd need. But what it did is, it gave me the foundation for it. Then, several years later, when I was older and really gambling, I got in it professionally the way I told you before.

I was going to tell you about one other caper. I'm quite proud of this one. They had a three-alarm fire out for me, trying to pick me up on a robbery charge. I was in the hotel in Corpus and had no way to get out of the hotel and beat it. I had been in the hotel for about two weeks. I can't get out of town and I can't get to my car because I know it's staked out. There's a whore working there in the hotel and she got to coming by my room to have a drink now and then, partying a little bit. I'm getting lower and lower on money. So I'm laying up there and now I haven't even got $100; I'm sitting there and I am broke. It wouldn't have been so bad being broke, but I didn't have any transportation and every police-man in the country's looking for me.

They had a head bellhop there and he and I were good friends. They brought my food and everything, and he kept changing my room. At night he'd register me in another room and I'd move.

Now, once before I had been in San Antonio and one weekend I had started to Mexico City. When I got to Corpus, the damn banks were closed and I couldn't get a check cashed, a good check, I mean. I went by my aunt's house and my aunt told me, "Just go by the hotel and cash a check, I'll call this lady." She mentioned the lady's name and I went on to the hotel, and when I got there, the lady cashed my check for $500 and I went on to Mexico on my vacation. See, they all know my family there and any bank in Corpus will cash checks for me. I don't give bad checks to the bank. In fact, I don't do much of anything in Corpus that's illegal; I just live there.[6]

Well, I'm staying up there in my hotel room and I was trying to think, Where can I cash some checks? I can't get out in the streets and be going from place to place writing checks because everybody knows me and they're going to pick me up. I picked up the newspaper and I looked over in the society column and an oilman that is a friend of my family had a picture in there—he and his wife were sailing on the *Queen Mary*, going to Europe on a vacation. Actually, they were leaving Corpus that day, and there was a group of them going.

I got to thinking about this other hotel. So I picked up the phone and called that lady at the hotel like my aunt had. For some reason, I don't know why, because I'm real bad about remembering names, I remembered the old gal's name. I also remembered that whenever I had cashed a check at that hotel, I had had to go up to the assistant manager's office. In the back of his office they had a big walk-in vault; they keep the money and records in there. They have about six or eight desks inside the vault where they all work. I called this lady by name and they connected me with her and I introduced myself to her as this oilman. He had offices in the hotel. Part of the hotel is office buildings; part of it is hotel. I told her that a little deal had come up and I was trying to get out of town and wanted to know if they'd cash a check for me, I had to put a cash deposit down on a land deal. And she said, "Why, certainly."

I said, "Well, I'll send my secretary down there in a few minutes." So I sent this whore down to the desk in the hotel where I was and got some blank checks and she came up and I wrote out a check and I sent her over to the other hotel. I said, "Now, when you get there, just go on up to the assistant manager's office and go back in there." I explained where the vault was and told her, "When you get there, ask for this lady." Then, this lady had to come up, but that was more convincing because this gal knew right where to go. This whore's a real pretty-looking girl and I made her put on a coat, and the woman gave her the money. The first check was for $580. She came on back. She's coming down the street from that hotel and I can get out in the hall and watch her all the way down. Living in this town as long as I have, I know every policeman there, so I just got up there and watched her, and when she came, I saw there was no policeman following her.

She came up and gave me my money. Now the girl thinks that the checks are good; she thinks they're under an assumed name. Whores are very simple-minded or they wouldn't be in the profession they're in. Once in a while you'll get a smart one; maybe they're not so simple as they just don't give a damn. Well, I sat there that night and we had a few drinks and I got to thinking about how good it was. So early the next morning I called up again and I sent the girl back up there. This time the check was for about $700. She brought me the money down, and I waited two or three hours and I called that lady again. Then I started getting $1,500.

This started on Friday and I hit them all day Saturday and Sunday. On Sunday I sent the girl up there and she came back with ones, fives, and tens. She told me, "Baby, they can't cash any more of your checks."

I said, "Why?"

"They don't have any more money."

She had a whole pocketful of money. Knocked them clean out. She said, "There's not even money left in the drawers there in the safe."

Now that is what this idiot woman did. I don't see how they can give you all that money. But she went up there and completely cleaned out the safe. Of course, now, the assistant manager lost his job and that lady lost her job and they had a hell of a shake-up. A man just came in there and took all their money.

How much did you get?

About $7,000.

How did you get out of the hotel?

After I got all this money, the head bellhop there—the one that's in charge of all the whores and everything (actually you can get a gal from the rest of the porters, but they had to give a little cut because he's running it)—when he got off Monday night, he took me to a town about forty miles from Corpus and I caught a bus there to San Antonio. Before I got into San Antonio, I got off the bus out in the suburbs and went over to a character joint where they have a bunch of trailer houses. I stayed in the trailer house two or three days and went down and caught the train and went to El Paso on the train, and from El Paso I caught the plane to Vegas. I stayed out in Vegas for about three or four weeks; then I went to Los Angeles and I stayed in Los Angeles for a couple of years.

They knew who did it, but they can't prove it. I wasn't in any way connected with it. That woman says she remembers my voice and everything. They know who did it. But that gal, you know how whores drift around, there's no telling where she is, so they didn't have any real way to prove it.

The only thing that was really bad about it was my uncle owned a big shop there in the hotel and they threatened to cancel his lease and everything. They got real mad about that, but they never did prove it. The assistant manager and the old gal in charge of bookkeeping, they both lost their jobs. I can't think of any other repercussion on it.

NOTES

THE CHECK BUSINESS

1. Like the police, most characters tend to underestimate the importance of the really successful convert thief, the *rara avis* who is rarely or never trapped. These do not go off on sprees, do not run with characters, do not make themselves known to thieves like Sam. I know of one in Houston, for example, who has been a check writer for twenty-five years; in all that time he was convicted once and served a one-year sentence. He now owns a house, appears to his neighbors to be quite conventional (as, essentially, he is), and makes his living cashing checks not too close to home.

   For more on the writing of checks as a professional activity, see Edwin H. Lemert, *Human Deviance, Social Problems and Social Control* (Englewood Cliffs, 1967), pp. 109-118 ("The Behavior of the Systematic Check Forger"), and pp. 119-134 ("Role Enactment, Self and Identity in the Systematic Check Forger").

2. In 1967, San Antonio had twenty-seven assistant district attorneys and eleven investigators. One investigator and five clerks were assigned (full time) to checks.

3. He is talking about passing forged company payroll checks.

4. The only critical point in this sort of operation is to make sure one cashes the good check from the resale before the bad purchase fails to clear.

5. *I.e.,* that the checks appear authentic when compared to a legitimate check.

6. One thief who knows Sam well wrote here, "Bullshit. His family has picked up two tons of bad paper in Corpus."

6 · The Big Bitch

□ □ □

ABOUT the habitual criminal act.

Say you get arrested for something, no matter what it is. The law reads that if you have two previous convictions less than capital, then upon the third conviction it constitutes a habitual criminal. Then they can try you on a separate charge as a habitual and give you life if you're convicted.

Take me. When I came to the penitentiary this time, I had, I don't know, twenty-five convictions against me. No, more than that, probably forty-five convictions. For every time I burglarized a place, when my partner copped out, he copped out on everything. Even places we *thought* about burglarizing but hadn't. For every time we had busted a drugstore safe, for example, they would get us for felony destruction of private property and for breaking into the building; then they would get us for burglary, breaking into a private house with an intention of burglarizing; thirdly, they would get us for stealing the narcotics and would file possession on us; and fourth, they would file felony theft on us because we would steal over $50.

They can take one crime, indict you, and, by doing it on each count separately, send you to the penitentiary for life.

Now they don't *do* that. What they usually do, the lawyers and the district attorneys, is consider every time you go to the penitentiary as counting once for the habitual.

Not always. I've got a friend in Central who was on the Ramsey that's doing a life sentence, and this is just the second time he's been to the penitentiary. When he came the first time he had two counts against him, and they used both of those; then he made a phone call to a girl—they say he did—to try to get her to be a prostitute, and they got him for attempting to procure and they gave him a life sentence as a habitual criminal. And he had only been in the penitentiary one time before and that was for breaking and entering and felony theft.

One reason for all of this is somebody like me. They know that my lawyers are bought and paid for before I ever get in jail. As soon as I get in jail, the lawyers are burning up the highway looking for me—throwing writs, calling the governor, and all that. What they do is carry me to a justice of the peace and set a $10,000 bond on each case, so for each burglary that's $40,000. In a short period of time, you've got a half million dollars' worth of bonds. You can't make them. It takes $50,000 to make a half-a-million-dollar bond, and if you had that kind of money, you wouldn't be stealing it anyway. That's what they do.

Now, after they've got you in jail, they still haven't gotten you in the penitentiary. Say they're going to have a confession if they want one bad enough. But say that they can't get a confession, or say that they even have a confession but they feel like it's going to cause a big stink. This boy's got good lawyers and they're going to fight it and there's going to be an investigation—nothing will come of it, but still it's publicity maybe right before election time or something. So they say, "Well, I'll tell you what. We'll let you cop for the maximum, less than a habitual." In other words, in Texas, where burglary carries two to twelve years, they'll let you cop for the twelve years, or they'll put the bitch on you. And there you are. They use it as a hammer.

There's some cases before the Supreme Court. One in

California; the inmates up there got up over $300,000 to take a case up there. Hired the best legal minds in the country and they're trying to get it outlawed.

If they do outlaw that, plus the fact that they can't beat a confession out of you and they have to abide by the law themselves, then you've got a free roll at them.

But I don't say that it's an unfair roll because it's the law. It's no more unfair than for me to go out and be treated like a dog by them. I mean, what's right's right and what's wrong's wrong. I don't think that they should be able to take part of the law and apply it to themselves and what they don't want throw it away. Let it be hard on them; the federal government does it. They make cases.

The Rangers and people like that, they don't do any *detective* work. They get a suspicion—that's right—that you're the one that did it and they take you out there and they beat you to death. You know, you can only stand so much. You can can only stand so much. People say that "I can't be brought." Well, I was brought and I'm about a half nut anyways when it comes to being stubborn, and I made up my mind that they weren't going to bring me. And they already had confessions signed by everybody against me. And you know that was enough, but I still made up my mind that I wasn't going to sign one.

And I finally had to. They finally just whipped me till I just couldn't get there anymore. They had me for three weeks. Three weeks. That's without seeing a lawyer, without using a telephone, without shaving, without anything. And that's just the way they operate.

Now if they take that beating out and the habitual criminal law, then it's something else. Then they can come up and they can find you dead guilty—no, I mean to say that if they bust you in a place, you still can deal with them because they don't have the habitual criminal law and you know the maximum they can give you is twelve. You just take your lawyer, go up, have them impanel you a jury—pick your jury and go up there—then your lawyer says, "Now this boy is a member of such-and-such a church, he is employed by so-and-so, he has a wife and three children, or whatever it might be, and doesn't anyone make a mistake *some*time in their life? Why not give him three years? Let him come out and support his family." They're not allowed to tell them that you've already been in the penitentiary five or six times or that you've been arrested 150 times or whatever it might be.

Of course Goldberg is the one who was the convict's friend. Now that he's gone, they're liable to never pass another minority-group law. Goldberg was the man. He became ambassador to the United Nations and, boy, I hated that. I was *sick* when I heard he was going to take it. He is the most foremost thinking justice that they ever had.

If they should outlaw the habitual, won't it encourage criminals like you?

No, we're going to steal anyway.

But the thing is, those new criminals coming up—it will give the public a chance to rehabilitate those people. The way it is now, once you get in trouble and you see what they are and what they can do to you, you become so bitter that nothing can change you.

I'm not proud of what I've done. I'm ashamed of what I am. But I won't tell anyone—especially my family. I'd have liked for things to have been different. But they weren't.

Take the first time I got in trouble. Man, if they'd have carried me up there and tried me and put me on one of these farms for one day and turned me loose—man, I never would have done anything for the rest of my life. But after you're here and you see that you can take anything that they can dish out, and you find out how sorry they are, how absolutely utterly sorry, well, it knocks you out. Then you just say, "What the hell." And when you get out on the streets the first time something's gone wrong and you need a little money, you say, "Well, them sorry sons of bitches, I'll teach them to whip me." And you just go to stealing something.

But if you arrest a boy, and treat him right, explain the rights and wrongs to him and take him to court, give him probation, and show him that the law is good . . . I've never seen anything about the law that's good. Nothing, absolutely nothing. And I think it would be a help.

But you can't change people like us.

That's wrong to say that. I don't know—if I could get out and get me a good job, if there was some respect went with it. . . . I'm not going to get out and work in a service station or work in a drive-in grocery store or sell peanuts or something like that. I'm just not going to do it. I've had some good jobs in my life, but I could never get one again, I'm getting too old now. When I was a kid, I had some real good jobs. But if I could get a good job with a future to it, I'd probably square up. But now when I get out, I'm going to be forty years old—I'm thirty-seven now—and when I get out, I can't wander around from filling station to filling station. I've got to get out and make me some money. Try to get in business for myself.

A POSTSCRIPT:

THE TWO-D MASKS AND THE COLD AT TOPKNOT'S

I READ through Sam's conversations and my introduction and the notes supplied by several of us, and it seems to me that a thing or two more should be said, things that are a little hard to put exactly, hard because they have to do more with the flavor or texture of the experiences Sam describes than with the facts of them. I will go at it obliquely in two ways. For the first I'll use words that sociologists would call "soft" terminology: "soft" terminology is metaphor that hasn't yet had time to become jargon.

You might consider the relationship between a lawyer and his client as *two-dimensional*. It is an extremely uncomplicated form of human relationship; there is really no interaction, for all contact is sequential. Man A comes into the room and says, "I have this problem," and Man B says from behind his desk, "With certain knowledge at my command and certain incentives supplied by you [*e.g.*, a check, or bills, or any coin of the realm] I can do these things for you." The assumption somehow gets made that people are dealing with people, but that is no more than a convenient fiction, one with which I suppose we are all adequately familiar.

Perhaps necessarily so: there would be neither time nor

energy left to brush one's teeth if we tried to put depth into even half the potential relationships that present themselves in any twenty-four-hour period. I remember John Berryman telling me that Saul Bellow once asserted he never read the papers because he identified with everyone in them and spent a whole day getting through the news. That is an opposite extreme of sorts.

What it means is that we frequently agree, by unspoken mutual contract, to act as if the surface self we present each other were something that exists in other relationships as well and really *is*, rather than barely represents, us, that it is something like a real human being, and that while we are in one another's presence we will introduce no styles of behavior complicating that contract.

When you are indicted for first-degree murder, you don't sit down with your lawyer and discuss disk brakes, and he does not invite you to play squash after lunch while you are out on bail, if you are out on bail. He perceives you as a certain kind of question, and you accept him as a certain possible answer. The analogy of courtroom to stage play has often been made, and with good reason: though personalities are sometimes involved, they are not nearly so important as personae, and the personae are all surface, two-dimensional. Each actor has his assigned role, and although he may be permitted to exercise a range of freedom within that role, he may not engage in anything that penetrates the borders. The system would collapse, and one would be faced with the terror of having to deal with human beings.

The lawyer, for example, may not step out of character and say, "My client is guilty as hell, but I am sharper than the D.A. and I will get my client off, and the D.A. knows it, the judge knows it, and the jury knows it, so why don't we all save ourselves a lot of trouble and ennui and go golfing now?"

In the character world, we have the same sort of drama; the only difference is there is more of it. The life style is even less real because the half-life of the various articulations of role are so brief and intermittent. Almost no relationship survives its own exercise. Residence, save in prison, is highly transitory; business relationships are ephemeral; personal involvements are assiduously avoided. Women are there to be rented, to be fucked, to be loaned, to be used. Characters deal with one another in a surface world that offers one splendid advantage: if you deal with someone that way, he is compelled to deal with you that way also, and you are both safe from each other.

Prison, of course, is more of that; it is almost entirely masks. The problem in prison is either getting caught with your mask down or with two on at once, and because of the proximity of everyone to everyone else and the likelihood that one must use more than one mask in an agonizingly confined area, that risk is high.

That part of the problem is less troublesome in the character world on the streets: contacts are so transitory, so predetermined, and movements are so discontinuous, that it is possible to maintain the two-dimensional multiplicities with relative ease.

A specific agent or actor is different in different situations; to an extent he has to be. You are not the same set of responses with your wife, your boss, your body servant, your imaginary dream Love. This is no fresh insight, and many writers have discussed it in many ways (Hermann Hesse in *Steppenwolf* and Erving Goffman in *The Presentation of Self in Everyday Life*, for example). Never does one bring all the selves or masks into play at one time, nor does one even bring very many of them in at one time; that creates a three-dimensional human situation, and most of our systems do not tolerate that very well, just as the court does not tolerate it if the lawyer, who has played poker with the judge every Thursday for twenty-six years, says "Harry" rather than "Your Honor."

I said the character world was extremely two-dimensional. That is not so extraordinary in itself, for so are politics and show business and selling. But there is a difference and I suspect it lies in the fact that those other people—the pols, the stars, the hucksters—get to go at least a little naked

when they're off duty, while for the character there is *no*
off-duty time. Sam says somewhere that stealing is a full-
time business; he's wrong, it's only part-time, but being a
character *is* full-time. It is there night and day, while passing
a check or cracking a safe or fading the beef, while hustling
a woman or having a meal or buying some Stacy Adams.
Sam talks also about how hard it is to break check writers
because the scores are so tempting and available; I think it
is harder to break a character of being a character, because
the world he avoids seems so chaotic. We sometimes talk
about peeling off the outer layers of show to get to the real
self; I don't know about other people, but I can tell you that
the character like Sam is no onion; there is only one outer
layer, and it is composed of that set of masks Sam tells you
about, and it is one without which the character never con-
fronts anyone or anything.

But masks do not exist by themselves; this kind you cannot tack to your wall. They need their contexts to become
visible. Sam told you of some; there are others.

I remember one night when we drove around the back
roads of the sparsely inhabited outskirts of Houston looking
for a country bar where Sam was to deliver a message to the
girl friend of a man still in prison. We went back and forth
across old U.S. 75 on one empty road after the other; we
asked directions and were given them and found they were
bad and asked again; and finally, fifty or a hundred miles
later, we found the place and realized we had started out
with bum directions, for we were now on the far side of town
near U.S. 59.

There was a girl getting out of an old car as we pulled up.
Her breath made clouds in front of her face as she went to
the entrance. Inside, we found out she was the one we were
looking for; had we been on time, she would have been an
hour late. The joint was almost as cold as outside; few places
down there were ready for the rare cold snaps, and this
wasn't one of them. The girl's name was Harriet, and she
bore too much make-up on a hatchety face, and under her
coat she wore a purple sweater. She told us she worked as

a B-girl in a downtown stripjoint and made $400 a week, most of it from commissions on hustling drinks.

It was a small square building with four tables, a short bar, a pool table dominated by one man about forty in a Texas A&M sweat shirt, a jukebox, and a stripper who performed for three 45 r.p.m. singles every thirty minutes. The stripper was a pretty blond with a sad piquant mouth that didn't go very well with the rest of her face, which wasn't very sad or very much of anything. The expression didn't change; it was cast. When she came out, she wore a satin robe that came off pretty quick. By the middle of the second record of each set she got down to pasties and panties. She had saggy breasts, which surprised me, because the rest of her was lithe and young. On the third song she swung her pastied breasts, one at a time, and for a finale got them going in opposite directions simultaneously. Her mouth kept not quite smiling. When the girl finished her set, Harriet left the table and Sam said, "She drove up in that 1955 Ford. Four hundred a week, my ass."

Harriet came back from the can and complained about the owner, an attractive woman of thirty-eight who looked about thirty. We were told that the owner had had silicone injections but hadn't massaged as the doctor instructed and she now had lumpy breasts. "I'm just a 32-C, but I'm proud of it." Harriet puffed out her pride. "You come down to the joint and you can tell which ones have used that shit. Their tits stick straight out."

The next night Sam and I drove out of Houston along Texas Route 35. We passed Ramsey, Retrieve, and some of the other prison farms ("Probably we're more class-conscious here than you are on the streets . . ."), through Bay City, and into Palacios ("The sheriff said, 'Cut it out; if you have to do that, take him out in the country and do it.'"), where the road was black and shining in the dark and we passed squashed cadavers of large dead birds. Sometimes ducks with what seemed broken legs tried to scurry out of the headlights, and Sam told me that in the night they mistook the blackness of the road for quiet water and zoomed in to a big surprise. Then through Port Lavaca and into Corpus Christi ("I had a little ole whorehouse and it got closed down . . ."). After a while we were on the road again, still heading southwest, this time on Texas 44 through Alice ("And I never did get it. It never did give. If it gave a sixteenth of an inch, I could get it, but I never could get a sixteenth of an inch.") to Freer in Duval County, where we picked up U.S. 59 and a lot more speed. In the moonlight there was nothing but mesquite and rabbits (coming back another day, I found that there was nothing but mesquite and rabbits in daylight either) for the sixty-five miles to the Mexican border.

And there we wound it up after I don't remember exactly how long as the only window not painted or boarded over in the place we were in went from nighttime black to morning blue. It was cold, cold as I can remember there, and in Mexico they are less prepared for cold than in Houston. The bartender kept giving us phony Pedro Domecq brandy—which puzzled me because you'd expect people to confine counterfeiting at least to something potable—and in between fiddling with the large brown butane space heater that never, for all his fiddling, threw out one perceivable calorie of warmth. The blue went gray as we sat there in that frozen whorehouse bar in Nuevo Laredo talking over big scores and high rollers with Topknot, the Mexican gambler who owned the joint. Topknot looked like Sidney Greenstreet. He was looking for an American to handle the dice action, he said, because if a Mexican ran it, the American tourists wouldn't bet. The bartender rounded the table again with the Pedro Domecq surrogate; it didn't warm. He put the bottle down and again fiddled with the space heater and made us move our chairs to get where the heat was; it wasn't. He asked us if we wanted any girls. We looked at him like he was crazy: it was frozen and we were *talking*. "I don't," I said; "maybe he does." The bartender went out without asking Sam the question. He came back a few minutes later and said, "She's getting up." We drank and talked. A while later Topknot said, "This man is my guest. What happened to the girl?" The bartender went out again and came back in ten minutes.

"She's too drunk to get up." Sam didn't seem to mind: he was happy talking over the high rollers with Topknot.

The gray window showed streaks of rain. The day brought no warmth. Nothing did. About 7 A.M. some women came in. I won't try to describe them: there is nothing in the world quite like the 7 A.M. shift in a Mexican whorehouse. Sam and Topknot ignored them; they had the bottle of brandy between them, almost gone now, and the words were still of old scores, great games, and someplace else where the women were polished and the action fast and the money big. I went outside and sloshed through the muddy street to the car and drove awhile, crossed the border to Laredo, and went to the motel to shower and change clothes. In the room were two steak-and-egg breakfasts, still hot, that Sam had ordered for us the night before. That meant it was 9 or 10 A.M. I consumed all of one and part of the other, realizing we'd been drinking a lot but hadn't eaten for a long time.

What I think I'm trying to tell you here is that somewhere behind all those separate deals and busts and hustles and parties and women there is something like a person, and it has gone through all those things that Sam told you about, it makes a kind of sense of those experiences that we—you and I—cannot, it gets them into terms that are human. I thought if I told you *that*, as obvious as it must be, and showed you a little bit about one ride we took, you might get some of the feeling, and when you think back on what you've read, you may find it means something to you too.

Cambridge-Houston-Buffalo
1965-1969